TAKE EAT,
TAKE DRINK

TAKE EAT, TAKE DRINK

The Lord's Supper through the Centuries

ERNEST BARTELS

CONCORDIA PUBLISHING HOUSE · SAINT LOUIS

To my wife, Lois, my beloved partner and helpmeet for more than 53 years, for the encouragement, inspiration, and support she gave me as I was writing this book about the Lord's Supper.

Manufactured in the United States of America

Library of Congress Cataloging-in-Publication Data

Bartels, Ernest.
Take eat, take drink : the Lord's Supper through the centuries / Ernest Bartels.
p. cm.
Includes bibliographical references (p.   ).
ISBN 0-7586-0037-2
1. Lord's Supper— History. I. Title.
BV823.B362 2004
234'.163'09—dc22
2004000978

1 2 3 4 5 6 7 8 9 10   13 12 11 10 09 08 07 06 05 04

CONTENTS

PREFACE

*T*ake Eat, Take Drink has been written for Christian pastors and laity alike. Pastors will find this book to be of value as a handy one volume reference tool. It will be especially helpful in answering the questions of concerned, interested, and inquiring laypersons. This book has also been designed to be employed as a resource for study groups of pastors and laity in learning more about the important and mysterious subject of the Lord's Supper. The author envisions that with the aid of the study helps that are incorporated into the book it will be profitably used for this purpose.

In *Take Eat, Take Drink* there is information about the Sacrament that is not otherwise available except in scattered form in many separate books and other writings. The answers to a wide variety of pertinent questions about the Lord's Supper are to be found in this unique and one of a kind book.

There are reasons why numerous questions about the Lord's Supper surface in the minds of confessional Lutherans and other Christians. This widely observed communal meal has been much controverted among the churches of Christendom. Despite widespread attempts at consensus, considerably divergent views are held regarding its nature and intent. Although the words used in some unity documents would suggest agreement, there is instead what faculty members of two Missouri Synod Lutheran seminaries call "woolly language" and "studied ambiguity."[1] Robert McAffee Brown of Union Theological Seminary once observed, "The Lord's Table is where Christians should be most united. They are not. The Lord's Table is the place where they are the most divided.... Division here is a scandal in the life of Christendom."[2] In *Take Eat, Take Drink* the "scandal" is examined in the belief that a clear delineation of differences and an explanation of how the present situation came to be will be useful to concerned persons, and an aid to understanding. The approach in this study is primarily historical. Materials from the disciplines of symbolics and systematics are woven into the text where appropriate.

Persons like myself who are simply interested and fascinated by the Lord's Supper will enjoy this book. For those who wish to have a deeper understanding of what their own church teaches, and desire to learn more about their neighbor's faith regarding this sacred repast, the study of *Take Eat, Take Drink* will be a learning experience. Christians who struggle with questions about the diversity of beliefs concerning the Lord's Supper will find this book to be a helpful source.

All Scripture quotations are from the King James Version of the Bible, except where otherwise noted. Important dates of individuals mentioned are mainly taken from *Lutheran Cyclopedia* edited by Erwin L. Lueker and *Lives of the Popes* by Richard F. McBrien. When known to the writer, brief denomination and/or academic information about authors quoted is given at least once in the text of the book.

As I wrote this study of the Lord's Supper, my daughter Nancy J. Bartels assisted me in locating and gathering important information from various sources. Professors James L. Codling and David P. Meyer gave excellent suggestions as I developed the manuscript. Editors Charles P. Schaum, Kenneth C. Wagener, Dawn M. Weinstock, and Laura L. Lane provided valuable professional help in preparing the manuscript for publication. For the benefit of those who wish to use *Take Eat, Take Drink* as the basis of a twelve- or fifteen-week adult class, Rev. Charles P. Schaum has authored study questions and indicated points to consider for further study. Individuals who loaned or gave me informative materials include: Robert A. Bartels, Reuben M. Brownlee, Randall E. Gehring, Peter M. Glock, Harvey G. Henderson, Robert J. Jastram, Howard D. Lyons, William J. Stottlemyer, and Dale G. Young. Ernest W. Bernet, Ronald R. Carnicom, Howard J. Jording, and Robert E. Smith were also helpful to me. I thank these persons and all others who assisted me in any way.

May the Lord who instituted this Supper use this volume to His glory and for the spiritual enrichment of those who read and study it.

Rev. Ernest Bartels, D. Min., D. R. S., Ph.D.

NOTES

1. "The Porvoo Declaration in Confessional Perspective," Concordia Theological Quarterly 61, no. 1–2 (1997): 41.
2. Robert McAffee Brown, *The Spirit of Protestantism* (New York: Oxford University Press, 1965), 156.

INTRODUCTION

AIDS TO READING AND STUDY

This resource covers the doctrine and practice of the Lord's Supper from the institution and mandate of our Lord circa A.D. 30 to the present day. The main focus has been given to the period from the events chronicled in the New Testament to the Reformation for two reasons: First, the time from Jerusalem to Wittenberg contains the doctrinal controversies and events that establish the fundamental Christian understanding of the Lord's Supper. Second, Luther's Small Catechism, which remains an indispensable tool of catechesis for both children and adults, deals readily with the material covered here, allowing this work to serve as further reading for those wanting to "dig deeper." The final chapter and conclusion show "where the rubber hits the road" by bringing the discussion from the Reformation to the present.

The reader will encounter some degree of philosophical language in this work, especially that of Plato and Aristotle. That is unavoidable because the church has deemed it necessary to engage the great thinkers of this world in order to present and defend the Word of God in a winsome dialogue. The church succeeds in this effort when using philosophical language in support of God's Word. Failure in the church results from letting worldly ideas take hold of and rule over God's Word. Helpful reference works to use with this presentation include the *Lutheran Cyclopedia*, Mortimer Adler's *The Great Ideas: A Lexicon of Western Thought*, the *Cambridge Dictionary of Philosophy,* and the *Oxford Companion to Philosophy*.

This resource may also be used as the basis for a twelve- to fifteen-week Bible study. Unit I might last three weeks, Unit II five weeks, and Unit III might encompass three weeks. Unit IV could vary, depending on the level of detail desired. Each week might focus on a major unit (chapter or part) in the text. Unit I gives the foundation, the words of our Lord, that we hold fast to—that is where Jesus has placed the sure and binding promise of our eternal salvation. All other ground is sinking sand. Units II and III discuss how some have ably confessed the scriptures and how some have failed in that regard. Unit IV helps show the current state of affairs. The conclusion gives perspective to it all.

May our Lord bless you and guide you as you read
and study onward!

THE LORD'S SUPPER
IN THE APOSTOLIC ERA

1 | THE INSTITUTION
OF THE LORD'S SUPPER

Christians throughout the world regularly celebrate a rite which they call the Lord's Supper, Holy Communion, the Eucharist, the Lord's Table, the Breaking of Bread, the Cup of Blessing, the Holy Supper, the Divine Liturgy, the Mass, the Oblation, the Present, the Consecration, the New Testament Passover, the Foot Washing, or the Thanksgiving.[1] Some of the names originate from the New Testament, while churches have coined others. Some terms arise from the words, the nature, or the circumstance of the meal. This study will primarily use the term Lord's Supper for this sacred meal because the apostle Paul uses the expression in 1 Corinthians 11:20.

The accounts regarding Christ's institution of the Lord's Supper appear four times in the Bible. While the authors differ in the order and amount of information supplied, all four provide the same words of institution: "This is My body; this . . . is My blood." The first three accounts are recorded by the authors of the Synoptic Gospels, whose narratives strongly resemble each other: Matthew 26:26–28, Mark 14:22–24, and Luke 22:19, 20. St. Paul also gives witness to the Lord's Supper in 1 Corinthians 11:23–25. Since Paul's letter predates the Gospels, his writing of the Lord's words is considered the earliest of the four versions.[2] Martin Luther (1483–1546) harmonized Christ's words of institution, adapting them from an ancient liturgy for use in his Small Catechism:[3]

> Our LORD Jesus Christ, on the night in which he was betrayed, took the bread, gave thanks, and broke it and gave it to his disciples and said, "Take; eat; this is my body which is given for you. Do this in remembrance of me."
>
> In the same way he also took the cup after the supper, gave thanks, and gave it to them and said, "Take, and drink of it, all of you. This cup is the New Testament in my blood, which is shed for you for the forgiveness of sins. Do this, as often as you drink it, in remembrance of me."[4]

Jesus gave bread to the disciples to eat (Matthew 26:26; Mark 14:22; Luke 22:19; 1 Corinthians 11:24), and gave fruit of the vine to drink (Matthew 26:29; Mark 14:25). This brief meal, which some, including Lutherans, call a sacrament and others call an ordinance, came at or near the conclusion of a larger meal (Matthew 26:26; Mark 14:22).

There is no unanimity among Christian church bodies today as to the exact nature of the "bread" and "fruit of the vine" drink served by Jesus to His disciples. Many Christian churches, believing the original meal to be a celebration of the Passover, say that the "bread" was unleavened Passover bread.[5] The Greek word used is *artos*, which means "bread" or "loaf of bread."[6] Lutheran commentator R. C. H. Lenski describes this as "a thin sheet of unleavened bread, pieces of which were broken off for the purpose of eating."[7] The Greek language has a word specifically for unleavened bread. This word, *azumos*, is not found in any of the New Testament accounts of the Lord's Supper.[8] Those who do not consider the Lord's Supper to be a true Passover meal think that the bread was leavened.[9] Regarding the "fruit of the vine" drink, some say it was wine,[10] some believe it was wine mixed with water,[11] and others hold that it was unfermented grape juice.[12] Still others suggest a raisin drink,[13] raisin tea, and diluted grape syrup.[14] Professor Joachim Jeremias states that it was red Passover wine in distinction from Palestinian black or white wine.[15] Although *oinos*, the Greek word for wine, is not used in the Bible when speaking of the cup blessed and given by Jesus and His disciples, Lutheran commentator Paul E. Kretzmann writes that " 'fruit of the vine' was the technical term of the Jews for the wine of the Passover."[16]

Matthew, Mark, and Luke tell us that the meal in which the institution of the Lord's Supper occurred was a celebration of the Passover by Jesus and his disciples (Matthew 26:17–20; Mark 14:12–17; Luke 22:7–14). John also gives an account of this evening in his Gospel, yet he does not mention the institution of the Lord's Supper. New Testament scholar Norman Perrin has remarked, "We have no idea why the Eucharistic words are missing."[17] Some believe that, according to John's text, the meal was not on or during the Passover, but that it happened before the beginning of the Passover. John introduces the account of this evening with the words "Now before the feast of the passover, when Jesus knew that His hour was come that He should depart out of this world unto the Father, having loved His own which were in the world, He loved them unto the end" (John 13:1). Later, in telling of Jesus being taken to Pilate's judgment hall, John says of the Jewish religious leaders, "They themselves went not into the judgment hall, lest they should be defiled; but that they might eat the passover" (John 18:28).

Those that interpret the above passages from John to imply a meal prior to the Passover suggest a number of alternative meals. Some call it a preliminary meal as part of the sequence of events connected with the Passover.[18] Some advance theories that it may have been a sanctification type of a weekly pre-Sabbath meal,[19] an Essene cultic meal,[20] or a kind of Jewish religious meal that a group of friends might hold whenever they felt the need.[21] Others hold that there are plausible explanations for the words in John 13:1 and 18:28. Jeremias says that the time reference in 13:1 "simply asserts that Jesus already knew before the Passover that his death was imminent."[22] About the phrase "eat the passover" (18:28), Lenski holds that this need not be applied or restricted only to the meal with the paschal lamb, but may also mean the other sacrificial feasts during the seven day long celebration.[23]

Bible scholars have proposed a wide variety of possible explanations for seeming differences between John and the other three evangelists. One such suggestion is that Jesus arranged for an earlier Passover meal because He knew that His death would occur at the time of the official sacrifice.[24] A variation of this argument states that the last meal may not have been the regular Passover meal, but it came to be interpreted in that way.[25] Another view is that the Galileans or the Pharisees ate the Passover on Thursday evening, while the Judeans or the Sadducees ate the Passover on Friday evening.[26] English scholar Donald Guthrie feels that both the Synoptic Gospels and John are likely correct.[27] He speaks of the general idea that there were two calendars that fixed the Passover by different methods, and there is a possible answer in "this theory of divergent calendars."[28] In a summary statement, Guthrie remarks, "The historical and chronological differences may well be capable of an interpretation which does not involve contradictions or corrections."[29] Bible scholars have made other plausible suggestions regarding the dating and authenticity of this Paschal meal.[30] These proposals notwithstanding, the record of the Synoptic Gospels leads us to confess that this evening meal, in all likelihood, was eaten on Thursday, the fourteenth of the Jewish month Nisan.[31] The authors of *Peloubet's Bible Dictionary* say that this corresponds to the sixth of April in the year A.D. 30 in our calendar.[32]

This writer believes that the meal in the Upper Room was indeed a Passover observance by Jesus and His disciples. Like all faithful Jews, Jesus annually celebrated the commemorative Passover meal.[33] Of this particular Passover, Jesus said to His disciples, "With desire I have desired to eat this passover with you before I suffer" (Luke 22:15). He explicitly instructed two of His disciples to make arrangements and preparations for this meal that He called "the passover" (Mark 14:14). Lutheran author Adam Fahling considers it decisive that "Jesus Himself calls it Passover."[34]

During the time of Jesus, Passover preparations consisted in doing the necessary things regarding the paschal lamb (from procuring to roasting), providing the unleavened bread and other requisites for the feast, and preparing the table, sofas, and pillows for the dining room.[35] Jesus had instructed Peter and John to go into a house, then say to the "goodman of the house," "The Master saith, Where is the guestchamber where I shall eat the passover with My disciples? And he will shew you a large upper room furnished and prepared: there make ready for us" (Mark 14:14–15; Luke 22:11–12). The two disciples did as Jesus directed. Continuing with the assumption that Jesus on that night truly celebrated the Passover, it would be well to mention some of the essential features of a Paschal meal in Jesus' day.

One such feature is that the Passover lambs were slain in various sections of Jerusalem. They were then taken to the priests for the presentation of their sacrificial portions at the altar in the temple. The remaining portions were taken to the houses where the meals would be celebrated. A group of not less than ten men and not more than twenty ate one animal.[36] A communal group like Jesus and His disciples could observe the Passover together as though they were a family unit.[37] Bitter herbs, intended to remind the participants of the bitterness of Egypt, were eaten. They also ate unleavened cakes dipped in a sweet reddish-brown sauce, or gravylike soup, made of raisins, dates, vinegar, and several other ingredients.[38] Four cups of red wine[39] or wine mixed with water[40] were drunk. The father (or leader, as in the case of Jesus) blessed the first cup, and it was passed around. Then, in a family situation, the oldest son asked the meaning of the Passover, and the father told the story of the institution of the Passover. Psalms 113 and 114 were sung. The second cup was drunk, and the meal was eaten followed by a prayer of thanksgiving. The third cup was blessed. During the passing of the fourth cup Psalms 115 through 118 were sung.[41]

The Lord's Supper was probably instituted at the third cup, which was called the cup of blessing,[42] or the cup of thanksgiving.[43] The ancient Jewish prayer over the bread at this point was "Blessed be Thou, our God, King of the universe, who bringest forth bread out of the earth."[44] St. Paul says, "The Lord Jesus the same night in which He was betrayed took bread: And when He had given thanks, He brake it . . . " (1 Corinthians 11:23b, 24a). Jesus took one of the cakes of unleavened bread, broke it, and gave it to His disciples.[45] He said of the Passover bread, "Take; eat; this is my body which is given for you."[46] Jesus' words gave the unleavened bread a new character. Then, passing the cup, He told them, "Take, and drink of it, all of you. This cup is the New Testament in my blood, which is shed for you for the forgiveness of sins."[47]

Christians have interpreted the words "This is My body," and "This cup is the new testament in My blood," in various ways.[48] Today the Orthodox and Roman Catholic churches believe that by these words Jesus meant that the bread was literally changed into His body and the wine into His blood, so that the disciples actually did not receive bread and wine, but only body and blood.[49] This belief in the changing of the elements is known as "transubstantiation." Some use the term "real presence" to speak against this change. The first recorded use of the term "real presence" was in the Roman Catholic doctrine of the Lord's Supper in the bull *Transiturus* by Pope Urban IV that instituted the Corpus Christi feast in 1264.[50] The Lutheran confession is that "the true body and blood of Christ are truly present under the form of bread and wine."[51] Lutherans speak of the bread and wine given in a natural way and the body and blood given in a supernatural way.[52] American Lutherans appear to have used the term "real presence" in 1820, while European Lutherans did not use the term until about 1875.[53] Protestants in the tradition of John Calvin (1509–1564) believe that Jesus meant the "real presence" of His body and blood to be spiritual rather than physical. They also believe that the bread and wine are received in a natural way and His body and blood received in a spiritual manner.[54] Other Protestants agree with Ulrich Zwingli (1483–1531) who taught that Jesus was simply saying that the bread and wine memorialized, pictured, symbolized, or signified His body and blood as reminders of His sacrifice for salvation.[55] Although the language of "supernatural" and "spiritual" and "symbolic" can seem to blur together in modern usage, the words meant very different things during the Reformation and the years following. Some of that change arises from the philosophies of René Descartes, Immanuel Kant, Friedrich Schleiermacher, Georg Hegel, and others. Since many groups use the term "real presence" differently, we must go examine closer what various groups are saying.

The words "This is the new testament in My blood" regarding the cup were Jesus' fulfillment of the wonderful prophecy of a new covenant in the presence of His disciples. Through the prophet Jeremiah God had said, "Behold, the days come, saith the Lord, that I will make a new covenant with the house of Israel, and with the house of Judah" (Jeremiah 31:31). It was not by chance that Jesus instituted the Lord's Supper in the context of the Passover observance. His selection of the Passover "clothes the institution of the Lord's Supper with Israel's history."[56] There is a definite connection between the Passover and the Lord's Supper.[57] Baptist evangelist Harold F. Hunter tells us of at least fourteen parallels between them.[58] For example, the Passover commemorates the deliverance of God's people from the bondage of slavery in Egypt. The Lord's Supper is a deliverance from the bondage of sin by the shed blood and sacrificial death of the Lord Jesus, the true Paschal Lamb. When Jesus instituted the Lord's Supper, He lifted the cup after the Passover meal and said, "This cup is the new testament in My blood" (Luke 22:20). In a sense Jesus instituted a new rite. In another sense He reinterpreted an old rite.[59]

Some question why Jesus ordained bread to be used in the Lord's Supper and not a lamb. Canon Walsham How gave this opinion: "Because the types and shadows were to cease when the real Sacrifice was come. There must be nothing which might cast a doubt upon the all-sufficiency of *that*."[60] Another suggestion is that Jesus chose bread because it is more easily provided, and therefore could more easily be used in a universally celebrated rite.[61]

The Old Testament Passover had been an annual observance. Jesus gave no rule as to the time and frequency of the new Lord's Supper.[62] He simply said, "This do in remembrance of Me" (Luke 22:19; 1 Corinthians 11:24, 25). St. Paul suggested frequency in participation in the Lord's Supper when he wrote, "For as *often* as you eat this bread, and drink the cup, you proclaim the Lord's death until He comes" (1 Corinthians 11:26, ESV). A Lutheran pastor, Herbert F. Juneau, once said to this author, "Notice that St. Paul didn't say, 'As *seldom* . . .' "[63]

Methodist professor Laurence H. Stookey has pointed out that seven steps are involved in Jesus' command, "This do . . ." (Luke 22:19; 1 Corinthians 11:24, 25). He outlines the steps as

follows: "Take bread. Give thanks over the loaf for God's gra-
ciousness. Break the bread. Give the bread to the people of Christ.
Take the cup. Again, give thanks to God. Then give the cup to the
congregation."[64] Some Christian groups follow the seven steps in
this exact order. Others have combined the steps into what they
call "the fourfold action,"[65] or revised the order somewhat while
still retaining what they refer to as "the sacramental action"—
consecration, distribution, and reception.[66]

Another debate is whether Judas was present and participated when Jesus broke and distributed the bread and passed the
cup for His disciples to drink. Jesus announced at some time during this evening that one of the disciples would betray Him
(Matthew 26:21; Mark 14:18). Luke mentions this announcement
as occurring after the institution of the Lord's Supper (Luke
22:21, 22). Many scholars believe the verses are misplaced here.
None of the Synoptic writers tells of the departure of Judas from
the Upper Room. John wrote that Judas left immediately after
receiving a morsel from Jesus (John 13:21–30). Mark seemed to
imply that this happened before the institution of the Lord's Supper (Mark 14:18–21). Due to complexities in the biblical text, the
question of Judas's reception of the Lord's Supper will remain a
debated question.[67]

It is interesting to note that Matthew, Mark, and Paul all say
that Jesus first gave the bread to His disciples, and then the cup.
Luke reverses the order and says that He first gave the cup, and
then the bread. The Lukan order of first the wine and then the
bread was followed in at least a part of the early church, as the
second-century *Didache* confirms.[68] Southern Baptist professor
Malcolm O. Tolbert writes that in common practice that individual cups were used in the celebration of the Passover, and that in
the Last Supper all the disciples drank from the cup of Jesus. St.
Luke says, "And He took the cup, and gave thanks, and said, 'Take
this, and divide it among yourselves'" (Luke 22:17). Tolbert states
that the disciples drinking from Jesus' cup emphasizes the unity

of their fellowship in Him and with one another. Tolbert also says that it reminds the disciples that they are all to drink of the same cup of which Jesus drank, that is, to share in His sufferings.[69] About a week earlier Jesus had asked the disciples, "Can ye drink of the cup that I drink of? . . . And they said unto Him, We can. And Jesus said unto them, Ye shall indeed drink of the cup that I drink of . . . " (Mark 10:38, 39).

However, there are those who do not believe that Jesus ate the Passover meal with His disciples. Some say this because they hold that the meal in the Upper Room was not the real Passover meal,[70] as touched on earlier in this chapter. Others say that while this was indeed the Passover meal, Jesus abstained from partaking. In his book *The Eucharistic Words of Jesus*, Joachim Jeremias states that the instruction given by Jesus to the disciples, "Take this, and divide it among yourselves" (Luke 22:17), should probably indicate that Jesus did not drink of the cup. Jeremias is of the opinion that Jesus probably fasted completely, neither eating of the Passover lamb, nor drinking of the wine. He thinks it highly unlikely that Jesus would have eaten bread which He spoke of as His body, or that He would have drunk the wine that He referred to as His blood.[71] The authors of the *Orthodox Study Bible*, along with others, are of a different opinion. In regard to the question of whether Jesus drank of the wine, they say, "Jesus Himself drinks of the cup, His own blood, in order to lead the disciples into participation in the heavenly mysteries."[72]

Commenting on the verse where Jesus says, "With desire I have desired to eat this passover with you before I suffer" (Luke 22:15), Kretzmann identifies Jesus as the true Passover Lamb and says that now He was about to be "brought to the slaughter." Thereby He would gain the joys of eternal life for sinners. The reason Jesus had intense longing to eat the Passover with His disciples was because it would introduce His suffering and death. Kretzmann writes, "As the Savior of sinners He was consumed with eagerness to earn salvation for all sinners."[73] At a very early date the Lord's Supper completely replaced the Passover in the Christian church.[74]

The outward features of the Lord's Supper have changed over the centuries. When Jesus celebrated the first Lord's Supper with His disciples, it was in the upper chamber of a private house. It was at night, with the participants reclining around a table. Women were excluded, and only the "ordained apostles" of Jesus were admitted.[75] As far as externals are concerned, there are no churches in Christendom that observe the Lord's Supper in exactly the same manner as did Jesus with His disciples "the same night in which He was betrayed" (1 Corinthians 11:23). However, to this day Christian churches throughout the world continue reverently to observe this solemn rite, each in their own way, and according to their own confession. The words of Lutheran professor Robert W. Jenson regarding the Lord's Supper are interesting and inclusive. He states, "It is exactly as old as the gospel itself, and its centrality in the church's life is uninterrupted."[76]

NOTES

1. Sources listing these names include M. J. Bosma, *Exposition of Reformed Doctrine: A Popular Explanation of the Most Essential Teachings of the Reformed Churches*, 5th ed. (Grand Rapids: Zondervan, 1927), 274; Heinrich Heppe, *Reformed Dogmatics Set Out and Illustrated from the Sources*, rev. ed. trans. G. T. Thomson (London: George Allen & Unwin Ltd., 1950), 628; Robert W. Jenson, *Visible Words: The Interpretation and Practice of Christian Sacraments* (Philadelphia: Fortress, 1978), 62; David L. Kimbrough, *Taking Up Serpents: Snake Handlers of Eastern Kentucky* (Chapel Hill, N.C.: University of North Carolina Press, 1995), 78; Edward W. A. Koehler, *A Short Exposition of Dr. Martin Luther's Small Catechism, edited by the Evangelical Lutheran Synod of Missouri, Ohio, and other States, with Additional Notes for Students, Teachers, and Pastors* (River Forest, Ill.: Koehler, 1946), 291; Eugene LaVerdiere, *The Eucharist in the New Testament and the Early Church* (Collegeville, Minn.: Liturgical Press, 1996), l; J. Gordon Melton, ed., *American Religious Creeds* (New York: Triumph Books, 1991), 2:265; Madeline S. Miller and J. Lane Miller, *Harper's Bible Dictionary* (New York: Harper, 1952), 401; Francis Pieper, *Christian Dogmatics* (St. Louis: Concordia, 1953), 3:292; Max Thurian, ed., *Churches Respond to BEM: Official Responses to the "Baptism, Eucharist and Ministry" Text* (Geneva: World Council of Churches, 1986–88), 3:7, 28; 4:31.

2. Miller and Miller, *Harper's*, 400.

3. Adam Fahling, *The Life of Christ* (St. Louis: Concordia, 1936), 600.

4. Robert Kolb and Timothy J. Wengert, eds., *The Book of Concord: The Confessions of the Evangelical Lutheran Church* (Minneapolis: Fortress, 2000), 362.

5. John D. Davis, *The Westminster Dictionary of the Bible*, rev. Henry Snyder Gehman (Philadelphia: Westminster Press, 1944), 363; F. N. Peloubet, ed., assisted by Alice D. Adams, Peloubet's Bible Dictionary (Philadelphia: John C. Winston, 1947), 369.

6. F. Wilbur Gingrich, *Shorter Lexicon of the Greek New Testament* (Chicago: University of Chicago Press, 1965), 29.

7. R. C. H. Lenski, *The Interpretation of St. Matthew's Gospel* (Columbus, Ohio: Wartburg Press, 1943), 1023, 1024.

8. *Theology and Practice of the Lord's Supper* (Commission on Theology and Church Relations, The Lutheran Church—Missouri Synod, 1983).

9. Joachim Jeremias, *The Eucharistic Words of Jesus*, trans. Norman Perrin (London: SCM, 1966), 21.

10. Clifton J. Allen et al, ed., *The Broadman Bible Commentary* (Nashville: Broadman, 1969–1972), 8:234; Fahling, *Life*, 602; *Theology and Practice*, 16.

11. Davis, *Westminster*, 363; R. C. H. Lenski, *The Interpretation of St. Luke's Gospel* (Columbus, Ohio: Wartburg Press, 1946), 1051; Lenski, *Matthew*, 1028; Pieper, *Dogmatics*, 3:354; Johann M. Reu, *Two Treatises on the Means of Grace* (n. d.; reprint, Minneapolis: Augsburg, 1952), 89.

12. John R. Rice, *The King of the Jews: A Verse-by-Verse Commentary on the Gospel According to Matthew* (Murfreesboro, Tenn.: Sword of the Lord Publishers, 1955), 433, 434, 436; *Seventh-Day Adventists Believe: A Biblical Exposition of 27 Doctrines* (Washington, D.C.: Ministerial Association, General Conference of Seventh-day Adventists, 1988), 200.

13. *Seventh-Day Adventists Believe*, 204.

14. R. C. H. Lenski, *The Interpretation of St. Mark's Gospel* (Columbus, Ohio: Wartburg Press, 1946), 2.

15. Jeremias, *Eucharistic Words*, 53.

16. Paul E. Kretzmann, *Popular Commentary of the Bible, New Testament* (St. Louis: Concordia, 1921–1922), 1:147.

17. Norman Perrin, *The New Testament, an Introduction; Proclamation and Paronesis, Myth and History* (New York: Harcourt Brace Jovanovich, Inc., 1974), 243.

18. John R. Rice, *The Son of Man, A Verse-by-Verse Commentary on the Gospel According to Luke* (Murfreesboro, Tenn.: Sword of the Lord Publishers, 1971), 506.

19. Peter M. Glock, "Early Developments of the Eucharist" (Wahpeton, N.Dak. Pastoral Conference, 1994), 2, 3; Jeremias, *Eucharistic Words*, 26–29.

20. Jeremias, *Eucharistic Words*, 31, 32.

21. Charles J. Evanson, "New Directions," *Logia* 4, no. 1 (1995): 4; Jeremias, *Eucharistic Words*, 29, 31.

22. Jeremias, *Eucharistic Words*, 80.

23. R. C. H. Lenski, *The Interpretation of St. John's Gospel* (Columbus, Ohio: Lutheran Book Concern, 1942), 1213, 121.

24. Charles Pfeiffer et al, ed., *Wycliffe Bible Encyclopedia* (Chicago: Moody Press, 1975), 2:1053.

25. Donald Guthrie, *New Testament Introduction* (Downers Grove: InterVarsity, 1990), 313.

26. Guthrie, *New Testament*, 313; Harold F. Hunter, *The Passover: Old Truths for Today's World* (Jacksonville, Fla.: Harold Hunter, 1984), 30.

27. Guthrie, *New Testament*, 312.

28. Guthrie, *New Testament*, 313.

29. Guthrie, *New Testament*, 313.

30. Fahling, *Life*, 3, 591, 592; Kretzmann, *Popular Commentary*, 1:145, 384; Pfeiffer, *Wycliffe*, 2:1051, 1052.

31. Fahling, *Life*, 591, 592; Lenski, *Luke*, 1033, 1036; Lenski, *Matthew*, 1014.

32. Peloubet, *Dictionary*, 368.

33. Kretzmann, *Popular Commentary*, 1:384.

34. Fahling, *Life*, 592.

35. Kretzmann, *Popular Commentary*, 1:145.

36. Kretzmann, *Popular Commentary*, l:241; Miller and Miller, *Harper's*, 528.

37. Pfeiffer, *Wycliffe*, 2:1284.

38. Kretzmann, *Popular Commentary*, 1:242.

39. Miller and Miller, *Harper's*, 528.

40. Davis, *Westminster*, 4533; Lenski, *Luke*, 1051; Lenski, *Matthew*, 1028.

41. Miller and Miller, *Harper's*, 528.

42. Alfred Edersheim, *The Life and Times of Jesus the Messiah* (Grand Rapids: Eerdmans, 1950), 2:511; Peloubet, *Dictionary*, 369; Gaylin Schmeling, "The Theology of the Lord's Supper," *Lutheran Synod Quarterly* 28, no. 4 (1988): 6.

43. Kretzmann, *Popular Commentary*, 1:146.

44. Kretzmann, *Popular Commentary*, 1:146.

45. Peloubet, *Dictionary*, 369.

46. Kolb-Wengert, *Concord*, 362

47. Kolb-Wengert, *Concord*, 362.

48. Allen, *Broadman*, 9:167.

49. Daniel B. Clendenin, ed., *Eastern Orthodox Theology: A Contemporary Reader* (Grand Rapids: Baker, 1995), 27; Bennet Kelley, *Saint Joseph Baltimore Catechism: The Truths of Our Catholic Faith Clearly Explained and Illustrated*, rev. ed. (New York: Catholic Book Publishing Co., 1969), 164; Pieper, *Dogmatics*, 3:294, 295.

50. Albert Collver, "Real Presence: An Overview and History of the Term," *Concordia Journal* 28, no. 2 (2002): 144.

51. Kolb-Wengert, Concord, 44.

52. Koehler, *Short Exposition*, 293, 300; Olaus Swebellus, *Dr. Martin Luther's Catechism with Explanation*, trans. Andrew and Mary Mickelsen (1852; reprint, Apostolic Lutheran Church of America, 1966), 114–116.

53. Collver, "Real Presence," 151; Virgilius Ferm, *The Crisis in American Lutheran Theology: A Study of the Issue between American Lutheranism and Old*

Lutheranism (1927; reprint, St. Louis: Concordia, 1987), 67–68.

54. James Montgomery Boice, *Foundations of the Christian Faith: A Comprehensive and Readable Theology* (Downers Grove: InterVarsity, 1986), 604; Charles Hodge, *Systematic Theology* (Grand Rapids: Eerdmans, 1997), 3:650.

55. Ronald Q. Leavell, *Studies in Matthew: The King and the Kingdom* (Nashville: Convention Press, 1962), 130; Miller and Miller, *Harper's*, 401; Robert G. Witty, *Signs of the Second Coming* (Nashville: Broadman, 1969), 74.

56. *Theology and Practice*, 6.

57. Philippe Larere, *The Lord's Supper: Toward an Ecumenical Understanding of the Eucharist*, trans. Patrick Madigan (Collegeville, Minn.: The Liturgical Press, 1993), 9; Carl A. Volz, *Faith and Practice in the Early Church: Foundations for Contemporary Theology* (Minneapolis: Augsburg, 1983), 110.

58. Hunter, *Passover*, 31.

59. Hunter, *Passover*, 32–33.

60. Peloubet, *Dictionary*, 369.

61. Peloubet, *Dictionary*, 369.

62. Pieper, *Dogmatics*, 3:393.

63. Herbert F. Juneau, conversation with author, Eau Claire, Wis., n.d.

64. Laurence Hull Stookey, *Eucharist: Christ's Feast with the Church* (Nashville: Abingdon, 1993), 29.

65. Stookey, *Eucharist*, 29.

66. C. F. W. Walther, *Walther's Pastorale, that is, American Lutheran Pastoral Theology*, trans. and abridged by John M. Drickhamer (1906; New Haven, Mo.: Lutheran News, Inc., 1995), 144.

67. Edersheim, *Life and Times*, 2:55; Fahling, *Life*, 597, 598; Lenski, *Matthew*, 1022; *The Orthodox Study Bible: New Testament and Psalms* (Nashville: Nelson, 1993), 72; Giovanni Papini, *Life of Christ*, trans. Dorothy Canfield Fischer (New York: Harcourt, 1923), 301; Ewald M. Plass, *What Luther Says: An Anthology* (St. Louis: Concordia, 1959), 2:810; Rice, *Luke*, 506; Philip Schaff, *The Creeds of Christendom with a History and Critical Notes*, rev. by David F. Schaff (Grand Rapids, Mich.: Baker, 1966), 3:431; Philip Schaff, *History of the Christian Church* (n.p.; Charles Scribner's Sons, 1958–1960), 3:499; Walther, *Pastorale*, 148.

68. Allen, *Broadman*, 8:384.

69. Allen, *Broadman*, 9:167.

70. Lenski, *John*, 1213, 1214; John R. Rice, T*he Son of God: A Verse-by-Verse Commentary on the Gospel According to John* (Murfreesboro, Tenn.: Sword of the Lord Publishers, 1971), 259, 260, 353.

71. Jeremias, *Eucharistic Words*, 208, 209, 212.

72. *Orthodox Study Bible*, 72.

73. Kretzmann, *Popular Commentary*, 1:384.

74. Pfeiffer, *Wycliffe*, 2:1284.

75. Peloubet, *Dictionary*, 370.

76. Jenson, *Visible Words*, 62.

STUDY QUESTIONS

1. Why do we use the term "Lord's Supper" and in what Bible verse do we see it used?

2. In what Bible passages do we find the four accounts in which Jesus institutes and mandates the Lord's Supper?

3. What words are common to and essential to these four accounts? What do we call these essential words?

4. On what evidence from which Gospels do we find that Jesus mandated and instituted the Lord's Supper with His disciples on the day that is now commemorated as Holy Thursday or Maundy Thursday?

5. Who calls the Lord's Supper a "Passover," thus revealing it as the fulfillment of the ancient feast and signaling the great sacrifice of the Lamb for the salvation of all? Where in the Gospels is this found?

6. True or false: The term "real presence" used in describing the presence of the body and blood of Christ in the Lord's Supper was first used by the Pope in 1264. It has been subsequently used by various groups to mean different things.

7. Who among Lutherans appears to have used the term "real presence" first, those in Europe or those in the United States?

8. Summarize the Roman Catholic, Lutheran, Calvinist, and Zwinglian teachings about the Lord's body and blood in the Supper.

9. Why must we seek to learn the appropriate, contextual meanings of terms like real, symbol, figure, substance, sign, spiritual, and the like? How can false understandings of these terms result in a misunderstanding of the Bible?

10. Do changes in the external aspects of the Lord's Supper (place of celebration, time of day, use of altar versus table, and so forth) change the essential parts of the Lord's Supper? What does have such a potential for change?

2 | THE BREAD OF LIFE IN THE GOSPEL ACCORDING TO JOHN

The apostle John, author of the fourth Gospel in the New Testament, was present and participated in the Last Supper with Jesus and the disciples in the Upper Room in Jerusalem. While John's Gospel gives more information concerning events that evening than the other three evangelists combined, he makes no mention at all of the institution and first celebration of the Lord's Supper. Scholars have attempted to account for this omission with various theories. German scholar Rudolph Bultmann contended that John was either anti-sacramental or uninterested in the sacraments and did not consider them of primary importance in the life of the church.[1] Other scholars believe that John was silent because he desired to conceal knowledge of this sacred rite and the words and actions connected with it from the uninitiated.[2] Others think that John may have regarded the narrative too sacred to be written down.[3] Still others claim that John did not associate the institution of the Lord's Supper with the meal in the Upper Room but with the feeding of the five thousand recorded in chapter six of his Gospel.[4] This writer believes that John simply saw no need to mention the celebration of the Supper in the Upper Room because others had already given a full account in their writings. By the time John wrote his Gospel, four reports of the institution of the first Lord's Supper (Matthew, Mark, Luke, and 1 Corinthians) were already being circulated in the churches.[5]

Portions of John's Gospel are considered by some to be related to the Lord's Supper. The first of these is the account of Jesus turning water into wine during the wedding at Cana in Galilee (John 2:1–11). Since the time of the early church fathers, some have considered this miracle to be an allusion to the Lord's Supper.[6] Eastern Orthodox Christians have referred to this event as "an anticipation" of what takes place in the Supper.[7] Roman Catholic authors have called it "a possible reference to the Lord's Supper"[8] and an "indirect or secondary reference to the Eucharist."[9] British Protestant writer A. J. B. Higgins says Jesus turning water into wine is "a sign pointing forward to the Lord's Supper." He states, "The wine represents the eucharistic wine, the blood of Christ which cleanses from sin, and replaces the purificatory water and washings of Judaism."[10]

John's sixth chapter is sometimes viewed as the center of his teaching regarding the Lord's Supper. Thus Roman Catholic author Johannes H. Emminghaus has asserted, "John's teaching on the Eucharist . . . is . . . found . . . in his sixth chapter.[11] Other Catholic scholars agree.[12] For example, professor Eugene LaVerdiere believes that, "John's chapter 6 . . . represents the highest point in the Eucharistic theology of the New Testament."[13] Two Reformation era Protestant figures, Casper Schwenkfeld (1489/90–1561) and Valentin Krautwald, held that the words of institution spoken by Jesus in the Upper Room must be explained in light of the sixth chapter of John's Gospel.[14] Both Ulrich Zwingli and John Calvin based much of their teaching about the Lord's Supper on material found in this chapter.[15] Zwingli did not base his doctrine of the Lord's Supper on the words of institution but on the words "The flesh profiteth nothing" (6:63).[16] Calvin said that the Lord's Supper is "a spiritual feast, at which Christ attests that he is the living bread, Jn. 6, on which our souls feed unto true and blessed immortality."[17]

In his treatise *The Babylonian Captivity of the Church*, Martin Luther strongly disagrees with those who find a basis for or a reference to the Lord's Supper in John chapter six. He says, "John 6 must be set aside entirely, since not a single syllable of it refers to the Lord's Supper."[18] Lutheran scholar J. Michael Reu (1869–1943) echoes what Luther said. His statement is "today it should no longer be necessary to prove that John 6 cannot be used as the basis for a Biblical doctrine of the Lord's Supper."[19]

John tells in the first 14 verses of chapter six about Jesus feeding five thousand people by dividing and multiplying a little boy's lunch of five barley loaves and two small fish. The denominational affiliations of individuals who consider this event to be related to the Lord's Supper are varied. They range from Orthodox, to Roman Catholic, to Lutheran, to Protestant.[20] LaVerdiere, who espouses this view, makes a clear and emphatic statement when he says, "The story of Jesus giving bread to eat to a crowd of some five thousand is the most Eucharistic in the whole gospel."[21] He further states that this "breaking of bread . . . transforms all the meals in Jesus' gospel story and relates them to the Eucharist."[22]

As John relates the story of Jesus feeding the multitude he appears to insert a side thought into the narrative. In verse four he states, "And the Passover, a feast of the Jews was nigh." Some think that the mention of the proximity of the Passover indicates that John regarded the feeding of the five thousand as Eucharistic.[23] They observe the fact that the Passover was also the setting of the Last Supper and the death of Jesus.[24] Some suggest that by this remark John intended to convey the thought that Jesus intended to supplant the Jewish Paschal feast with a better Bread of Life feast, which would typify the Lord's Supper.[25] Lenski states that John mentioned the impending Passover for a reason that had nothing to do with the Lord's Supper.[26]

Church of England professor H. R. Reynolds suggests another Passover-Lord's Supper link in the story of the feeding of the five thousand in connection with verse eleven where John relates that "Jesus then took the loaves; and having given thanks he distributed to them who were set down." Regarding the first part of the verse, "Jesus then took the loaves; and having given thanks . . . ," Reynolds remarks, "The Eucharistial expression corresponds with the function of the head of a household at the Paschal feast."[27] He contends that this is a hint of relation with the Passover.[28] Commenting on the latter part of verse eleven, ". . . he distributed to them who were set down," Reynolds states that this has been thought "to show that the narrative is a glorification of the Eucharistial meal, at which Jesus gave to his disciples the bread which he brake."[29]

Higgins remarks, "The most important source for Johannine Eucharistic doctrine is the discourse on the bread of life in the sixth chapter."[30] Likewise, Stookey states, "Of greatest importance is the long discourse on the bread of life."[31] The Bread of Life discourse, or sermon, which Jesus delivered in the synagogue at Capernaeum, as reported by John, reads, in part:

> I am the bread of life: he that cometh to Me shall never hunger: and he that believeth in Me shall never thirst . . . Verily, verily, I say unto you. He that believeth in Me hath everlasting life. I am that bread of life . . . This is the bread which cometh down from heaven, that a man may eat thereof and not die. I am the living bread which came down from heaven: if any man eat of this bread, he shall live forever: and the bread that I will give is flesh, which

I will give for the life of the world (John 6:35, 47–48, 50–51).

Verily, verily, I say unto you, Except ye eat the flesh of the Son of man, and drink His blood, ye have no life in you. Whoso eateth My flesh, and drinketh My blood, hath eternal life; and I will raise him up on the last day. For My flesh is meat indeed, and My blood is drink indeed. He that eateth My flesh, and drinketh My blood, dwelleth in Me, and I in him. As the living Father hath sent Me, and I live by the Father: so he that eateth Me, even he shall live by Me. This is the bread which came down from heaven not as your fathers did eat manna, and are dead: he that eateth of this bread shall live forever (John 6:53–58).

There is a broad range of opinion among Christians as to whether or not Jesus is speaking of the Lord's Supper in this discourse. Some believe that he is.[32] Others do not.[33] However, some of the latter, considering the entire New Testament context, do make applications to the Lord's Supper from these words of Jesus, especially in sermons and devotional writings.[34]

Roman Catholic author Philippe Larere raises the question as to what type of food is being spoken of in the Bread of Life discourse. He asks, "Is this the bread of the Eucharist, or is it rather the bread of the Word?"[35] Citing verses 35, 43, and 63 Larere states, "That this food is that of the Word leading to faith is clearly affirmed three times."[36] He also says, "That this food is that of the Eucharist seems clearly stated in verses 48 to 59."[37] Lutheran scholar Hermann Sasse also divides the Bread of Life discourse into two parts. He says that the first part of the discourse (verses 35–51a) is the Scriptural foundation for the doctrine of the spiritual eating of Christ in faith. But Sasse warns against reading this meaning into the second part of the discourse (verses 51b–58). He says that here the heavenly bread is no longer Christ's person but His flesh. The transition is abrupt: from spiritual eating of

Christ by faith to sacramental eating and drinking of His flesh and blood.[38] Catholic commentator Jerome Kodell reports that due to this sudden change, some feel that verses 51b–58 were either inserted by John, or by someone in the Johannine school, and were meant "to carry the point about the bread of life through to its eucharistic conclusion."[39] Others contend that a redactor added verses 51b–58.[40]

Sasse remarks that "here two lines of thought about the bread of life stand next to each other that at first seem to contradict each other."[41] He explains that both are true of Jesus. He is the bread from heaven. His flesh is the bread of heaven. Eating Him as the true bread of heaven occurs in faith. And eating Jesus' flesh and drinking His blood happens in the Lord's Supper. Sasse says, "Both of these truths belong together in such a way that one cannot reduce one of them to the other."[42] The authors of the *Orthodox Study Bible* state in reference to verses 51–59, "The eucharistic significance of this passage is indisputable."[43] They go on to say that by Jesus' own declaration He is the living bread that brings us to life. His intention is "to reveal the eucharistic feast."[44] Their point of reference for this statement is verse 53, "Most assuredly, I say to you, unless you eat the flesh of the Son of Man and drink His blood, you have no life in you." Then the authors declare, "These words refer directly to the Eucharist, the mystery of Christ in our life. . . . To receive everlasting life, we must partake of His Eucharistic *flesh* and *blood*."[45]

Some authors believe they find glimpses of the words of institution of the Lord's Supper in verse 51, "The bread that I will give is My flesh." Some note the closeness of these words to those in Luke 22:19, "This is My body which is given for you."[46] Others compare the words in verse 51 with Paul's rendering of the words of institution in 1 Corinthians 11:24, "This is My body which is broken for you."[47] Jeremias remarks, "John . . . although he does not mention the institution of the Lord's Supper introduces the word of interpretation to the bread in the context of a discourse by Jesus."[48] In verses 54, 56, and 57 Jesus speaks of eating His flesh. He says, "Whoso eateth My flesh" (verse 54), "he that eateth My flesh" (verse 56), and "eateth Me" (verse 57). The ordinary Greek word for "eat" is *esthein*. Rather than using *esthein* John uses the word *trogein,* which Kodell says may have the "vulgar connotation of 'gnaw.'"[49] Sasse states that this word is "extremely harsh sounding."[50] Additionally, John speaks of "flesh," *sarx* in Greek, rather than "body," which is *soma* in Greek. Elsewhere in the New Testament, Jesus, the other evangelists, and Paul all use the word *soma.* The words used here by John occur nowhere else in the New Testament with reference to the Lord's Supper. This has caused some to conclude that John could not here be speaking of the Lord's Supper.[51] Both Kodell and Sasse suggest that a reason why John used the word for "flesh" instead of the word for "body" is because his principal antagonists were the Gnostics, who were emerging on the Christian scene by the time he wrote. They regarded Jesus Christ as a divine being who had a heavenly body, but no body of flesh. John needed to specify so the Gnostics could not exploit what he wrote to promote their heresy.[52]

Those who hold that in the John 6 discourse Jesus was not speaking of the Lord's Supper say that instead it is a spiritual eating and drinking to which Jesus invites. An unnamed Wisconsin Synod Lutheran author comments, "To 'eat and drink' his 'flesh and blood' is to believe in the crucified Christ with all of one's being. It is a union of the most intimate kind."[53] Another Lutheran, F. R. Zucker, states, "The Bible does speak of a spiritual eating and drinking in John 6:53–56. That is faith."[54]

Those who believe that Jesus did not have the Lord's Supper in mind when He spoke the words of the discourse advance a number of arguments. They feel that it is unlikely that Jesus would command the sacramental partaking of His body and blood before He had instituted the Lord's Supper.[55] Martin Luther asked, "Why should Christ here have in mind that Sacrament when it was not yet instituted?"[56] Charles Haddon Spurgeon

(1834–1892), an English Baptist preacher, states, "Our Lord Jesus did not in this passage allude to the Lord's Supper . . . there was no Lord's Supper at the time to allude to."[57] In verse 53 Jesus said, "Except ye eat the flesh of the Son of man, and drink his blood, ye have no life in you." Of this verse Zucker writes, "This passage is wrongly applied to the Lord's Supper . . . since it speaks of an eating and drinking without which no one can have eternal life.[58]

Jesus said in verse 54, "Whoso eateth my flesh and drinketh my blood, hath eternal life." He also makes the promise of eternal life in such passages as Mark 16:16 and John 3:16. The unnamed Wisconsin Synod author states of verse 54 that the Bible contains no guarantee of eternal life to anyone who partakes of the body and blood of Jesus in the Lord's Supper. He refers to 1 Corinthians 11:29 where the statement is made that a person who receives the Sacrament unworthily eats and drinks damnation on himself.[59]

Presbyterian dogmatician Charles Hodge (1797–1878) states in his *Systematic Theology* that the leading Reformed theologians hold that what is said in John 6 of eating the flesh and drinking the blood of Jesus has to do with "the appropriation of his sacrificial death by the act of believing."[60] He writes that in John 6 Jesus interchanged the words "eating" and "believing."[61] Hodge says, "It is by believing that we eat his flesh and drink his blood."[62] He quotes John Calvin who wrote, "There is no eating but by faith, and it is impossible to imagine any other."[63] Hodge says that his position is consistent with that of all the leading Reformed confessional writings.[64] For example, it is stated in the *Zurich Confession*, "Eating is believing, and believing is eating."[65] The *Helvetic Confession* says that this eating takes place often and whenever one believes in Christ.[66] Baptist evangelist John R. Rice is forthright in stating his conviction in this matter. He writes that it is a "sinful perversion of the Gospel" when "Rome teaches that this refers to the mass." Instead, Rice says, "To eat the flesh and drink the blood of Jesus is simply to trust in him for salvation."[67]

In the Upper Room, on the night when He instituted the Lord's Supper, Jesus washed the feet of His disciples (John 13:4, 5). Thinking is divided as to the relationship the foot washing may or may not have to the Lord's Supper. Some believe that the foot washing represents the Lord's Supper. Bultmann considers this idea to be "grotesque." He holds that there is no sacramental reference to the Lord's Supper in the foot washing.[68] Yet foot washing has been seen by some as an allegory of the Lord's Supper. For instance, Higgins remarks, "The injunction that the disciples follow his example in washing one another's feet . . . corresponds . . . to the command to repeat the Eucharist."[69] It has also been thought of as "a symbolic act" which John used to comment homiletically on Jesus' Last Supper and the Eucharist.[70] Pastors often use the story of Jesus washing His disiples' feet in relation to the Lord's Supper. Thus, in a sermon based on John 13:1–15 Frederick G. Kuegele, a Lutheran country preacher, spoke of the foot washing as an occurrence that took place in connection with the Lord's Supper and which "in a very simple manner, teaches us what to do and how to conduct ourselves before, during and after communion."[71]

Some Pentecostals,[72] Baptist,[73] and Anabaptist[74] sub-groups regularly include foot washing as an integral part of their Lord's Supper services. Among some groups participation in the foot washing is a prerequisite for partaking of the Lord's Supper. One Old Regular Baptist group includes foot washing in its definition of the Lord's Supper.[75] Some Pentecostals also have tied the two so closely together that they designate both as the "Foot Washing." Independent scholar David L. Kimbrough reports of some early day Pentecostals, "The word would go through the community 'We are having a foot washing at Church tonight.' Everyone knew it was the Lord's Supper."[76]

Several items in the farewell discourse which Jesus spoke to the disciples in the Upper Room are considered by some students of Scripture to be related to the Lord's Supper. It is felt by some that the clearest of these references is in chapter 15 where Jesus says, "I am the vine" (John 15:5). Both Protestant Higgins and Catholic Kodell see a connection between these words of Jesus and the Lord's Supper.[77] This section (John 15:1–17) is thought to correspond to material found in the Bread of Life discourse in chapter 6, with the emphasis in chapter 6 being on the bread in the Lord's Supper,[78] while here in chapter 15 the emphasis is on the wine.[79] In chapter 6 Jesus said, "I am the bread of life" (verse 35). Here in chapter 15 He states, "I am the true vine" (verse 1). Another parallel is seen in the words "My Father is the husband-man" (vinedresser, RSV) (John 15:1), and the words "My Father giveth you the true bread from heaven" (John 6:32). Jesus says, "He that eateth My flesh and drinketh My blood dwelleth in Me, and I in him" (John 6:56). He also says, "Abide in Me, and I in you. As the branch cannot bear fruit of itself, except it abide in the vine; no more can ye, except ye abide in Me" (15:4). The vine was a recognized symbol of the Lord's Supper at an early date. We know this from a Eucharistic prayer in the *Didache*. There we read, "And concerning the Eucharist, hold Eucharist thus: First concerning the Cup, 'We give thanks, Our Father, for the Holy Vine of David your child, which you made known to us through Jesus your child . . . ' "[80]

In the account of the crucifixion John relates that the Jews asked Pilate that the legs of the three who had been crucified might be broken to hasten their deaths. Pilate ordered his soldiers and they broke the legs of the two malefactors. But when they came to Jesus they did not break His legs, because they saw that He was already dead. "But," says John, "one of the soldiers with a spear pierced His side, and forthwith came there out blood and water" (John 19:34). Since the days of the church fathers the blood and the water that flowed from the side of Jesus have been considered by some to have symbolic significance regarding the Lord's Supper and Baptism. Both Chrysostom (ca. 345–407) and Augustine (354–430) believed this. Chrysostom spoke of "the mysteries of baptism and of the flesh and blood." Augustine saw in the water and the blood, "the laver and the cup."[81] Fahling writes that this passage quite naturally lends itself to symbolical interpretation. The cleansing water and the redeeming blood spring forth from the riven side of Jesus. He then says, "The beautiful saying has come down from the Fathers that from the side of Jesus, as from the open door to life, have flowed forth the holy Sacraments of the Church."[82] Kodell states, "At Jesus' death, blood and water flowed from his side, symbols of baptism and Eucharist, now the channels of salvation and life in the Church."[83]

The final section of John's Gospel, thought by some to have a relationship to the Lord's Supper, is the post-resurrection account of a breakfast the risen Jesus served to seven of His disciples beside the sea of Tiberias (John 21:1–14). The disciples were on the sea fishing as the story began. When they first saw Jesus on the shore they did not know who He was. Upon landing they found that Jesus had already prepared a charcoal fire, with fish and bread lying on it. Jesus invited them to come and eat. John then reports, "Jesus then cometh, and taketh bread, and giveth them, and fish likewise" (John 21:13). LaVerdiere says that this story "comes closest to the story of Jesus' giving bread to the five thousand."[84] From his Catholic perspective he contends that the seashore breakfast relates the Lord's Supper to the apostolic church and to Peter's special role in the life of the church. Several authors see this breakfast by the seashore as a parallel to the Emmaus meal recorded in Luke (24:29–32).[85] Stookey states that "the risen One is known in the familiar act of eating with the disciples."[86] Lenski has said that the critics have made a Eucharistic meal of this breakfast that Jesus provided for the disciples. He questions the soundness of such criticism and declares this evaluation of the meal of bread and fish to be unhistorical.[87] We see from the foregoing that little unanimity exists in the church as to what material in the Gospel of John does or does not relate to the Lord's Supper.

NOTES

1. A. J. B. Higgins, *The Lord's Supper in the New Testament* (London: SCM, 1952), 74.

2. Higgins, *Lord's Supper*, 74.

3. Norman Perrin, *The New Testament, an Introduction; Proclamation and Paronesis, Myth and History* (New York: Harcourt Brace Jovanovich, Inc., 1974), 243.

4. Higgins, *Lord's Supper*, 74.

5. Henrietta C. Mears, *What the Bible Is All About*, rev. ed. (Ventura, Calif.: Regal Books, 1983), 396; Henry Clarence Thiessen, *Introduction to the New Testament* (Grand Rapids: Eerdmans, 1943), 171, 172.

6. *The Orthodox Study Bible: New Testament and Psalms* (Nashville: Nelson, 1993), 207.

7. *Orthodox Study Bible*, 215.

8. Jerome Kodell, *The Eucharist in the New Testament* (1988; reprint, Collegeville, Minn.: Liturgical Press, 1991), 120.

9. Eugene LaVerdiere, *The Eucharist in the New Testament and the Early Church* (Collegeville, Minn.: Liturgical Press, 1996), 115.

10. Higgins, *Lord's Supper*, 78, 79.

11. Johannes H. Emminghaus, *The Eucharist: Essence, Form, Celebration*, trans. Matthew J. O'Connell. (Collegeville, Minn.: Liturgical Press, 1978), 2i.

12. Joseph M. Champlin, *Special Signs of Grace: The Sacraments and Sacramentals* (Collegeville, Minn.: Liturgical Press, 1986), 51.

13. LaVerdiere, *Eucharist,* 119.

14. Johann M. Reu, *Two Treatises on the Means of Grace* (n. d.; reprint, Minneapolis: Augsburg, 1952), 75.

15. Heinrich Heppe, *Reformed Dogmatics Set Out and Illustrated from the Sources*, rev. ed. trans. G. T. Thomson (London: George Allen & Unwin Ltd., 1950), 627; Reu, *Two Treatises*, 75.

16. Francis Pieper, *Christian Dogmatics* (St. Louis: Concordia, 1953), 3:332.

17. Heppe, *Reformed Dogmatics*, 627.

18. Ewald M. Plass, *What Luther Says: An Anthology* (St. Louis: Concordia, 1959), 2:802.

19. Reu, *Two Treatises*, 75.

20. Paul A. Feider, *The Sacraments: Encountering the Risen Lord* (Notre Dame, Ind.: Ave Maria Press, 1986), 35; J. Robert Jacobson, *Besides Women & Children: A Guide for Parents & Pastors on Infant & Child Communion*, rev. ed. (Camrose, Alberta: Concord Canada, 1981), 14; Kodell, *Eucharist*, 120; LaVerdiere, *Eucharist*, 104, 115, 116, 119, 120; *Orthodox Study Bible*, 207; Laurence Hull Stookey, *Eucharist: Christ's Feast with the Church* (Nashville: Abingdon, 1993), 38.

21. LaVerdiere, *Eucharist*, 115.

22. LaVerdiere, *Eucharist*, 104.

23. Higgins, *Lord's Supper*, 79, 80.

24. Kodell, *Eucharist*, 122.

25. R. C. H. Lenski, *The Interpretation of St. John's Gospel* (Columbus, Ohio: Lutheran Book Concern, 1942), 430.

26. Lenski, *John*, 430.

27. H. D. M. Spence and Joseph S. Exell, ed., *The Pulpit Commentary* (Grand Rapids, Mich.: Eerdmans, 1950), 17:1:251.

28. Spence and Exell, *Pulpit*, 17:1:251.

29. Spence and Exell, *Pulpit*, 17:1:251.

30. Higgins, *Lord's Supper*, 75.

31. Stookey, *Eucharist*, 38.

32. Philippe Larere, *The Lord's Supper: Toward an Ecumenical Understanding of the Eucharist,* trans. Patrick Madigan (Collegeville, Minn.: The Liturgical Press, 1993), 11; *Orthodox Study Bible*, 229; Hermann Sasse, *We Confess the Sacraments*, trans. Norman Nagel (St. Louis: Concordia, 1985), 2:78, 79.

33. Charles Hodge, *Systematic Theology* (Grand Rapids: Eerdmans, 1997), 3:643; Theodore Laetsch, ed., *The Abiding Word: An Anthology of Doctrinal Essays* (St. Louis: Concordia, 1946–1960), 2:434; John R. Rice, *The Son of God: A Verse-by-Verse Commentary on the Gospel According to John* (Murfreesboro, Tenn.: Sword of the Lord Publishers, 1971), 153; Ernest H. Wendland and G. Jerome Albrecht, ed., *Sermon Studies on the Gospels (ILCW Series B)* (Milwaukee: Northwestern, 1987), 295.

34. J. Sheatsley, *Sermons on the Eisenach Gospels* (Columbus, Ohio: Lutheran Book Concern, 1915), 207.

35. Larere, *Lord's Supper*, 11.

36. Larere, *Lord's Supper*, 11.

37. Larere, *Lord's Supper*, 11.

38. Sasse, *Sacraments*, 780.

39. Kodell, *Eucharist*, 124.

40. Joachim Jeremias, *The Eucharistic Words of Jesus,* trans. Norman Perrin (London: SCM, 1966), 107; Kodell, *Eucharist*, 124.

41. Sasse, *Sacraments*, 78.

42. Sasse, *Sacraments*, 78, 79.

43. *Orthodox Study Bible*, 229.

44. *Orthodox Study Bible*, 229.

45. *Orthodox Study Bible*, 229.

46. Kodell, *Eucharist*, 125.

47. Jeremias, *Eucharistic Words*, 108.

48. Jeremias, *Eucharistic Words*, 108.

49. Kodell, *Eucharist*, 1250

50. Sasse, *Sacraments*, 79.

51. Wendland, *Sermon Studies*, 295.

52. Kodell, *Eucharist*, 125; Sasse, *Sacraments*, 79.

53. Wendland, *Sermon Studies*, 295.

54. Laetsch, *Abiding Word*, 2:434.

55. *Augsburg Sermons: Gospel Series B* (Minneapolis: Augsburg, 1975), 218; Lenski, *John*, 502; Pieper, *Dogmatics*, 3:330; Wendland, *Sermon Studies*, 295.

56. Wendland, *Sermon Studies*, 295.

57. C. H. Spurgeon, *The Metropolitan Tabernacle Pulpit* (London: Passmore & Alabaster, 1908), 2:205.

58. Laetsch, *Abiding Word*, 2:434.

59. Wendland, *Sermon Studies*, 295.

60. Hodge, *Systematic*, 3:643.

61. Hodge, *Systematic*, 3:668.

62. Hodge, *Systematic*, 3:643.

63. Hodge, *Systematic*, 3:644.

64. Hodge, *Systematic*, 3:643.

65. Hodge, *Systematic*, 3:643.

66. Hodge, *Systematic*, 3:643.

67. Rice, *John*, 153.

68. Higgins, *Lord's Supper*, 85.

69. Higgins, *Lord's Supper*, 84, 85.

70. LaVerdiere, *Eucharist*, 116.

71. Frederick Kuegele, *Country Sermons: Sermons on the Gospels for the Church Year* (Crimora, V.I.: Augusta, 1908), 4:267.

72. Dennis Covington, *Salvation on Sand Mountain: Snake Handling and Redemption in Southern Appalachia* (Reading, Mass.: Addison-Wesley, 1995), 115–121; Paul F. Gillespie, ed., *Foxfire 7* (Garden City, N.Y.: Anchor Press/Doubleday, 1982), 14, 66, 97, 353; David L. Kimbrough, *Taking up Serpents: Snake Handlers of Eastern Kentucky* (Chapel Hill, N.C.: University of North Carolina Press, 1995), 114.

73. Howard Dorgan, *Giving Glory to God in Appalachia: Worship Practices of Six Baptist Subdenominations* (Knoxville: University of Tennessee Press, 1987), 126–128, 133–135, 137–139, 142–146; Gillespie, *Foxfire*, 14, 14, 66, 97, 353.

74. Stephen Scott, *The Amish Wedding and Other Special Occasions of the Old Order Communities* (Intercourse, Pa.: Good Books, 1988), 58, 59, 73–75.

75. Dorgan, *Appalachia*, 114.

76. Kimbrough, *Taking up Serpents*, 78.

77. Higgins, *Lord's Supper*, 85; Kodell, *Eucharist*, 126.

78. Higgins, *Lord's Supper*, 86; Kodell, *Eucharist*, 126.

79. Higgins, *Lord's Supper*, 85; Kodell, *Eucharist*, 126.

80. Kodell, *Eucharist*, 126.

81. Spence and Exell, *Pulpit*, 17:2:433.

82. Adam Fahling, *The Life of Christ* (St. Louis: Concordia, 1936), 682.

83. Kodell, *Eucharist*, 119.

84. LaVerdiere, *Eucharist in the New Testament*, 115, 116.

85. LaVerdiere, *Eucharist in the New Testament*, 116.

86. Stookey, *Eucharist*, 38.
87. Lenski, *John*, 1414.

STUDY QUESTIONS

1. In what chapter of the Gospel According to St. John does one find the Bread of Life narrative?

2. What wedding miracle is said to anticipate the Lord's Supper?

3. Roman Catholic scholars, John Calvin, and Ulrich Zwingli all have a similar understanding regarding John 6 and the Lord's Supper. Luther and Lutherans have generally rejected this understanding. What is this belief regarding John 6?

4. How, in particular, has John 6 influenced Zwingli's theology of the Lord's Supper?

5. What reason might John have in using his Greek terms for "eat" and "flesh" in contrast with the terms used in the four instances of the Words of Institution?

6. What do Lutherans say of the spiritual eating and drinking in John 6?

7. How do Reformed theologians understand this spiritual eating and drinking?

8. What action of Jesus in the Upper Room recorded in John 13:1–15 gets interpreted as a sacramental act related to or included in the Lord's Supper by some Baptist, Pentecostal, and Anabaptist groups?

9. In addition to the Bread of life (John 15:1), Jesus also refers to Himself in language that recalls the wine in the Lord's Supper. What is that?

10. True or false: Few Christians have interpreted the reference to water and blood in John's account of the crucifixion (John 19:34) in relation to Baptism and the Lord's Supper.

11. What two New Testament meals following the resurrection of Jesus are considered by some to have significance with regard to the Lord's Supper, and where in the Scriptures may they be found?

3 | THE APOSTOLIC ERA

When Jesus instituted and celebrated the first Lord's Supper with His disciples in the Upper Room in Jerusalem He commanded them to continue observing this sacred rite. "This do in remembrance of Me" (Luke 22:19; 1 Corinthians 11:24). The disciples followed Jesus' injunction and not only celebrated the Lord's Supper among themselves but also included the growing church in this holy meal. To learn of the early Christian church's understanding of the Lord's Supper and to gain insight into how they practiced the Sacrament, we look to the Acts of the Apostles, written by St. Luke, and the First Epistle to the Corinthians, penned by St. Paul. Brief sections of the Gospels according to St. Luke and St. Matthew will also be considered.

The first mention of the Lord's Supper in the book of Acts is the passage "And they continued steadfastly in the apostles' doctrine and fellowship, and in breaking of bread and in prayers"

(2:42). The words in this passage that pertain to the Lord's Supper are "breaking of bread" which is what the Lord's Supper is referred to in the book of Acts. In denoting the Lord's Supper as "breaking of bread" the church adopted a terminology that was used contemporaneously among the Jews in at least two different ways.[1] In common daily household usage it might simply mean the action of breaking or "tearing"[2] the bread as the means of dividing for distribution to the eaters.[3] The rite by which a meal was opened was also referred to as "breaking of bread."[4] In Judaism "breaking of bread" never referred to a whole meal.[5] The shift in meaning occurred when the early Christians chose to call the Lord's Supper "breaking of bread."

Luke first mentions "breaking of bread" as he reports the events in the Upper Room and says of Jesus, "And He took bread, and gave thanks, and brake it, and gave it unto them" (Luke 22:19). He next speaks of Jesus breaking bread with the Emmaus disciples on the afternoon and early evening of the day of His resurrection (Luke 24:13–35). The disciples did not recognize Jesus as He walked with them and expounded the Scriptures to them. When they came to Emmaus they invited Jesus, saying, "Abide with us: for it is toward evening, and the day is far spent" (Luke 24:29). As they were at the supper table, Luke says, "He took bread, and blessed it, and brake and gave it to them" (Luke 24:30). The description of Jesus' action in the verse is virtually identical to what He said and did at the institution of the Lord's Supper.[6] As soon as Jesus had broken the bread the disciples recognized Him and He vanished out of their sight. The disciples' reaction is recorded in verse 35, "And they told how He was known of them in breaking of bread." Because of the similarity between the action of Jesus in the Upper Room and what occurred in the dwelling at Emmaus, Anglican scholar H. D. M. Spence writes, "It resembles too closely the great sacramental act in the upper room, when Jesus was alone with his apostles for us to mistake its sacramental character."[7]

Many New Testament scholars over the centuries have regarded the breaking of bread at Emmaus as a celebration of the Lord's Supper.[8] Chrysostom in the Eastern church and Augustine in the Western church so believed, as did Theophylact, a Bulgarian metropolitan in the late eleventh century. Theodore Beza, successor to John Calvin, was of the same opinion.[9] Kodell concurs with these earlier individuals, making the following statement: "At Emmaus, Jesus performs the ritual that is recognized as his signature and then, when he is recognized disappears. From now on, the Lord will be present in the breaking of bread, but he will no longer be visible."[10] Stookey speaks of "the Eucharist . . . the Emmaus meal of the risen Christ made known to us in the breaking of bread."[11] An Orthodox author comments that in the meal at Emmaus, the action of Christ and the experience of the two men image the Eucharist, and that when we continue to share the Lord's Supper, "the risen Christ comes to open our eyes to His mystical presence and to leave our hearts burning with His love."[12]

On the other hand there are those who do not believe that what happened at Emmaus was a celebration of the Lord's Supper. Lutheran pastor Otto W. Toelke says that the men at the table with Jesus were reminded of many previous occasions due to the way Jesus became the Host, asked the blessing, and broke the bread. Toelke contends that this was not necessarily a reminder of the Lord's Supper, because these two individuals had not been present at its institution by Jesus.[13] Fahling flatly says, "This is not a reference to the Lord's Supper."[14] A Wisconsin Synod Lutheran author writes of this meal, "Jesus was not celebrating Holy Communion. He wouldn't be there long enough to offer the cup. No, Jesus was simply serving the supper."[15] Lenski comments, "A strange sacrament, indeed—broken off in the very first act of it and never completed."[16]

In chapter two of Acts Luke supplies several details about the practice of the Lord's Supper in the Jerusalem church. Jeremias believes that when Luke wrote, "And they continued steadfastly in the apostles' doctrine and fellowship, and in breaking of bread and in prayers" (Acts 2:42), he was "giving the sequence of an early Christian service."[17] The four items mentioned in this verse then become four steps in their worship services. First there was the "apostles' doctrine," the teaching of the apostles. This was followed by "fellowship." Jeremias defines this fellowship as "table" fellowship, a fellowship meal.[18] Then came the "breaking of bread," the celebration of the Lord's Supper. Their worship together ended with "the prayers." This pattern of Christian worship in apostolic times can be corroborated from other literature of the era.[19]

For a time these early Jerusalem Christians continued to go to the temple and to worship with their fellow Jewish brethren. However, they supplemented what occurred in the temple with distinctly Christian worship, including the breaking of bread, which many believe to have been the celebration of the Lord's Supper.[20] These services were held in the homes of Christians. It was not that each family had its own private Communion service, but that they broke bread at the houses where the Christian assemblies were held.[21]

Luke tells us these supplemental services were "continuing daily with one accord in the temple, and breaking bread from house to house . . ." (Acts 2:46). Reformed historian Philip Schaff reports that the Lord's Supper was celebrated daily in the apostolic period.[22] Lutheran pastor Peter Glock asks the question about verse 46, "Does this breaking of bread necessarily refer to celebrations of the Eucharist?" He answers his own question thus, "While absolute proof is difficult, there is considerable evidence that this is indeed the case."[23] Some do not believe that these gatherings with breaking of bread were observations of the Lord's Supper. Because the breaking of bread occurred daily, Southern Baptist professor T. G. Smith questions whether this was an observance of the Lord's Supper. To him that seems too frequent to be likely.[24]

Early in the twentieth century German scholar Hans Lietz-mann theorized that in the beginning there were two distinct forms of the Lord's Supper, a Jerusalem form and Pauline form. He felt the Jerusalem form corresponded to the breaking of bread in Acts 2:42–46 in which there was emphasis on table fellowship and on the joy of celebrating in the presence of the risen Lord. According to Lietzmann, the Pauline concentrated on the death of Christ, eschatological anticipations, and sacrificial concepts, rather than on the joy of fellowship. He believed that eventually in the church the Pauline form displaced the Jerusalem form.[25] Lietz-mann based his conclusions on differences in two ancient litur-gies. One was the Roman liturgy which he traced to the "breaking of bread." The other liturgy was Egyptian. He felt this liturgy was based on Paul's teachings in 1 Corinthians 11. In response to Lietz-mann's conclusions, another European scholar, Oscar Cullman, recognized the differences in the liturgies, but contended that both had their origin in Jesus' Maundy Thursday institution.[26]

In Acts 20:7–12 Luke relates a story about a service in which the Lord's Supper was celebrated. It was on a Sunday that the Christians met in an upper chamber of a house[27] to "break bread." Rice says that by the wording, "upon the first day of the week, when the disciples came together to break bread" (verse 7), Luke was indicating that "in Troas at least, it was a custom to meet together to break bread, to take the Lord's Supper every Sunday."[28] It was an evening service.[29] Luke mentions, "There were many lights where they met" (verse 8). Anglican bishop A. C. Hervey feels that evening Communion, following the example of the first Lord's Supper, was the practice of the church at that time.[30] The apostle Paul was with them and delivered the sermon. A young man sitting on the sill of an open window fell asleep as Paul was preaching. He fell from "the third loft" window and "was taken up dead" (verse 9). Paul then raised him from the dead. When the service resumed, Paul broke bread and ate (verse 11). Of this event Reu emphatically writes, "There is only one passage in which the term 'to break the bread' can scarcely mean anything else than the celebration of the Lord's Supper, and that is Acts 20:11."[31] Commentators of all backgrounds agree that this was an authentic celebration of the Lord's Supper.[32]

In Acts 27:33–38 when the apostle Paul was being taken to Rome as a prisoner, the ship on which he was a passenger was wrecked in a violent storm. Due to their struggle with the storm, the sailors and others aboard had not eaten a regular meal for two weeks. They needed to take food if they wished to survive. Paul urged everyone to eat, and then "he took bread, and gave thanks to God in the presence of them all: and when he had broken it, he began to eat" (27:35). Encouraged by his example, the others also ate. Virtually all Bible scholars believe this was "probably" not a celebration of the Lord's Supper.[33] However, some say it is an "unmistakable reference to the Eucharist"[34] and that it has "Eucharistic overtones."[35]

In the New Testament, church fellowship meals known as the *agape*, or love feasts (Jude 12), were held in conjunction with the celebration of the Lord's Supper. Originally the Lord's Supper took place at the end of these social meals.[36] The first Lord's Supper was held at, or near, the end of a meal, the Passover. The early New Testament church adopted a non-Passover meal format as the setting for the Lord's Supper. In Jewish homes a weekly meal was held each Friday evening with the purpose of hallowing the beginning of the Sabbath. Scholars believe that among the Christians this meal was moved to Sunday, the Lord's Day, and became the setting in which the Lord's Supper was celebrated.[37] When possible, all members brought food and drink, rich and poor alike. All shared with each other to promote love among the believers, as an expression of that love.[38] Some of the bread and wine that had been brought for the *agape* meal was reserved for the Lord's Supper.[39]

In 1 Corinthians 11:17–22 we read that these love feasts were being desecrated by the congregation in Corinth. Instead of being expressions of Christian love and brotherhood, they had become occasions of division and gluttony. Paul writes words of reprimand to the congregation, saying,

> When ye come together therefore into one place, this is not to eat the Lord's Supper. For in eating every one taketh before other his own supper: and one is hungry, and another is drunken. What? have ye no houses to eat and to drink in? or despise ye the church of God, and shame them that have not? (1 Corinthians 11:20–22a).

The attitude reflected in persons bringing their own supper, sharing only with their friends, not with new converts or the poor who could not bring food, was not proper for people about to receive the Lord's Supper. The love that should exist among persons united as Christians was lacking. Lenski writes, "When the agape ceased to be an Agape, the Sacrament was also virtually impossible."[40] Rice says, "The fellowship was not complete as they took the bread and cup in memory of Christ's death."[41] British author C. Harold Dodd states that, "Under these conditions . . . it was quite impossible to eat a true 'Supper of the Lord.' "[42] Higgins says briefly that when they assembled as a church, it was not the Lord's Supper that they ate "because brotherly fellowship was absent."[43] Lenski thinks that the poor especially felt themselves excluded and ceased to commune.[44]

Paul seems to urge discontinuance of the love feast tied to the Lord's Supper. In verse 22 he asks, "What? have ye no houses to eat and drink in?" Then near the end of the chapter he advises, "If any man hunger, let him eat at home; that ye come not together unto condemnation" (verse 34a). Higgins thinks that by what he said here Paul was initiating a process that ended in the celebration of the Lord's Supper being separated from the community meal.[45] Commenting on this line of thought, Jeremias reports that "a rather convincing suggestion has been made: that the separation of Agape and Eucharist is already presupposed in 1 Corinthians."[46]

At Corinth there were some converts from paganism who did not consider it inconsistent with their confession as Christians to continue attending feasts of the heathen temples and partaking of sacrificial food and drink offered to idols. In 1 Corinthians 10:1–22 Paul censured them for this view. He told them that to continue eating at the table of pagan gods was to make a mockery of the Lord's Supper. Paul said, "The cup of blessing which we bless, is it not the communion of the blood of Christ? The bread which we break, is it not the communion of the body of Christ? For we being many are one bread, and one body, for we are all partakers of that one bread" (verses 16 and 17). Higgins comments, "The Lord, too, has a table and a cup, and by eating at his table we are brought into close communion with him."[47] Rice sees these words as a reminder that "the Lord's Supper is a constant plea for separation and holy living."[48] Baptist professor Raymond B. Brown states, "The communion with Christ involves communion with one another."[49]

After giving an account of the institution of the Lord's Supper in 1 Corinthians 11:23–25 the apostle told his readers, "For as often as ye eat this bread, and drink this cup, ye do shew (proclaim, NIV) the Lord's death till He come" (verse 26). Following this beautiful statement Paul gives instruction regarding the proper use of the Lord's Supper, His advise given has validity also for our day and time.

> Whoever eats the bread or drinks the cup of the Lord in an unworthy manner will be guilty of sinning against the body and blood of the Lord. A man ought to examine himself before he eats of the bread and drinks of the cup. For anyone who eats and drinks without recognizing the body of the Lord eats and drinks judgment on himself (1 Corinthians 11:27–29, NIV).

On the basis of Paul's injunction, Christians generally seem to recognize the need for self-examination and preparation before receiving the Sacrament.[50] Most would accept the statement that "we must prepare for so great and holy a moment."[51] They also take seriously Paul's words about the worthiness of the communicant, even though definitions of worthiness vary.[52]

At the conclusion of this paragraph of pastoral instruction Paul speaks of a person eating and drinking judgment upon himself because he is "not discerning the Lord's body" (11:29). Christians understand this phrase in two different ways. Some believe this to be a reference to the sacramental union of Christ's body and blood with the bread and wine in the Lord's Supper. Lenski says, "To discern the Lord's body means to perceive that in the Sacrament that body is really present and received."[53] Lutheran scholar Werner Elert states, "The unworthy communicant fails to 'discern the body,' that is, that he eats the bread as though he were thereby not receiving the body of Christ."[54]

The second way of understanding this passage is that eating and drinking without "discerning the body" means, as Higgins says, "Conduct at the Lord's Supper which is due to failure to recognize the Church for what it is, the Body of Christ, in which the living Christ is present."[55] Heidelberg professor Günther Bornkamm tells of the divided situation in Corinth in which the wealthy went ahead and ate, not bothering with the poor who came later and had nothing. He writes, "In Paul's view this was profanation of the 'body' of Christ, the church. . . . Paul was forced to appeal to them to celebrate the meal 'worthily' and not to begin without discerning the body (1 Cor. 11:29), that is respecting it as the body of Christ."[56]

Paul then writes of what is seen by some as a negative temporal effect of misuse of the Lord's Supper. "For this cause many are weak and sickly among you, and many sleep" (1 Corinthians 11:30). Kodell believes that Paul had a problem with the fact that some members of the Christian community had already died before the return of Christ. He says of Paul, "He seemed to interpret their death as a judgment on selfishness in the celebration of the Eucharist."[57] Lenski disposes of the idea that the body and blood act as poison which makes an unworthy communicant sick or kills him. Rather, "It is the sin of communing unworthily which, like other sins, entails the penalty of judgment."[58]

Some think that the Lord's Supper can be traced to Jesus feeding the five thousand (Matthew 14:15–21) and the four thousand (Matthew 15:32–39). This is not directly indicated by the biblical texts in question, but it is rather an inference that stands in contradiction to the Lutheran principle of letting the clear texts inform those less clear on a given doctrine. On the basis of these miraculous occurrences in Matthew's Gospel, some believe that infants and small children received the Lord's Supper in the New Testament church. In speaking of the numbers who ate of the miraculous meals Matthew wrote, "And they that had eaten were about five thousand men, beside women and children" (14:21) and, "Those who ate were about four thousand men, beside women and children" (15:38). For example, pastor J. Robert Jacobson is convinced that in these texts there is clear evidence that both women and children were included in the celebration of the Lord's Supper.[59] He contends that because in all the other principal models for the "Lord's Meal" only adult males were involved, "Matthew goes out of his way to point out that on both occasions . . . Jesus shared His Meal with women and children as well as men."[60] Jacobson further comments, "One thing is certain: no baptized woman sitting in a Matthean congregation could hear these passages read aloud and conclude that the Lord's Meal was not for her and her children."[61] Regarding "infant communion," Jacobson writes:

> In a crowd of thousands we may be sure there were plenty of them. It's unthinkable to suppose they did not share in the Lord's bounty as the bread passed through their own mother's hands, just as unthinkable to suppose that women in Matthew's congregations, hearing of this, would have withheld the bread of the Eucharist from their little ones.[62]

Several designations of the Lord's Supper are found in, or can be traced directly to the New Testament. "Breaking of Bread" has already been discussed in this chapter. It was St. Paul who first called this Sacrament the "Lord's Supper" (1 Corinthians 11:21).[63] This sacred meal is often referred to as "Communion," derived from 1 Corinthians 10:16 where the apostle states, "The cup of blessing which we bless, is it not the communion of the blood of Christ? The bread which we break, is it not the communion of the body of Christ?" Paul also calls it the "Lord's Table"[64] in 1 Corinthians 10:21b, where he counsels, "Ye cannot be partakers of the Lord's table, and of the table of devils." Another widely used designation in the history of the church[65] and in current use today is "Eucharist." While this term did not originate in the New Testament,[66] its roots are traceable to the words of institution spoken by Jesus, and recorded by Luke and Paul (Luke 22:19; 1 Corinthians 11:24). They say of Jesus, as He began to celebrate the Sacrament for the first time, "having given thanks." These three words in English are one word in the Greek, *eucharistesas*.[67] All of these designations describe aspects of this holy meal.

In the eleventh chapter of 1 Corinthians Paul deals with the subject of the Lord's Supper. Immediately after his narrative of the institution of the Lord's Supper, and just before his instruction concerning partaking worthily of the Sacrament, he says, "As often as ye eat this bread, and drink this cup, ye do shew the Lord's death *till He come*" (1 Corinthians 11:26). The second advent of Christ is anticipated in the words "till he come."[68] Christians are to observe the Lord's Supper until that time.[69] The phrase "till he come" occurs in early Eucharistic liturgy. Otfried Hofius of Tübingen University in Germany writes that these words from Paul normatively establish and simultaneously reflect "the liturgical practice of the early Christian communities."[70]

When the early church celebrated the Lord's Supper it was in anticipation of sharing in full communion with Christ in the future banquet in the Kingdom of God.[71] German theologians

Hermann Sasse and Otto Knock (among others) believe that 1 Corinthians 16:22, "If anyone does not love the Lord—a curse be upon him. Come, O Lord" (NIV), is a prayer used in connection with the Lord's Supper. Not only does this prayer call for a curse upon persons who participate in the Supper without loving the Lord, but it is also seen as an invocation for Christ's presence in the Sacrament,[72] and as a cry of longing for His return in glory.[73] Hofius suggest that an inner relation exists between the words "till He come" in 11:26 and "Come, O Lord" in 16:22.[74] The Aramaic word which the New International Version translated "Come, O Lord" is *Maranatha*. It is left untranslated in the King James Version, just as Paul did not translate it into Greek when he wrote First Corinthians. This word also appears untranslated in a eucharistic prayer in the *Didache* (10:6), a second century church manual. Some consider the evidence that this was already used liturgically at Communion celebrations in the first century in Paul's day.[75] Swedish Lutheran bishop Gustav Aulen states, "The eschatology of the Lord's Supper is . . . characterized by waiting: '*Maranatha*; Our Lord, come' (1 Corinthians 16:22) is its constant refrain. The Lord's Supper celebrated on earth is a foretaste of the 'great supper in heaven.'"[76] Michael Plekon, an Eastern Orthodox priest, says, "The Eucharist is always a 'foretaste of the feast to come,' *an eschatological experience*."[77]

The writers of the three Synoptic Gospels all report that on the night when Jesus instituted the Lord's Supper He spoke of drinking the fruit of the vine at a future time (Matthew 26:29; Mark 14:25; Luke 22:18). Matthew's version reads as follows, "I will not drink henceforth of this fruit of the vine, until that day when I drink it new with you in My Father's kingdom." The German scholar, Ernst Sommerlath, in commenting on these words, states,

> Every time we celebrate this Sacrament our horizon is widened and our sights are raised to reach into eternity itself . . . The table fellowship offered in the Lord's

Supper shall one day be completed in the communion of eternal life. Every communion celebration is directed toward the consummation of all things and has eschatological significance.[78]

St. Luke also relates that prior to instituting the Lord's Supper Jesus said to His disciples, "With desire I have desired to eat this Passover with you before I suffer: For I say unto you, I will not anymore eat thereof, until it be fulfilled in the kingdom of God" (Luke 22:15–16). R. C. H. Lenski remarks, "This is the last Passover on earth for Jesus until he partakes of the fulfillment in heaven."[79] He expresses the opinion that Jesus' statement regarding a future heavenly eating of the Passover and drinking of the fruit of the vine is figurative in nature.[80]

There are differences of opinion among Christians as to when and where Jesus intended to eat and drink at a future meal. Some think He was speaking of when He would eat and drink with His followers after He rose from the dead.[81] They cite as an example the evening of Easter day when Jesus "sat at meat" with the Emmaus disciples and "took the bread, and blessed, and broke, and gave to them" (Luke 24:30, RSV). Also mentioned is when on Easter night Jesus' followers were meeting behind locked doors, and he appeared among them and asked, "Have you any meat? And they gave Him a piece of broiled fish, and of an honeycomb. And He took it, and did eat before them" (Luke 24:41b–43). He also served breakfast to seven disciples who had been fishing. John writes, "Jesus then cometh, and taketh bread, and giveth them, and fish likewise" (John 21:13). Also cited are the words of Peter as recorded in Acts 10:41, "Not to all the people, but unto witnesses chosen before of God, even to us, who did eat and drink with Him after He rose from the dead." The ancient church father, Chrysostom, favored this view.[82]

Premillennialists believe that this eating and drinking will be in a literal material kingdom on earth.[83] They speak of the Messianic banquet which Jesus will share with His disciples at the end of the age.[84] Southern Baptist professor Frank Stagg states, "The Last Supper is not a farewell but a pledge that the *Father's kingdom* will prevail and that Jesus' people will be reunited in the messianic banquet under that sovereign rule."[85]

At the Last Supper Jesus drank of the fruit of the vine for the last time "in this life," but after the resurrection, when the kingdom is established, He will "drink it new." Based on the "fruit of the vine" verses in the accounts of the meal in the Upper Room, premillenialists believe that Christ will drink with His saints in the coming kingdom on earth. Baptist evangelist John R. Rice says that this will be "grape juice."[86] Both the Lord and His people will have physical bodies, as real as those of Adam and Eve in the Garden of Eden.[87] Ezekiel 47:9–12 and Revelation 22:2 are cited in support of the idea that Christians in resurrected bodies will eat such things as fish and fruit. The belief is that these foods will be provided for Christ's followers in the coming age when He says He will drink the fruit of the vine "new with you in My Father's kingdom."[88]

Others, including this author, confess that the future eating and drinking spoken of by Jesus in connection with the Lord's Supper will take place in the glorious kingdom of His Father in heaven,[89] at the great marriage supper of the Lamb.[90] It is suggested that Jesus was speaking of this heavenly feast when, after having healed the centurion's servant, He said, "And I say unto you, That many shall come from the east and west, and shall *sit down* with Abraham, and Isaac, and Jacob, in the kingdom of heaven" (Matthew 8:11).[91] In the book of Revelation, John tells of a vision in which he heard a voice coming out of the throne in heaven say, "Write, blessed are they which are called to the marriage supper of the Lamb" (Revelation 19:9a). Luke tells us that shortly after Jesus celebrated the first Lord's Supper with His disciples He told them, "And I appoint unto you a kingdom, as My Father hath appointed unto Me; that ye may eat and drink at My table in My kingdom, and sit on thrones judging the twelve tribes of Israel" (Luke

22:29–30). Based on Luke 22:15–16, one concludes that the feast in heaven will be the heavenly fulfillment of the Passover and the Lord's Supper.[92] Georg Stöckhardt (1842–1913), who taught at Concordia Seminary in St. Louis, stated,

> As the first paschal meal strengthened the Israelites for the journey which lay before them, through the desert to Canaan, so the Lord's Supper is for the children of the New Covenant food upon the way, for the time of their earthly journey. And it . . . points forward, just like the Passover meal, to the end of the Journey, to the meal of eternity, when the Lord will drink it with us in His Father's kingdom.[93]

Stöckhardt speaks of "the meal of eternity." Figuratively speaking, it will be an eternal, never-ending meal.[94] According to Matthew, Jesus said, "I will not drink henceforth of this fruit of the vine, until that day when I drink it new with you in My Father's kingdom (Matthew 26:29). In the original Greek the tense of the word translated "drink" in the King James version is the present subjunctive ("be drinking") indicating that the feast will never end.[95] In a confessional address, Lutheran professor W. A. Poehler said the Lord's Supper is "a type or symbol of that perfect Joy in heaven, where He will give us to eat of His pleasure forevermore."[96]

In a Eucharistic hymn, Thomas Aquinas said it prayerfully this way, "O Christ, whom now beneath a veil we see May what we thirst for soon our portion be, To gaze on thee unveiled, and see thy face, The vision of thy glory and thy grace."[97] Hermann Sasse summarized it thus, "The Sacrament . . . is the remembrance of the terrific hour when the Lamb of God was slain, and at the same time it is the joyful looking forward to the day when our redemption will be accomplished at the Supper of the Lord."[98] Henry E. Jacobs (1844–1932) wrote, "Lord Jesus Christ, we humbly pray To keep us steadfast to that day That each may be Thy welcomed guest. When thou shalt spread Thy heavenly feast."[99]

Notes

1. Joachim Jeremias, *The Eucharistic Words of Jesus,* trans. Norman Perrin (London: SCM, 1966), 120.

2. Jeremias, *Eucharistic Words,* 120.

3. R. C. H. Lenski, *The Interpretation of the Acts of the Apostles* (Columbus, Ohio: The Wartburg Press, 1944), 116.

4. Peter M. Glock, "Early Developments of the Eucharist" (Wahpeton, N.Dak. Pastoral Conference, 1994), 5; Jeremias, *Eucharistic Words,* 120; Eugene LaVerdiere, *The Eucharist in the New Testament and the Early Church* (Collegeville, Minn.: Liturgical Press, 1996), 103.

5. Jeremias, *Eucharistic Words,* 119, 120.

6. *The Orthodox Study Bible: New Testament and Psalms* (Nashville: Nelson, 1993), 202.

7. H. D. M. Spence and Joseph S. Exell, ed., *The Pulpit Commentary* (Grand Rapids, Mich.: Eerdmans, 1950), 16:2:272.

8. LaVerdiere, *Eucharist,* 104; Spence and Exell, *Pulpit,* 16:2:272; Laurence Hull Stookey, *Eucharist: Christ's Feast with the Church* (Nashville: Abingdon, 1993), 36, 37, 98, 130.

9. Spence and Exell, *Pulpit,* 16:2:272.

10. Jerome Kodell, *The Eucharist in the New Testament* (1988; reprint, Collegeville, Minn.: Liturgical Press, 1991), 111.

11. Stookey, *Eucharist,* 130.

12. *Orthodox Study Bible,* 202.

13. *The Concordia Pulpit* (St. Louis: Concordia, 1929–1989), 55:142.

14. Adam Fahling, *The Life of Christ* (St. Louis: Concordia, 1936), 696.

15. Richard D. Balge and Roland Cap Ehlke, ed., *Sermon Studies on the Gospels (ILCW Series A)* (Milwaukee: Northwestern, 1989), 154.

16. R. C. H. Lenski, *The Interpretation of St. Luke's Gospel* (Columbus, Ohio: Wartburg Press, 1946), 1192.

17. Jeremias, *Eucharistic Words,* 119.

18. Jeremias, *Eucharistic Words,* 119.

19. Jeremias, *Eucharistic Words,* 119.

20. Lenski, *Acts,* 120; Spence and Exell, *Pulpit,* 18:1:55.

21. Paul E. Kretzmann, *Christian Art in the Place and in the Form of Lutheran Worship* (St. Louis: Concordia, 1921), 21; Spence and Exell, *Pulpit,* 18:1:550.

22. Philip Schaff, *History of the Christian Church* (n.p.; Charles Scribner's Sons, 1958–1960), 1:473.

23. Glock, "Early Developments," 5.

24. Clifton J. Allen et al, ed., *The Broadman Bible Commentary* (Nashville: Broadman, 1969–1972), 10:32.

25. Kodell, *Eucharist,* 25.

26. Glock, "Early Developments," 5.

27. Paul E. Kretzmann, *Popular Commentary of the Bible, New Testament* (St. Louis: Concordia, 1921–1922), 1:636.

28. John R. Rice, *Filled with the Spirit: Verse-by-Verse Commentary on the Acts of the Apostles* (Murfreesboro, Tenn.: Sword of the Lord Publishers, 1963), 438.

29. Kretzmann, *Popular Commentary*, 1:636.

30. Spence and Exell, *Pulpit*, 18:2:143.

31. Johann M. Reu, *Two Treatises on the Means of Grace* (n.d.; reprint, Minneapolis: Augsburg, 1952), 95.

32. Duane W. H. Arnold and C. George Fry, *The Way, the Truth and the Life: An Introduction to Lutheran Christianity* (Grand Rapids: Baker Book House, 1982), 179, Kretzmann, *Popular Commentary*, 1:636; LaVerdiere, *Eucharist*, 109; Lenski, *Acts*, 826; Ben F. Meyer, ed., *One Loaf, One Cup: Ecumenical Studies of 1 Cor. 11 and other Eucharistic Texts* (Macon, Ga.: Mercer University Press, 1993), 2, 3; Rice, *Acts*, 438.

33. Jeremias, *Eucharistic Words*, 133; Kodell, *Eucharist*, 111; LaVerdiere, *Eucharist*, 109, 110.

34. LaVerdiere, *Eucharist in the New Testament*, 109, 110.

35. *Orthodox Study Bible*, 332.

36. John D. Davis, *The Westminster Dictionary of the Bible*, rev. Henry Snyder Gehman (Philadelphia: Westminster Press, 1944), 363; R. C. H. Lenski, *The Interpretation of St. Paul's First and Second Epistles to the Corinthians* (Columbus, Ohio: The Wartburg Press, 1946), 458.

37. Aidan Kavanagh, "Repeating the Unrepeatable," *Christian History* 12, no. 1 (1993): 38.

38. Davis, *Westminster*, 363; F. N. Peloubet, ed., assisted by Alice D. Adams, *Peloubet's Bible Dictionary* (Philadelphia: John C. Winston, 1947), 371.

39. Lenski, *Corinthians*, 458.

40. Lenski, *Corinthians*, 459.

41. John R. Rice, *The Church at Corinth: A Verse-by-Verse Commentary on 1 and 2 Corinthians* (Murfreesboro, Tenn.: Sword of the Lord Publishers, 1973), 110.

42. C. Harold Dodd, *The Meaning of Paul for Today* (Glasgow: William Collins Sons and Co. Ltd., 1958), 1580.

43. A. J. B. Higgins, *The Lord's Supper in the New Testament* (London: SCM, 1952), 71.

44. Lenski, *Corinthians*, 459.

45. Higgins, *Lord's Supper*, 71.

46. Jeremias, *Eucharistic Words*, 121.

47. Higgins, *Lord's Supper*, 68.

48. Rice, *Corinthians*, 102.

49. Allen, *Broadman*, 10:349.

50. *Catechism of the Catholic Church* (Vatican City: Liberia Editrice Vaticana 1994, trans. Collegeville, Minn.: Liturgical Press, 1994), 350; Edward W. A. Koehler, *A Short Exposition of Dr. Martin Luther's Small Catechism, edited by the Evangelical Lutheran Synod of Missouri, Ohio, and other States, with Additional Notes for Students, Teachers, and Pastors* (River Forest, Ill.: Koehler, 1946), 309, 310; Lenski, *Corinthians*, 480; Rice, *Corinthians*, 114;

Philip Schaff, *The Creeds of Christendom with a History and Critical Notes*, rev. by David F. Schaff (Grand Rapids, Mich.: Baker, 1966), 3:522; Olaus Swebellus, *Dr. Martin Luther's Catechism with Explanation*, trans. Andrew and Mary Mickelsen (1852; reprint, Apostolic Lutheran Church of America, 1966), 118.

51. *Catechism of the Catholic Church*, 350.

52. Allen, *Broadman*, 10:359; Ernest H. Falardeau, *One Bread and Cup: Source of Communion* (1987; reprint, Collegeville, Minn.: Liturgical Press, 1990), 59; Bennet Kelley, *Saint Joseph Baltimore Catechism: The Truths of Our Catholic Faith Clearly Explained and Illustrated*, rev. ed. (New York: Catholic Book Publishing Co., 1969), 117; Koehler, *Short Exposition*, 12; *Orthodox Study Bible*, 394; Swebellus, *Catechism with Explanation*, 1180.

53. Lenski, *Corinthians*, 482.

54. Jeffrey A. Gibbs, "An Exegetical Case for Close(d) Communion: I Corinthians 10:14–22; 11:17–34," *Concordia Journal* 21, no. 2 (1995): 159.

55. Higgins, *Lord's Supper*, 72, 73.

56. Günther Bornkamm, *Paul*, trans. D. M. G. Stalker (New York: Harper & Row, 1971), 73, 193.

57. Kodell, *Eucharist*, 121.

58. Lenski, *Corinthians*, 484.

59. J. Robert Jacobson, *Besides Women & Children: A Guide for Parents & Pastors on Infant & Child Communion*, rev. ed. (Camrose, Alberta: Concord Canada, 1981), 17.

60. Jacobson, *Besides Women and Children*, 18.

61. Jacobson, *Besides Women and Children*, 18.

62. Jacobson, *Besides Women and Children*, 18, 19.

63. Georgia Harkness, *Understanding the Christian Faith* (Nashville: Abingdon, 1992), 2.

64. Werner Elert, *Eucharist and Church Fellowship in the First Four Centuries*, trans. N. E. Nagel (St. Louis: Concordia, 1966), 1.

65. Tim Dowley, et al, ed., *Eerdmans Handbook to the History of Christianity* (Grand Rapids, Mich.: Eerdmans, 1977), 9.

66. LaVerdiere, *Eucharist*, 1, 2.

67. *The Greek-English New Testament: King James Version, New International Version, Greek Text, Literal Interlinear* (Washington, DC: Christianity Today, 1975), 249, 507.

68. Hermann Sasse, *This Is My Body: Luther's Contention for the Real Presence in the Sacrament of the Altar*, rev. ed. (Adelaide, South Australia: Lutheran Publishing House, 1977), 324.

69. B. H. Carroll, *Baptists and Their Doctrines,* ed. Timothy and Denise George (Nashville: Broadman & Holman, 1995), 92.

70. Meyer, *One Loaf*, 75.

71. Meyer, *One Loaf*, 9, 10.

72. Allen, *Broadman*, 10:397; Sasse, *Body*, 324, 325.

73. Allen, *Broadman*, 10:397; Meyer, *One Loaf*, 10; Sasse, *Body*, 325.

74. Meyer, *One Loaf*, 111.

75. Allen, *Broadman*, 10:397; Lenski, *Corinthians*, 789.

76. Gustaf Aulén, *Eucharist and Sacrifice*, trans. Eric H. Wahlstrom (Philadelphia: Muhlenberg Press, 1958), 351.

77. Michael P. Plekon, "Communion in the Holy Things: The Eucharist Makes the Church," *Lutheran Forum* 30, no. 4 (1996): 49.

78. Julius Bodensieck, ed., *The Encyclopedia of the Lutheran Church* (Minneapolis: Augsburg, 1965), 2:1342.

79. Lenski, *Luke*, 1042.

80. R. C. H. Lenski, *The Interpretation of St. Matthew's Gospel* (Columbus, Ohio: Wartburg Press, 1943), 1033.

81. Spence and Exell, *Pulpit*, 15:2:524; 16:2:198.

82. Spence and Exell, *Pulpit*, 15:2:524.

83. William E. Blackstone, *Jesus Is Coming: God's Hope for a Restless World* (Grand Rapids, Mich.: Kregel Publications, 1989), 126.

84. Allen, *Broadman*, 8:234; 9:167. See Louis A. Brighton, *Revelation* (St. Louis: Concordia, 1999) to find out why premillenialism is based on a false interpretation of the scriptures, especially of Revelation.

85. Allen, *Broadman*, 8:234.

86. John. R. Rice, *The King of the Jews: A Verse-by-Verse Commentary on the Gospel According to Matthew* (Murfreesboro, Tenn.: Sword of the Lord Publishers, 1955), 436.

87. Rice, *Matthew*, 436.

88. Rice, *Matthew*, 436.

89. Aulen, *Eucharist and Sacrifice*, 351; Lenski, *Matthew*, 1032.

90. Spence and Exell, *Pulpit*, 15:2:524.

91. Lenski, *Matthew*, 1032.

92. Lenski, *Matthew*, 1033.

93. Kretzmann, *Popular Commentary*, 1:147.

94. Lenski, *Matthew*, 1032,1033.

95. Lenski, *Matthew*, 1032.

96. *Concordia Pulpit*, 19:566.

97. Arnold and Fry, *The Way*, 146.

98. Sasse, *Body*, 324.

99. W. G. Polack, *The Handbook to the Lutheran Hymnal* (St. Louis: Concordia, 1942), 225.

STUDY QUESTIONS

1. What command of Jesus gives the basis for the regular celebration of the Lord's Supper in the church?

2. What term does Luke use to usually mean the Lord's Supper in the Gospel According to Luke and in Acts? In what five verses or groups of verses does he use this term?

3. In what instances within the five passages considered above have some questioned whether the Lord's Supper was indeed celebrated?

4. What adaptation of the Passover that preceded the celebration of the Lord's Supper did some churches adopt in the apostolic era, and where in the New Testament do we see evidence of its abuse?

5. In what passage in 1 Corinthians does Paul instruct the congregation to flee from idolatry, thus separating itself as God's people at the Lord's Table from those who are not of God's people, those who are seated at the table of demons?

6. In what passage does Paul instruct Christians regarding the worthy reception of the Lord's Supper?

7. In what two ways have Christians interpreted the discernment of the body of Christ in the Lord's Supper?

8. Against what principle of biblical interpretation does the interpretation of Jesus' miraculous feeding of the five thousand as the Lord's Supper stand?

9. From what Bible verse do we receive the term "Communion"?

10. From what Bible verse do we receive the term "Lord's Table"?

11. In what verse do we see the doctrine of the Lord's Supper as a sign of the Second Advent of Jesus Christ?

12. What Aramaic word meaning "Our Lord, come" was used commonly in the ancient church, as we see especially in

the King James Version of 1 Corinthians 16:22, echoed also in the petition of the church in Revelation 22?

13. What Gospel passages also support this eschatological or end-time understanding of the Lord's Supper as heralding the return of Christ and being the foretaste of the coming Marriage Feast of the Lamb?

THE LORD'S SUPPER IN ANCIENT AND MEDIEVAL TIMES

4 | THE EARLY CHURCH

From the beginning Sunday has been the Christian day of worship. Jesus rose from the dead on Sunday. On Easter night He appeared to His followers who were gathered together behind locked doors (Luke 24:36–49; John 20:19–23). A week later, also on Sunday, He came to them as they were similarly meeting (John 20:26–29). The day of Pentecost, the birthday of the Christian church, was on a Sunday fifty days after Easter.[1] By the time the apostle John wrote the book of Revelation, Sunday was called the Lord's Day (Revelation 1:10).

The church continued to observe Sunday as the day of worship after the apostles had died.[2] Celebration of the Lord's Supper was a regular and the most solemn portion of every Sunday service.[3] In various places Christians also followed the earlier practice of having the Lord's Supper on a daily basis.[4] Augustine (354–430) tells that in North Africa some people partook of the Lord's Supper every day, while others did so every Sunday. Still others communed less often. The people were urged to receive the Lord's Supper frequently, and especially exhorted to do so on high festival days. Augustine wrote, "The Eucharist is our daily bread."[5] At the time some interpreted the fourth Petition of the Lord's Prayer, "Give us this day our daily bread," as connected mystically to daily reception of the Lord's Supper.[6]

Until the time of Emperor Constantine's *Peace of the Church* in A.D. 313, Christians came together for worship, including the celebration of the Lord's Supper, in a variety of settings. In the first centuries, persecution began in various localities, but it increased after the fall of Nero until the two great persecutions under emperors Decius (reigned 249–251) and Diocletian (reigned 284–305). Christians chose their places of worship according to local circumstances and social conditions.[7] Justin Martyr says that in second century Rome Christians met in private homes in the same way they had done in the New Testament era, "breaking bread from house to house."[8] There is evidence that by the middle of the third century the interiors of private homes were structurally altered to serve as churches.[9] With Emperor Valerian in A.D. 260, the persecution of Christians ceased for a time and they began constructing spacious church buildings.[10] It was not until Constantine's peace that the practice of building impressive structures used for Christian worship, such as *basilicas*, the traditional form of Roman public buildings, became widespread.[11]

In the early centuries Christians also met in cemeteries for Communion services. In Rome and in other cities, including Naples and Syracuse, and in Syria, some of the cemeteries were underground catacombs.[12] At times feasts were held at graves because they wished to worship "in the company of the martyrs." Some considered cemeteries as places where the dead Christians slept, awaiting Christ's return, and that the martyrs, though with the Lord in spirit, were also sacramentally present in their remains.[13] Ambrose (340–397) relates that in such services the names and struggles of the martyrs buried there were recited before the bread and wine were consecrated. Eventually tables or altars for the celebration of the Lord's Supper were placed directly over the bodies of the martyrs.[14]

There are three key sources of information regarding services celebrating the Lord's Supper during the first centuries following the apostolic era. These are the *Didache*, or *Teachings of the Twelve*,[15] a second century Christian document; the writings of Justin Martyr, an unordained lay preacher who lived in the second century, and those of Hippolytus (ca. 170–ca. 235) of the third century. Three chapters of the *Didache* pertain to the Lord's Supper.[16] The oldest known Eucharistic prayers are found in the *Didache*. There are prayers of thanksgiving for the cup, the broken bread, and for all mercies.[17] It is this document that refers to the Lord's Supper as a sacrifice.[18] In Justin Martyr's *First Apology* he attempted to explain the Christian faith, including the Lord's Supper, to people of pagan background. In another writing, *The Testimony of the Dialogue with Trypho*, he tried to explain and justify the Lord's Supper to Jewish readers.[19] Hippolytus wrote a church order entitled *Apostolic Tradition*. This order has detailed directions for celebrating the Lord's Supper.[20] The earliest known prayer for the consecration of the bread and wine is preserved for us in his writings.[21] Much of his language exists in the Lord's Supper liturgies used today by Roman Catholics, Lutherans, Anglicans, Methodists, and Presbyterians.[22]

The basic format of early Christian worship services was rather simple. The service was divided into two parts. The first part was open to all: the baptized, the unbaptized, the catechumens, persons under penance, and the general public. Only the baptized were admitted to the second portion of the service when the Lord's Supper was celebrated.[23] The first section of the service consisted of a brief liturgy, scripture readings, a sermon, and prayers. At the end of this portion of the service a final prayer was said and a blessing given. After this one of the deacons announced, "Let all who are unbaptized leave."[24] The *Apostolic Constitutions*, compiled around A.D. 380,[25] directed, "Let none of the catechumens, none of the unbelievers, none of the heterodox, stay here."[26] At some point in this context, the deacon said, "Holy things for holy ones."[27] This pronouncement is based on the words of Jesus: "Give not that which is holy unto the dogs" (Matthew 7:6).[28] Lutheran professor Norman Nagel states that "the 'holy things' are the body and blood of our Lord ... The holy ones are the saints, the ones the Lord has made His own, the baptized."[29] After those not permitted to remain had left the room the doors were closed and guarded by deacons or subdeacons.[30] Those remaining participated in the celebration of the Lord's Supper. These early Christians practiced and rigidly enforced what we today call "closed communion."[31] In fact, the term "closed communion" derives from their practice of closing the doors.[32]

At Dura-Europos in Syria archaeologists discovered the remains of a home, the interior of which had been renovated for use as a Christian place of worship.[33] They found a separate room next to the sanctuary that was used for celebration of the Lord's Supper. The baptized would move from the regular meeting room to this room for the Communion part of the service. Persons who were not baptized were not permitted to enter this part of the building.[34] Behind the closed and guarded doors "the most sacred part of the service,"[35] the celebration of the Lord's Supper, followed. It began with the kiss of peace.[36] Justin Martyr said that before the bread and wine are brought forward "we salute one another with a kiss."[37] Augustine declared that the kiss of peace was good preparation for the Lord's Supper.[38] Only those who received and gave the kiss were permitted to receive the Sacrament.[39] The kiss of peace was given "cheek to cheek"[40] by men to men and women to women.[41] There is an account of an occurrence in a service where the kiss of peace suddenly stopped as it was being given and received all through the congregation. Apparently a certain member or members refused to kiss or to receive a kiss or kisses from another member or members. The celebrant left the altar and went to where the kiss of peace was blocked. He assisted in working through reconciliation, and only after this was accomplished did the kissing continue. The order of service was not carried forward until after the kiss of peace had been concluded all the way around.[42]

After the kiss of peace a number of steps were involved in the celebration of the Lord's Supper. These did not always occur in the same order, nor were all steps always carried out in every congregation. Ordinarily the first step after the kiss of peace was that bread and water mixed with wine were brought forward and presented to the presiding bishop. The bishop placed these elements on the altar table and spoke an *ex tempore* prayer.[43] In his *Apostolic Tradition* Hippolytus speaks of the prayer to be spoken by the bishop as he receives what he calls the "offering." He includes in the "offering" not only the bread and the cup of wine mixed with water but also milk and honey which have been mixed together and brought forward. Hippolytus explains the significance of the milk and honey, saying, "Milk and honey mixed together in fulfillment of the promise that was made to the fathers, in which he said, 'A land flowing with milk and honey.'"[44] Hippolytus refers to the promise God made to Israel recorded in Exodus 3:8.

The bread, wine, milk, and honey were considered offerings presented by the deacons on behalf of the congregation for use in the celebration of the Lord's Supper. The offering of the sacramental elements was called the "oblation."[45] Hippolytus supplies some details regarding the ceremonial handling of the items brought forward for use in the celebration of the Lord's Supper.

The bishop breaks the bread saying, "The bread of heaven in Christ Jesus." If enough presbyters are not present, deacons shall assist in holding the cups. One has the water, another the milk, and a third the wine. They shall taste of each of these three times in recognition of the Holy Trinity—Father, Son, and Holy Spirit.[46]

There were three distinct prayers, or sets of prayers, in the Lord's Supper portion of the service. The prayer of thanksgiving occurred at the time the elements and offerings were brought forward and presented. A prayer of consecration, sometimes combined with the prayer of thanksgiving, invoked the Holy Spirit upon the people and the sacramental elements. Justin Martyr considered the prayer of thanksgiving to be a consecration. He believed that the officiant's thanksgiving made the bread and wine no longer "common bread and common drink."[47] Usually the prayer of consecration was accompanied by the words of institution and the Lord's Prayer.[48] In some cases, the Lord's Prayer was used in place of the prayer of consecration. Pope Gregory I (pope 590–604) stated that it "was the custom of the Apostles to consecrate the oblation only by the Lord's Prayer."[49] Finally, intercessory prayers were spoken on behalf of all classes of people, for the living and for the righteous dead.[50]

Confession and reconciliation were also part of the services. As noted above, sometimes reconciliation was effected during the kiss of peace. In some instances it may have taken place later in the service. In the *Didache* the communicants were told to "break bread and give thanks after having confessed your sins."[51] After all the initial steps were completed, the bread and wine mixed with water were distributed to each person present. Methods of distribution varied. In the experience of Justin Martyr, "the deacons . . . gave to each of those present some of the blessed bread, and of the wine mingled with water."[52] In some cases the recipients came before the bishop who placed a small piece of bread in their hand, saying, "The heavenly bread of Jesus Christ." Then they would walk to where a deacon was standing with a cup and receive the wine mixed with water from him.[53] In time it became quite customary for the individual who was distributing to say, "The body of Christ," as he gave the bread, and to say, "The blood of Christ, the cup of life," as he distributed the wine mixed with water to each person.[54] At some point it became the practice for the bishop and the clergy to commune first.[55]

When all present had received the Lord's Supper, the deacons carried some portions of the sacramental elements to members of the congregation who were absent from the service. The persons to whom the deacons carried both the bread and the consecrated cup[56] included the sick,[57] those who were imprisoned[58] or incapacitated in some other way,[59] perhaps even those whose work schedules would not permit them to attend the service.[60] In some instances family members took the consecrated bread home so that those who could not attend the service could also partake of the Lord's Supper.[61]

An old custom was that of sending some of the consecrated elements to visiting bishops,[62] and to distant churches or bishops at Easter as a token of fellowship.[63] Lutheran scholar Martin Chemnitz (1522–1586) tells of a presbyter giving the Eucharist to a boy to take to Bishop Serapion in the Nile delta. He also relates that a certain Exuperius carried "the body and blood of the Lord" in a wicker basket and a glass.[64] There was a custom in about A.D. 250 in the church at Constantinople that when "a somewhat larger amount of the parts of the immaculate body was left" they sent for boys from the elementary school to eat the remnants.[65]

Some communicants also took consecrated bread home to be eaten at a later time. Tertullian (ca. 155–ca. 220) and Cyprian (ca. 200–258) both report that the Eucharist was given to women to carry home.[66] Christians in North Africa did so in order that they might celebrate the Lord's Supper every day with their families.[67] Sasse states, "There was also private communion insofar as the members of the church took along some consecrated bread to eat at daybreak before they partook of any other food."[68] In a sermon Cyprian spoke of "lapsed" Communion with the cup being offered to those present at the service, and from which they drank at the time. The bread, however, was given into their hands so that they could eat it at once, or take it home and eat it there. Thus, "they first drank the cup in the church but ate the body of the Lord afterward at home." This practice was abrogated and prohibited at the First Council of Toledo in A.D. 390.[69]

During the first three centuries, celebrations of the Lord's Supper became simple and brief due to widespread persecution from secular authorities and Jewish antagonists. Christians usually met in small groups, at times in secret.[70] Some of the persecution directly resulted from popular misconceptions and false rumors about the celebration of the Lord's Supper. It was apparently common knowledge that Christians drank wine when they met together, and that men kissed men and women kissed women in their gatherings. Therefore, Christians were accused of having homosexual drunken orgies.[71] Since those outside the church knew that they shared in eating "the body of Christ" they were thought to be a cannibalistic cult.[72] It was rumored of the Christians that at their meeting "they ate the flesh and drank the blood of babies."[73] One reason Justin Martyr wrote his *Apology* was to allay the charge of cannibalism. He said that Christians are not subversive to the government, are not idolaters, and they are not cannibals.[74] In connection with such rumors, Pope Sixtus II (Pope 257–258) was arrested and beheaded for leading a service in the catacombs at Rome.[75]

The secrecy of the Lord's Supper celebrations helped increase the suspicion surrounding Christians. They observed silence about what they considered the "secrets" of Christianity, especially the Creed, the Lord's Prayer, and the words of institution. After the fourth century the consecration of the sacramental elements was required to be whispered because the sacred words were too awesome to be heard by all.[76] Some believed that the rites concerning the Lord's Supper seemed similar to the secret worship of pagan mystery religions. Justin Martyr and other apologists realized this similarity.[77]

Beginning in the post-apostolic era and continuing over time, worship practices became increasingly formal. Clement, who was bishop of Rome at the end of the first century,[78] indicates that this was occurring in the church at his time. Set liturgical forms and prayers were being put into place. As bishop Clement insisted that the only worthy celebrations of the Lord's Supper were those which were conducted by called bishops and presbyters.[79] When Christianity was legalized in the early part of the fourth century, numerous churches were built in various major cities and their surrounding areas. All the congregations were considered to be under the direct pastoral care of a city's bishop. The local churches were extensions of the bishop's central church. In Rome the bishop himself would consecrate the elements for the Lord's Supper each Sunday, and then acolytes would carry these to the various churches in the city.[80] A variation of this was that a piece of bread consecrated by the bishop was taken to each of the extension churches. Then it was dropped into the chalice "as a symbol of unity."[81] The agape love feast had been separated from the celebration of the Lord's Supper early in the second century.[82] Abuses of the love feast resulted in its final elimination and prohibition in the fourth century.[83]

Quite early the Lord's Supper became the focal point of the entire liturgy. Also, the "holy Communion" was given increased significance as a sacrament. Ignatius of Antioch (martyred ca. 112) referred to the Lord's Supper as "the flesh of our crucified and risen Lord Jesus." He called it "a medicine of immortality, the antidote that we should not die, but live forever in Jesus Christ."[84] Justin Martyr theorized that the elements of bread and wine over which a prayer of thanksgiving had been spoken nourished the lives of Christians "by assimilation."[85] Increasingly the Lord's Supper was seen as a means of sacramentally sharing the "divine life." A form of prayer came into use that called upon the divine Word to come upon the bread and wine. The prayer later came to be called the *epiclesis*.[86] In his *Sacramentary*, a book written primarily for bishops, Serapion speaks of the Word being asked to come upon the bread and wine to make them "the body of the Word, the blood of Truth." According to this concept the bread on the altar was thought to become "the likeness of the holy body" of Christ.[87]

By the third century it was common practice for persons to receive the Lord's Supper only in one kind, either the bread or the wine. It has already been noted that from an early time Christians would take consecrated bread from the Sunday service to commune themselves with bread only during the week. As early as the third century the Lord's Supper, especially in exceptional cases, was administered to certain persons without bread, and with wine only.[88] This was done in the case of infants and individuals who were unable to consume the bread.[89] According to the Fourth Council of Carthage and the Council of Toledo, "The blood of Christ was given . . . to sick men who had difficulty swallowing."[90] There is a report of a little girl in Carthage becoming drunk from receiving the Lord's Supper in the form of wine only. She resisted and pinched her mouth shut with her lips. The deacon forcefully poured wine into her, apparently misjudging the amount, and it "burst from her polluted inwards shortly thereafter."[91] Catholic author Joseph H. Champlin remarks of the practice of one kind in the early church, "Even then Christians recognized that each kind, blessed bread and wine contained the whole Christ."[92] To our knowledge, giving the bread only to the laity, and withholding the cup from them *in regular Sunday services* did not occur in the early church. In the latter part of the fifth century attempts were made to do so, but that practice began much later in medieval times, and only dates from the twelfth and thirteenth centuries.[93]

It is not definite as to exactly when the custom of communing infants and small children began in the early church. The practice was likely widespread. Augustine, Cyprian, Dionysis, and Pope Innocent I (Pope 401–417) all justified infant Communion on the basis of the words of Jesus in John 6:53, "Except ye eat the flesh of the Son of man and drink His blood, ye have no life in you."[94] In a sermon Augustine said of babies, "They are infants, but they are his members. They are infants, but they receive his sacraments. They are infants, but they become participants at his table, so that they may have life in themselves."[95] Pope Innocent I held that little children should be given the Lord's Supper "in the liquid form of the Lord's Blood, or in the form of bread crumbled and mixed with water."[96] He said that some thought that little ones should not be given the Lord's Supper because they might vomit it up, and that it would not be profitable for them if they did not swallow it down, but "certain esteemed men" have said that "in the consuming of the Eucharist nothing is required, except to coax a taste and to sense the flavor."[97]

In the third century some Christians used Old Testament ideas of priesthood and sacrifice to interpret the Lord's Supper. Yale professor Williston Walker comments, "The Eucharistic gifts of bread and wine presented to God were viewed as the 'pure sacrifice' foretold by Malachi and as the Christian form of the Old Testament offerings of fine flour and firstfruits."[98] The "sacrifice" at first was essentially a matter of praise and thanksgiving, "the gifts of bread and wine" being viewed as a sacrificial thankoffering to commemorate the sacrifice of Christ on the cross.[99] This understanding was followed by the concept of the self-sacrifice of the worshipers themselves in return to Christ for His sacrifice on Calvary.[100] There was an evolution of the thought that the Lord's Supper is a sacrifice. That evolution resulted in the understanding that in the Lord's Supper an offering was made to God to gain forgiveness.

In the ancient church three distinct theories emerged regarding the relationship of the elements of bread and wine to the body and blood of Christ.[101] The first two of these three views were the realistic and the symbolic. Some of the fathers clearly identified with one understanding or the other. Others seem to have espoused both views. It appears that in the minds of some of the fathers the two positions frequently overlapped. The third view, the metabolic, appeared toward the end of the fourth century, somewhat later than the realistic and the symbolic. We should pause here to consider the philosophical weight of "realistic" and "symbolic." Since the word "real" did not exist until the later Middle Ages, these ancient fathers would not have called their own position "realistic."[102] It is a label that we use to categorize views, as is similarly the case with "symbolic." The terms are useful when they are well defined and serve the confession of God's Word. Here, "realistic" means something like "tangible" or "located in a certain place" whereas "symbolic" refers to a located, tangible object being a "means of access" or a "representation" of a higher reality or object.

We encounter in such terms the question of how something is "real" versus "unreal," "present" versus "absent," "effective" versus "ineffectual," and so forth. Behind all this is the concern of how Jesus imparts His gifts to His people. In considering these views we see different ways in which the church fathers tried to explain the sacred witness in the Scriptures using worldly categories and systems of understanding. If we want to speak of something as "real," then we are indebted to systems that describe reality. In the early church, those systems and categories tended to come from the works of Plato, Porphyry, and Plotinus. Taken together, this is called Neoplatonism, a modified understanding of Plato's concept of the Forms, ideal "realities" that do not change and are eternal, coupled with the changeable, temporal reflections or shadows of those forms, similar to shadows of objects cast by the dancing flames of a fire on the wall of a cave. In the medieval period, Aristotle's model became prominent. That model incorporates the Unmoved Mover; the Logos, who goes forth from the Unmoved Mover to determine the fate of the world; and the material world as a stage for causes to generate effects by using thoughts from the Logos and matter from the world.

The ancient world struggled with the contradiction between a permanent reality on the one hand and the changeable world in which they lived on the other. What was real, what was unreal, and how did good and evil figure into it? Dreams have a semblance of reality, but they pass away when you wake up. Will the world similarly pass away? Philosophy tried to describe how we got here, how natural laws work, and where we will go to eternally. In the long run, Aristotle's system won out as the basis for modern science. Do you see a conflict here between philosophy or science and the Bible? In looking at these systems, one does not see the need for the witness of Genesis and the personal interest of God in His creation. Genesis is just as much about how God loves His creation as it is about His creating it, as the commitment to a savior in Genesis 3:15 shows. If Jesus is central to both the Scriptures and to the Lord's Supper, He and His words, not some philosophical system, should be paramount. The best way to confess God's love toward us, which includes the Lord's Supper, is to confess the words that our Lord gives us in the Scriptures.

Among the early church fathers, Justin Martyr (ca. 100–ca. 165), Ignatius (martyred ca. 112), Irenaeus (died ca. 200), Tertullian (ca. 155–ca. 220), and Hesychius (ca. 300) clearly held to a realistic conception of "the sacramental union."[103] In his *Apology* Justin wrote of the bread and wine, "The food which is blessed by the word of prayer and by which our blood and flesh are changed and nourished, is the flesh and blood of Jesus who was made flesh."[104] Ignatius spoke of what is received in the Sacrament as, "the flesh of our crucified and risen Lord Jesus."[105] Irenaeus contended that in view of the act of the consecration the bread and wine "are pervaded by the body and blood of Christ." He stated that after the elements are consecrated there are "two realities, earthly and heavenly."[106] Hesychlus saw this presence as a mystery, saying, "He commands to eat flesh with bread, in order that we might understand that that is called a mystery, because it is at the same time bread and flesh."[107] Sasse says of Ambrose of Milan (340–397), "Ambrose is the great authority for the sacramental realism which prevailed more and more in the following centuries."[108] In the *Book of Sacraments* Ambrose wrote, "Bread is ordinary bread before the sacramental words, yet, when the consecration takes place, the bread becomes the body of Christ," and, "Wine and water are put into the cup, but it becomes blood by the consecration of the heavenly word."[109] He illustrated the change worked in the elements by referring to the transformation of the rod of Moses (Exodus 4:3) and the waters of the Nile (Exodus 7:20).[110]

Among the church fathers that held to the symbolic view were Origin (ca. 185–ca. 254), Cyprian (ca. 200–258), and Eusebius (ca. 260–ca. 339). Origin held that the only effectual thing in the Lord's Supper is the Word of Christ. In a sermon he said that eating Christ's body and drinking His blood means to receive His words. For Origin, the only difference between hearing God's Word and receiving the Lord's Supper is that in the Supper a symbol is added.[111] Cyprian called the wine an allegory of Christ's blood.[112] He felt the words of institution were to be interpreted symbolically. For Cyprian, the mixing of the water with the wine was essential, because this symbolized the union of Christ with the church. The wine represented Christ's blood. The water represented the people.[113] Eusebius spoke of the Lord's Supper as being a memorial of Christ's sacrifice "by symbols both of the body and of the saving blood."[114]

Augustine is difficult to categorize, either with the realistic or symbolic thinkers. This is because he used the language of both interchangeably.[115] On the one hand, he spoke realistically when he stated, "The bread which you see on the altar, sanctified by the Word of God, is Christ's body. The cup, or rather the contents of that cup, sanctified by the Word of God, is Christ's blood."[116] He also spoke symbolically, saying that the elements were "visible signs of an invisible grace."[117] When he used the term "sacrament" he explained himself by writing, "A sacrament is a sacred sign."[118] Augustine claimed to believe that Christ's body was not actually present in the Sacrament, because he felt that according to His human nature Christ "is some place in heaven." According to His divine nature Christ is everywhere entirely present.[119] On one occasion Augustine represented Christ as saying, "You must understand what I have said in a spiritual sense. You are not going to eat this body which you see or drink that blood which those who crucify me are going to shed."[120] Schaff has stated, "From his immense dogmatic authority, Augustine has been an apple of contention among the different confessions in all controversies on the doctrine of the Supper."[121] Athanasius also spoke both ways. He emphatically repudiated the idea of partaking of real flesh and blood, and spoke rather of a "spiritual participation."[122] But he also declared, "When the great and wondrous prayers have been recited, then the bread becomes the body and the cup the blood of our Lord Jesus Christ."[123]

Proponents of the third view, the metabolic, included such church fathers as Cyril of Jerusalem (ca. 315–ca. 386), Gregory of Nyssa (ca. 331–ca. 396), and John Chrysostom (ca. 345–407). The metabolic view was connected with the symbolic, and had to do with a change of the elements into Christ's body and blood in a spiritual sense. Cyril of Jerusalem set forth the idea of a *metabole*, a spiritual "transformation of the bread and wine into the body and blood of Christ."[124] He plainly taught a supernatural connection between the elements and the body and blood of Christ, but he did not teach transubstantiation.[125] What Cyril had in mind was not a change in substance, but a spiritual change, whereby Christ became miraculously present in the consecrated elements. Chrysostom speaks of the body of Christ actually being present in the Lord's Supper, but he, too, does not think of a change in substance, but says that the consecrated bread "is worthy to be called the appearance of the Lord's body although the nature of bread remains in it."[126]

Whether realistically, symbolically, or metabolically, all parties asserted that the body and blood of Christ are present in the Sacrament. This perhaps led to the development of transubstantiation, a change in the substance of bread and wine into the body and blood of Christ. Although the term itself had not yet been coined, by A.D. 496 Pope Gelasius I condemned the root idea behind this theory in an *ex cathedra* (officially binding) statement. He pronounced, "The sacrament of the body and blood of Christ which we receive is a divine thing, because bread and wine do not cease to be and assuredly the image and the similitude of the body and blood of Christ are celebrated in the performance of the mysteries."[127]

About A.D. 440 a heretical group known as the Manichaeans advocated the introduction of giving only bread at the Lord's Supper because they detested wine. In their heresy they taught that Christ's body was imaginary and had no real blood. Pope Leo I (Pope 440–461) called it a sacrilege if anyone refused to drink the cup.[128] Some 50 years later there was again a movement for bread only at the Sacrament. Those proposing this in the second attempt were people within the church who, for superstitious reasons, wished to abstain from the cup. In response to them, Pope Gelasius I stated, "Let them either receive the sacraments entire, or be excluded from the entire sacraments, for a division of one and the same sacrament cannot be made without great sacrilege."[129] He believed that people who abstained from taking the wine for superstitious reasons should be excommunicated.[130]

The sixth century marked the beginning of private Masses, those with only the priest present. With this innovation the sense of all the people participating in the celebrations of the Lord's Supper began to be lost. Originally these private services were held with the intention of praying for special needs. However, the practice detracted from the purpose of the Lord's Supper and would ultimately have a long-term effect on the observance of the Lord's Supper in the church.[131]

In 1 Corinthians chapter 5 the apostle Paul reproved the congregation at Corinth because a man among them was living in open sin, having his father's wife as his own, and the congregation had taken no action regarding this. As Paul spoke to them, telling them to deal with the situation, he said in verse 11 that they should not even eat with such a person. This obviously was a reference to the Lord's Supper.[132] The manifest and impenitent sinner was not to be permitted to join with the congregation in partaking of the Sacrament. Exclusion from the Lord's Supper and excommunication were synonymous for all practical purposes. Erlangen University professor Werner Elert says that "beyond doubt excommunication meant in practice exclusion from the Lord's Supper, and reconciliation readmission."[133] The early church took this very seriously. In the *Didache* the directive is given, "Let no one who has a dispute with a fellow Christian assemble with you until they are reconciled, so that your sacrament may not be defiled."[134] When the man who had lived in sin repented, St. Paul exhorted the Corinthians to receive him back (2 Corinthians 2:6, 7). In a similar way Corinthian bishop Dionysius (ca. 170) told congregations to receive again repentant persons who had been separated from the church because of their sins. However, a lengthy process was involved in their being received again at the Lord's Table. Penitent sinners had to pass through penitential periods, sometimes as long as 27 years. There were even certain sins for which they could never again receive the Lord's Supper. The penitential period for an adulterer was five years. A believing wife who had left her husband because he committed adultery, and who married another man could not receive the Lord's Supper until her first husband had died. If a believer fell away and did not attend church for a long time, the penitential period was ten years. Basil gave the recommendation that if soldiers killed someone in war they should not commune for three years, but if a man had intentionally murdered someone he was to be excluded from the Lord's Supper for 20 years. At a Synod in A.D. 314 bishops were granted authority to lengthen or shorten penitential periods. In doing this they were to be guided by brotherly love. Exceptions to the penitential periods were made for those who were about to die. In deathbed cases penitential periods were to be set aside and such persons were to be granted the privilege of receiving the Lord's Supper before they died.[135]

Congregations in the early church practiced closed Communion. A fundamental tenet of this practice included the understanding of church fellowship, namely, that the church was one: "One Lord, one faith, one baptism" (Ephesians 4:5). This unity excluded external things such as ethnicity, wealth, poverty, gender, and other worldly distinctions when considering membership in the church (Galatians 3:28). This unity did not, however, serve to get rid of divine orders in the church, such as the Pastoral Ministry. Nor did this unity serve to blind individuals and churches to divisions in doctrine and to grievous sin (1 Corinthians 10–11). In observance of this unity and common obedience to Christ with respect to all scripture and all the doctrines taught therein (2 Timothy 3:16) the early church established means to regulate and express the fellowship that the congregations had in Christ and in each other. Christians could move about from one congregation to another and receive the Lord's Supper. To expedite this, certificates called "Letters of Peace" were given to Christian travelers and to Christians moving to a new location. The letters told those to whom they were issued whom they should seek fellowship with in a new place. If the person were changing residence, the letter served as a "transfer," using today's parlance, to a congregation in the new community. The Letters of Peace were also expressions of fellowship between congregations and between the bishops of these several congregations.[136]

NOTES

1. Fred L. Precht, ed., *Lutheran Worship: History and Practice* (St. Louis: Concordia, 1993), 134.
2. Justin Martyr, "How We Christians Worship," trans. Everett Ferguson *Christian History* 12, no. 1 (1993): 12.

3. Willy Rordorf, et al, *The Eucharist of the Early Christians*, trans. Michael J. O'Connell (New York: Pueblo Publishing Co., 1978), 3; Philip Schaff, *History of the Christian Church* (n.p.; Charles Scribner's Sons, 1958–1960), 2:236; Carl A. Volz, *Faith and Practice in the Early Church: Foundations for Contemporary Theology* (Minneapolis: Augsburg, 1983), 102.

4. Schaff, *History*, 2:236, 3:516.

5. Schaff, *History*, 3:516.

6. Schaff, *History*, 3:516.

7. Laurence Hull Stookey, *Eucharist: Christ's Feast with the Church* (Nashville: Abingdon, 1993), 69.

8. Christopher Haas, "Where Did Christians Worship?" *Christian History* 12, no. 1 (1993): 33, 34.

9. Haas, "Christians," 33, 34.

10. Haas, "Christians," 35.

11. Joseph M. Champlin, *Special Signs of Grace: The Sacraments and Sacramentals* (Collegeville, Minn.: Liturgical Press, 1986), 52; Stookey, *Eucharist*, 70.

12. Paul E. Kretzmann, *Christian Art in the Place and in the Form of Lutheran Worship* (St. Louis: Concordia, 1921), 22.

13. Haas, "Christians," 35.

14. Martin Chemnitz, *Examination of the Council of Trent: Part Two*, trans. Fred Kramer (St. Louis: Concordia, 1978), 501.

15. Volz, *Faith and Practice*, 970.

16. Rordorf, *Early Christians*, 2–17.

17. Schaff, *History*, 2:236.

18. Volz, *Faith and Practice*, 98.

19. Rordorf, *Early Christians*, 71, 77.

20. David P. Wright, "Early Glimpses," *Christian History* 12, no. 1 (1993): 23.

21. Williston Walker, *A History of the Christian Church*, rev. C. C. Richardson, W. Pauck, and R. Handy (New York: Scribner, 1959), 90.

22. Stookey, *Eucharist*, 69.

23. Tim Dowley, et al, ed., *Eerdmans Handbook to the History of Christianity* (Grand Rapids, Mich.: Eerdmans, 1977), 35; Schaff, *History*, 2:232; Stookey, *Eucharist*, 80; Walker, *Christian Church*, 153.

24. Norbert Engebrecht, *How the Church Grew* (St. Louis: Concordia, 1966), 13; Martyr, "Christians Worship," 12.

25. Rordorf, *Early Christians*, 195.

26. Charles P. Krauth, *The Conservative Reformation and Its Theology* (1871; reprint, Minneapolis: Augsburg House, 1963), 752; Schaff, *History*, 2:232.

27. Norman Nagel, "Closed Communion: In the Way of the Gospel: In the Way of the Law," *Concordia Journal* 17, no. 1 (1991): 20.

28. Nagel, "Closed Communion," 22; Rordorf, *Early Christians*, 2.

29. Nagel, "Closed Communion," 21.

30. Werner Elert, *Eucharist and Church Fellowship in the First Four Centuries*, trans. N. E. Nagel (St. Louis: Concordia, 1966), 75; Edward A. Engelbrecht,

Open, Close, Closed?: Lutheran Communion Practice (Roanoke, Ill.: Angel Bright Publication, 1996), 10.

31. Paul McCain, e-mail letter to Robert J. Jastram, et al, 10 September 1998; Nagel, "Closed Communion," 20.
32. Engelbrecht, *Closed?*, 10.
33. Haas, "Christians," 34; Engelbrecht, *Closed?*, 10.
34. Engelbrecht, *Closed?*, 10.
35. Walker, *Christian Church*, 153.
36. Dowley, *Handbook*, 127; Schaff, *History*, 2:237.
37. Martyr, "Christians Worship," 14; Schaff, *History*, 2:235.
38. Precht, *Lutheran Worship*, 430.
39. Nagel, "Closed Communion," 22.
40. Luther D. Reed, *The Lutheran Liturgy: A Study of the Common Service of the Lutheran Church in America* (Philadelphia: Muhlenberg Press, 1947), 343.
41. Martyr, "Christians Worship," 14; Schaff, *History*, 2:235.
42. Nagel, "Closed Communion," 22, 23.
43. Dowley, *Handbook*, 128; Schaff, *History*, 2:235.
44. Wright, "Early Glimpses," 23.
45. Schaff, *History*, 2:237.
46. Wright, "Early Glimpses," 23, 24.
47. Martyr, "Christians Worship," 13.
48. Schaff, *History*, 2:237, 238.
49. Schaff, *History*, 2:238.
50. Schaff, *History*, 2:238; 3:575.
51. Peter M. Glock, "Early Developments of the Eucharist" (Wahpeton, N.Dak. Pastoral Conference, 1994), 6; Wright, "Early Glimpses," 22.
52. Schaff, *History*, 2:235.
53. Engebrecht, *Grew*, 14.
54. Schaff, *History*, 2:238.
55. Schaff, *History*, 3:515.
56. Chemnitz, *Examination*, 369.
57. Chemnitz, *Examination*, 251.
58. Schaff, *History*, 3:515.
59. Stookey, *Eucharist*, 65.
60. Stookey, *Eucharist*, 65.
61. John O. Gooch, "Did You Know?" *Christian History* 12, no. 1 (1993): 3.
62. Chemnitz, *Examination*, 251.
63. Schaff, *History*, 3:517.
64. Chemnitz, *Examination*, 286.
65. Chemnitz, *Examination*, 286.
66. Chemnitz, *Examination*, 286.
67. Gooch, "Did You Know?" 30.

68. Hermann Sasse, *This Is My Body: Luther's Contention for the Real Presence in the Sacrament of the Altar*, rev. ed. (Adelaide, South Australia: Lutheran Publishing House, 1977), 51.

69. Chemnitz, *Examination*, 305, 306, 419, 420.

70. Champlin, *Special Signs*, 52; Paul Johnson, *A History of Christianity* (London: Weidenfeld and Nicolson, 1976), 71.

71. Johnson, *History of Christianity*, 71; Stookey, *Eucharist*, 64.

72. Dowley, *Handbook*, 72; Johnson, *History of Christianity*, 71; Krauth, *Conservative Reformation*, 752; Hermann Sasse, *We Confess the Sacraments*, trans. Norman Nagel (St. Louis: Concordia, 1985), 80; Stookey, *Eucharist*, 64.

73. Engebrecht, *Grew*, 11.

74. Nagel, "Closed Communion," 21.

75. Martyr, "Christians Worship," 15; Richard P. McBrien, *Lives of the Popes: The Pontiffs from St. Peter to John Paul II* (San Francisco: Harper, 1997), 51.

76. Volz, *Faith and Practice*, 96.

77. E. Glenn Hinson, "Worshiping Like Pagans?" *Christian History* 13, no. 1 (1993): 16.

78. Erwin L. Lueker, ed., *Lutheran Cyclopedia: A Concise In-Home Reference for the Christian Family*, rev. ed. (St. Louis: Concordia, 1975), 43; Malachi Martin, *The Decline and Fall of the Roman Church* (New York: Putnam, 1981), 30.

79. Dowley, *Handbook*, 126.

80. Dowley, *Handbook*, 181; Paul A. Feider, *The Sacraments: Encountering the Risen Lord* (Notre Dame, Ind.: Ave Maria Press, 1986), 41.

81. Feider, *Sacraments*, 41.

82. Dowley, *Handbook*, 126.

83. Schaff, *History*, 2:239.

84. Dowley, *Handbook*, 126; Schaff, *History*, 2:241.

85. Dowley, *Handbook*, 126; Schaff, *History*, 2:242.

86. Dowley, *Handbook*, 126.

87. Dowley, *Handbook*, 128.

88. Schaff, *History*, 2:239; 3:516, 517.

89. Champlin, *Special Signs*, 55.

90. Chemnitz, *Examination*, 366.

91. Chemnitz, *Examination*, 366; Schaff, *History*, 3:516, 517.

92. Champlin, *Special Signs*, 55.

93. Chemnitz, *Examination*, 353, 420, 421; Schaff, *History*, 3:517.

94. Johann Gerhard, "Whether the Eucharist Should be Given to Infants," trans. Ronald B. Bagnall, *Lutheran Forum* 30, no. 4 (1996): 14; Schaff, History, 3:516.

95. Saint Augustine, "Infants Become Partakers of His Table that They May Have Life," trans. Ronald B. Bagnall, *Lutheran Forum* 30, no. 4 (1996): 11.

96. Gerhard, "Infants," 14.

97. Gerhard, "Infants," 14.

98. Walker, *Christian Church*, 90.

99. Dowley, *Handbook*, 9; Schaff, *History*, 2:245.

100. Schaff, *History*, 2:245, 246.

101. E. H. Klotsche, *The History of Christian Doctrine*, rev. J. Theodore Mueller and David P. Scaer (1945; reprint, Grand Rapids: Baker, 1979), 105.

102. Albert Collver, "Real Presence: An Overview and History of the Term," *Concordia Journal* 28, no. 2 (2002): 144.

103. Chemnitz, *Examination*, 271; Klotsche, *Doctrine*, 105.

104. Dowley, *Handbook*, 127.

105. Schaff, *History*, 2:241.

106. Klotsche, *Doctrine*, 105; Walker, *Christian Church*, 90.

107. Chemnitz, *Examination*, 271.

108. Sasse, *Body*, 19.

109. Krauth, *Conservative Reformation*, 675.

110. Krauth, *Conservative Reformation*, 106

111. Klotsche, *Doctrine*, 106.

112. Schaff, *History*, 2:244.

113. Klotsche, *Doctrine*, 106.

114. Klotsche, *Doctrine*, 106.

115. Volz, *Faith and Practice*, 109.

116. Volz, *Faith and Practice*, 109.

117. Klotsche, *Doctrine*, 106.

118. Sasse, *Body*, 20.

119. Sasse, *Body*, 20.

120. Volz, *Faith and Practice*, 109.

121. Schaff, *History*, 3:498.

122. Klotsche, *Doctrine*, 106; Schaff, *History*, 3:496.

123. Volz, *Faith and Practice*, 108.

124. Klotsche, *Doctrine*, 107.

125. Schaff, *History*, 3:493.

126. Klotsche, *Doctrine*, 107.

127. Klotsche, *Doctrine*, 108.

128. Chemnitz, *Examination*, 420.

129. Chemnitz, *Examination*, 353.

130. Chemnitz, *Examination*, 421.

131. Feider, *Sacraments*, 42.

132. Elert, *Fellowship*, 84.

133. Elert, *Fellowship*, 94.

134. Wright, "Early Glimpses," 22.

135. Elert, *Fellowship*, 93, 95–97, 101.

136. Elert, *Fellowship*, 138, 139.

STUDY QUESTIONS

1. How frequently, and at least on what day, was the Lord's Supper celebrated in the ancient church?

2. By the end of the apostolic era when John wrote Revelation, what name had been given to Sunday and, by extension, to the worship on that day?

3. What was generally the first setting for Christian worship and the reception of the Lord's Supper?

4. Under what Roman emperor's *Peace of the Church* in A.D. 313, strengthened by his later favor and conversion, did Christians finally begin to build churches on a wide scale without fear of persecution?

5. Where were some celebrations of the Lord's Supper in "the company of the martyrs" located?

6. From which sources do we receive the oldest prayers, liturgical forms, and teachings regarding the Lord's Supper following the apostolic era?

7. True or false: The early church practiced closed Communion, even to the extent that all catechumens, all unbelievers, and all holding to heterodox teachings were ushered out of the sanctuary before the celebration of the Supper began.

8. What action began the ancient Communion liturgy that demonstrated the peace and unity of the congregation as they prepared to receive the Lord's Supper?

9. Although many congregations today consider the "offering" to be that of money given for the support and work of the congregation and the greater church, of what did the "offering" consist in the ancient church?

10. True or false: There has always been some kind of witness to an act of consecration and prayer before the administration of the Lord's Supper, so that the elements were no longer common food and drink.

11. True or false: Congregations never shared their consecrated elements with other congregations or bishops, even on Easter.

12. True or false: There existed a number of traditions regarding private Communion in the early church.

13. What two groups, by means of persecution, caused early Christian worship to be simple, brief, and secretive? What two falsehoods were commonly said of Christians and their celebrations of the Lord's Supper?

14. True or false: Worship in the first four centuries of the early church remained informal and bishops had no real central authority.

15. True or false: The Lord's Supper quickly became the centerpiece of the Sunday liturgy and grew in sacramental importance as a participation in the divine life.

16. True or false: Although some began receiving the Lord's Supper in one kind as early as the third century, the mandated reception in one kind at regular Sunday services did not begin until the medieval period.

17. True or false: Infant Communion was not widespread in the early church.

18. True or false: The false doctrine of the Sacrifice of the Mass finds its origins in the application of Old Testament concepts of sacrifice to the elements of the Lord's Supper made by some Christians in the third century.

19. The three main understandings of the Lord's Supper that developed in the ancient church are categorized as the realistic, the symbolic, and the metabolic. Briefly explain how each view considered the body and blood of Christ in the Sacrament.

20. How did Augustine's positions on the Lord's Supper lay the ground for division in the medieval and early modern church?

21. True or false: A heretical group known as the Manicheans was one of the first major groups to advocate giving only the bread in the Lord's Supper, prompting Pope Leo I to insist that both kinds be distributed.

22. True or false: Private Masses began in the sixth century.

23. True or false: Penance for those who lapsed into sin and were prevented from receiving the Lord's Supper could endure for more than twenty years, with an exception for deathbed communion.

24. True or false: Early Christians practiced closed Communion and signified altar fellowship and those of true doctrine and good standing with "Letters of Peace" that allowed one to join a congregation in a different area.

5 | EASTERN ORTHODOXY: THE LORD'S SUPPER AS LITURGY

The history of Eastern Orthodoxy begins with the establishment of the Christian church in Asia Minor and the Eastern Mediterranean area. In reality, the early history of the Christian church in that area is the same as the beginning chapters of Eastern Orthodoxy. This includes the missionary endeavors in the apostolic era, the accounts of many Christian martyrs, and the teachings of the earliest church fathers.[1]

Fathers of the Eastern church held a variety of views regarding the Lord's Supper. Ignatius of Antioch was a realist, holding to the "real presence" of Christ's body and blood in the Lord's Supper.[2] Athanasius sometimes seemed to accept a realistic view of the Lord's Supper, and sometimes the symbolic.[3] Origin embraced the symbolic view, believing that the only effectual thing in the Lord's Supper is Christ's Word.[4] Eusebius, like Origin, had a symbolic conception of the Lord's Supper.[5] Macarius the Elder (ca. 300–ca. 390) also viewed the Lord's Supper symbolically, calling the bread and wine types of Christ's body and blood.[6] A *type* (Greek *typos*) is something that either foreshadows or represents something else. Gregory of Nyssa taught that those partaking in the Lord's Supper are united with and incorporated into the God-man.[7] Gregory of Nazianzus (ca. 330–ca. 390) spoke of the consecrated bread and wine as symbols and types of the great mysteries, but ascribed saving virtues to them.[8] Basil the Great (ca. 330–ca. 379) tended to spiritualize the role of the elements in the Lord's Supper.[9] Cyril of Jerusalem (ca. 315–ca. 386) declared, "When the invocation is made, the bread becomes the body of Christ and the wine his blood"[10] and that "by partaking of the body and blood of Christ . . . we become partakers of the divine nature."[11] Chrysostom called the Lord's Supper "the very body and blood of Christ,"[12] and taught that those who participate in the Lord's Supper progress in sanctification as members of the mystical body of Christ.[13] Although the church fathers tried to explain the Scriptures using worldly categories of understanding, we need to remember that the best confession of the Lord's Supper remains in the Scriptures themselves.

The Orthodox church today uses the term "transubstantiation" when speaking of the relationship between the bread and wine and the body and blood of Christ in the Lord's Supper. The church traces the concept of transubstantiation back to the great dogmatician, John of Damascus (perhaps ca. 675–750), whose doctrine of a real change became the common property of the Orthodox church. John taught that the bread and wine become the body and blood of Christ, truly present in the Lord's Supper:

> It is truly that Body, united with Godhead, which has its origin from the Holy Virgin; not as though that Body which ascended came down from heaven, but because the bread and wine themselves are changed into the Body and Blood of God. But if thou seekest after the

manner how this is, let it suffice thee to be told that it is by the Holy Ghost; in like manner as by the same Holy Ghost, the Lord formed flesh to himself, and in himself, from the Mother of God; nor know I aught more than this, that the Word of God is true, powerful, and almighty, but its manner unsearchable."[14]

John wrote extensively on the Lord's Supper and compared the words of institution to the words of God spoken at creation. He likened the miracle of the Lord's Supper to the miracle accomplished by the Holy Spirit when Jesus was conceived. John said that Christ's body in the Lord's Supper is identical with the body born of the Virgin Mary. The Holy Spirit works the miracle of transforming the bread and wine into the Lord's body and blood.[15] John did not claim to be able to discern how the bread and wine are changed into the body and blood, but said, "We know nothing more than that the Word of God is true, effective and almighty, but the *how* is past finding out."[16] He compared the transforming of the bread and wine in the Lord's Supper with the transforming of food and drink in our bodies.[17]

The Orthodox church has retained John's doctrine. In the Eastern liturgy the prayer of consecration reads, in part, "Make this bread the precious body of Christ . . . and the contents of this chalice the precious blood of Thy Christ, changing them through Thy Holy Spirit."[18] Like John, the authors of the *Orthodox Study Bible* say, "The bread is truly His Body, and that which is in the cup is truly His Blood, but one cannot say *how* they become so."[19] Orthodox professor John Karmiris writes, "The elements of bread and wine are changed into body and blood in such a way that he is hypostatically and essentially present in the sacrament."[20] Orthodox teaching attributes this change to the direct invocation of the Holy Spirit,[21] not by repeating the words of institution. Orthodox theologian Paul Meyendorff says, "The Orthodox believe that, through the Holy Spirit, Christ descends to give us his body and blood."[22] It is taught that the real presence of Christ's body and blood remains in the consecrated elements after the Communion.[23] Karmiris speaks of "the permanent presence of the whole Lord in every part of the elements."[24]

In their use of the word "transubstantiation" the Orthodox differ from the Roman Catholic Church, which also uses the same term. According to Orthodox theologians, the Roman Church was pressed by rationalists to define *how* transformation takes place. They say, "The sacrament which only faith can comprehend, was subjected to a philosophical definition."[25] They declare that when Jesus said, "This is My body," and, "This is My blood" He was referring to the bread and wine that He was offering to the disciples as His own body and blood. Then they state, "Orthodox teaching has always affirmed the truth of Jesus' words, no more and no less, but without scrutinizing or theorizing about this great mystery of faith."[26]

There are seven "sacraments" or "mysteries" in the Holy Liturgy of the Orthodox churches.[27] Many Orthodox prefer to use the term mysteries, rather than sacraments.[28] The term "mystery" carries a sense of "secret" and "secret truths"[29] and provokes a feeling of awe for that which is holy. They hold that through these mysteries God enters the world to transform it and enters persons to make them divine.[30] The seven mysteries are Baptism, Unction with Chrism (anointing with oil mixed with balm, signifying confirmation), Holy Communion (or Eucharist), Penance, Orders, Matrimony, and Unction with Oil (of the sick or dying).[31] The Holy Communion is the chief mystery in the Holy Liturgy.[32]

During the iconoclastic controversy in the eighth and ninth centuries there were numerous images or pictures of Jesus, the apostles, martyrs, and saints in many churches. Many who bowed down before them or kissed them venerated these images. Sometimes scrapings of coloring matter from these images or pictures were mixed with the bread and wine in the Lord's Supper.[33] Icons figure prominently in Orthodox worship. It is considered that a proper icon should consist of the same substance as that for which it stands.[34] During the iconoclastic controversy Emperor Constantine V (Emperor 741–745) contended that the consecrated elements of the Lord's Supper are the true icon of Christ. He apparently believed that these elements are identical in substance with the body and blood of Christ.[35]

In the *Liturgy of Chrysostom* four reasons are given that explain why Orthodox believers partake of the Lord's Supper: "For the purification of the soul, for the remission of sins, for the fellowship of the Holy Spirit, and for the fulfillment of the kingdom of heaven."[36] Karmiris mentions a two-fold sacramental purpose of the Lord's Supper. He says that in the Lord's Supper the communicant's soul is purified and sanctified. Through partaking the person is spiritually nourished and "mystically rendered incorruptible." He also states that participants receive "the seed of incorruption, resurrection, immortality and eternal life." By taking in "the very body and blood of Christ" those communing progress in sanctification as members of Christ's church, His "mystical body."[37]

The Orthodox church also views the Lord's Supper as a true and propitiatory sacrifice of Christ offered for both the living and the dead.[38] It is taught as a continuation of Christ's sacrifice on the cross. In the Lord's Supper, Christ as both priest and victim offers His body and blood to the Father under the forms of bread and wine.[39] His offering is "for the whole world, for the holy, catholic, and apostolic church."[40] This includes all Orthodox Christians—those living today and those who have died and await the resurrection to eternal life. The sacrifice will not be complete until judgment day. In the Lord's Supper nothing is believed to be added to Christ's sacrifice on the cross. The benefits of that sacrifice are communicated to those who receive the Lord's Supper. His death on the cross is not repeated.[41]

Receiving the Lord's Supper is believed to be necessary for salvation.[42] It is considered to be equally important with the sacrament of Baptism.[43] Infants and little children should also be baptized and receive the Lord's Supper. However, Orthodox professor Thomas Hopko qualifies what some have said regarding the necessity of infants receiving the sacraments in order to be saved. He states, "What happens ultimately to those" who die without Baptism "is known to God alone who sees and judges every life."[44] It naturally follows that what he says of those not baptized, applies also to those not receiving the Lord's Supper, for in Orthodoxy only baptized persons may commune.

Infants have long received the Lord's Supper in Eastern churches.[45] In early days it was given in the form of wine only.[46] It is customary for infants to be given their first Lord's Supper on the day they are baptized. Hopko writes, "To baptize anyone, according to the Orthodox understanding, without Chrismation and Holy Communion following immediately is like being born without living."[47] Communing infants is justified on the basis of John 6:53–54. Babies are baptized, anointed with chrism, and receive the Lord's Supper for the first time on about the fortieth day after their birth. Hopko says that "in the case of infants the portion of the Lord's Body is obviously very small."[48] They continue to receive the Lord's Supper at each celebration of "the mystical supper" in their growing years.[49]

Orthodox communicants prepare for reception of the Lord's Supper by self-examination, fasting, and prayers. The self-examination includes the confession of sins in the presence of a priest, who visibly represents Christ. Being reconciled to one another is also part of the preparation.[50] The Supper is believed to have an effect whether the individual partaking has faith and is prepared or not. For the person who does not have faith and is not prepared the consequence of communing is negative and harmful. Only those who receive in faith and are rightly prepared are blessed through the mystery of the Lord's Supper. Therefore communicants are exhorted to prepare themselves so that it may be personally efficacious for them.

Ordinarily the Lord's Supper is celebrated only once a day in an individual church.[51] Sunday has been and is still accepted as the usual day for the celebration. The authors of the *Orthodox Study Bible* note that in Acts 20:7 it is stated that the disciples came together to break bread on the first day of the week, which is Sunday. They say that occasional Communion is without New Testament precedence.[52] Communion only on Sunday and major feast days remains the practice in normal parish churches, but some cathedrals and large monasteries celebrate the mystery every day. Timothy (Kallistos) Ware, lecturer at Oxford University, reports that in Russia, where there have been few churches and many Christians have been required to work on Sunday, many town parishes observe the Lord's Supper on a daily basis.[53] All members of Orthodox churches are required to receive the Lord's Supper at least once a year.[54] Many meet this requirement either on Maundy Thursday or Easter Sunday.[55]

In Orthodox churches the Lord's Supper is the chief and most essential part of the divine service. At one time many local liturgical forms were used. There was also considerable variety to the prayers. Today almost all Orthodox churches use the *Liturgy of St. John Chrysostom* when they celebrate the Lord's Supper, also known as the *Byzantine Divine Liturgy*.[56] The services are conducted in the language of the people. All the services are chanted or sung.[57] The Lord's Supper must always be celebrated in a church on a special table that has been consecrated by a bishop.[58] The table is called a "throne" because they believe that on it Christ is mystically present as King.[59] Before the liturgy begins, the priest and the deacons are prepared for the service. This is done outside the sanctuary proper behind an *iconostasis*. An *iconostasis* is a wall on which there are depictions of Christ, the Virgin Mary, and several saints. There are three doors through the wall. In front of these doors the celebrants venerate the icons of Christ and Mary. Then they come into the sanctuary where they vest themselves. The vesting is accompanied by appropriate prayers, and followed by a hand-washing ritual of purification.

After an opening prayer the bread and wine are ceremoniously prepared. Prayers, the "Small Procession" which symbolizes Christ's entry into the world, hymns, and readings follow. This section of the service concludes with a prayer for the universal church, including petitions for the intentions of the faithful, and also the catechumens.[60] At this point the catechumens are dismissed as a deacon says, "Catechumens, depart; catechumens, depart; catechumens, depart; away with the catechumens."[61]

The Eucharistic portion of the service begins with prayers. Then there is the "Great Procession." The procession consists of the solemn bringing of the gifts to the table. The song of the cherubim is sung. After the incensing of the bread and wine the elements are surrounded by candles and carried in procession. Prayers and songs continue. A deacon says, "The Holy Spirit will celebrate with us all the days of our life."[62] Litanies are recited at the offering. The priest and those assisting him exchange the kiss of peace. They kiss each other on the left and right shoulders. The *Nicene Creed* is recited. This is followed by the priest shaking a veil over the bread and wine signifying the trembling of the angels around the altar.[63] The "*anaphora*" (Eucharistic prayer sequence), which may be quite lengthy, is spoken in a low voice. Included in this prayer series are the words of institution, the invocation of the Holy Spirit, and the blessing of the people.[64] In the *Larger Catechism* it is stated that at this time "the bread and wine are changed . . . into the very Body of Christ, and into the very Blood of Christ."[65] The Orthodox hold that in this act of consecration the Holy Spirit is the one who transubstantiates the bread and wine, doing so through the officiating priest.[66]

In celebration of the Lord's Supper the Orthodox use leavened bread.[67] They contend that by the examples of Jesus and all of the apostles, the only bread that should be used is pure wheat leavened bread.[68] The leavened bread signifies the life in Christ's body.[69] In some cases three rather thick loaves of bread are used. As part of the preparation of the bread for the Communion the loaves are dedicated: one to the Lamb, another to the Virgin Mary, and the third to John the Baptist. Then pieces are taken from the loaves in recognition of the apostles, the holy doctors of the church, the martyrs, and all the saints.[70] A variation of the preparation of the bread involves five loaves on the altar. Each of these is stamped with the sign of the cross and is inscribed, "Jesus Christ conquers." The priest selects one loaf to represent the sacrificial lamb. He makes a symbolic reference to the side of Jesus being pierced with a spear so that blood and water flowed forth. Then he cuts the loaf with a knife that is shaped like a lance.[71] After the bread has been made ready for use in the Communion it is collectively called "the Lamb." The reason it is so named is because it is the figure of Christ's suffering, as was the Paschal Lamb in the Old Testament.[72]

The wine used in the Lord's Supper is mixed with water as a reminder of Christ's sufferings.[73] The mixing of wine and water is considered essential to a proper celebration.[74] In the ritual form in which the priest cuts the bread symbolically with a lance-like knife, a deacon simultaneously mixes the wine and water by pouring them ceremoniously into a cup.[75] In the *Larger Catechism* it is stated that "the whole of this celebration is so ordered so as to figure forth the sufferings of Christ, and when he suffered there flowed forth from his pierced side *blood and water*."[76] Chrysostom said that in partaking of the Communion we are "drinking from His very side."[77]

Final preparations are made consisting of more prayers, including the Lord's Prayer. There is a proclamation, "Holy Things for Holy People, Only One is Holy, only One is Lord, Jesus Christ, for the glory of God the Father. Amen."[78] The bread is broken. After a Communion song those desiring to partake of the Lord's Supper come forward. Their hands are crossed over their chests and they receive the Lord's Supper standing. They give their baptismal name and then receive on their tongue a piece of the consecrated bread that has been dipped in the chalice. The celebrating priest or a deacon uses a golden spoon to place the bread into the communicant's mouth.[79] This method of distribution is called "intinction."[80] The service concludes with a ceremony that includes a blessing and distribution of the consecrated bread. Leftover bread is dipped in the chalice and saved for communing the sick.[81]

Similar to the ancient church, Orthodox churches observe closed Communion. They do not admit non-Orthodox persons to the Lord's Supper in their churches. Only in extreme cases and in extraordinary circumstances will they commune a person who is not Orthodox and who otherwise would be deprived of the Sacrament. When this is done it is "out of mercy."[82] Members of Orthodox congregations are not permitted to commune in churches of other denominations.[83]

NOTES

1. Julius Bodensieck, ed., *The Encyclopedia of the Lutheran Church* (Minneapolis: Augsburg, 1965), 1:742.

2. Willy Rordorf, et al, *The Eucharist of the Early Christians*, trans. Michael J. O'Connell (New York: Pueblo Publishing Co., 1978), 52.

3. E. H. Klotsche, *The History of Christian Doctrine*, rev. J. Theodore Mueller and David P. Scaer (1945; reprint, Grand Rapids: Baker, 1979), 106; Philip Schaff, *History of the Christian Church* (n.p.; Charles Scribner's Sons, 1958–1960), 3:496; Carl A. Volz, *Faith and Practice in the Early Church: Foundations for Contemporary Theology* (Minneapolis: Augsburg, 1983), 108.

4. Klotsche, *Doctrine*, 106.

5. Klotsche, *Doctrine*, 106.

6. Schaff, *History*, 3:497.

7. Daniel B. Clendenin, ed., *Eastern Orthodox Theology: A Contemporary Reader* (Grand Rapids: Baker, 1995), 26.

8. Schaff, *History*, 3:496.

9. Schaff, *History*, 3:497.

10. Charles P. Krauth, *The Conservative Reformation and Its Theology* (1871; reprint, Minneapolis: Augsburg, 1963), 675.

11. Clendenin, *Orthodox*, 26.

12. Clendenin, *Orthodox*, 27.

13. Clendenin, *Orthodox*, 27.

14. See the text from the Larger Catechism of the Orthodox Catholic, Eastern Church in Philip Schaff, *The Creeds of Christendom with a History and Critical Notes*, rev. by David F. Schaff (Grand Rapids: Baker, 1966), 2:498.

15. Hermann Sasse, *This Is My Body: Luther's Contention for the Real Presence in the Sacrament of the Altar*, rev. ed. (Adelaide, South Australia: Lutheran Publishing House, 1977), 11, 12.

16. Sasse, *Body*, 12.

17. Sasse, *Body*, 12.

18. Sasse, *Body*, 12.

19. *The Orthodox Study Bible: New Testament and Psalms* (Nashville: Nelson, 1993), 392.

20. Clendenin, *Orthodox*, 28.

21. Clendenin, *Orthodox*, 28.

22. Paul Meyendorff, "A Taste of Glory," *Christian History* 16, no. 2 (1997): 41.

23. J. L. Neve, *Churches and Sects of Christendom*, rev. ed. (Blair, Nebr.: Lutheran Publishing House, 1952), 62.

24. Clendenin, *Orthodox*, 28.

25. Clendenin, *Orthodox*, 28.

26. Clendenin, *Orthodox*, 122.

27. Neve, *Churches*, 61.

28. F. E. Mayer, *The Religious Bodies of America* (St. Louis: Concordia, 1954), 16; Sasse, *Body*, 19.

29. F. Wilbur Gingrich, *Shorter Lexicon of the Greek New Testament* (Chicago: University of Chicago Press, 1965), 141.

30. Mayer, *Bodies*, 16.

31. Neve, *Churches*, 61.

32. Neve, *Churches*, 61, 62.

33. Lars P. Qualben, *A History of the Christian Church*, rev. ed. (New York: Nelson, 1942), 152.

34. Tim Dowley, et al, ed., *Eerdmans Handbook to the History of Christianity* (Grand Rapids: Eerdmans, 1977), 247.

35. Dowley, *Handbook*, 247.

36. Clendinen, *Orthodox*, 26.

37. Clendinen, *Orthodox*, 26, 27.

38. Theodore Engelder, et al, *Popular Symbolics; The Doctrines of the Churches of Christendom and of Other Religious Bodies Examined in the Light of Scripture* (St. Louis: Concordia, 1934), 144; Neve, *Churches*, 62.

39. Mayer, *Bodies*, 17.

40. Clendenin, *Orthodox*, 28, 29.

41. Clendenin, *Orthodox*, 29.

42. Mayer, *Bodies*, 16.

43. Clendenin, *Orthodox*, 28.

44. Thomas Hopko, "Children and Holy Communion," *Lutheran Forum* 30, no. 4 (1996): 32.

45. Kevin Smyth, trans., *A New Catechism: Catholic Faith for Adults* (New York: Herder and Herder, 1967), 333.

46. Schaff, *History*, 2:239; Hopko, "Children," 32.

47. Hopko, "Children," 33.
48. Hopko, "Children," 34.
49. Hopko, "Children," 34.
50. *Orthodox Study Bible*, 394.
51. Neve, *Churches*, 62.
52. *Orthodox Study Bible*, 317.
53. Clendenin, *Orthodox*, 15.
54. Schaff, *Creeds*, 2:498.
55. Sasse, *Body* 5.
56. Philippe Larere, *The Lord's Supper: Toward an Ecumenical Understanding of the Eucharist*, trans. Patrick Madigan (Collegeville, Minn.: The Liturgical Press, 1993), 32.
57. Clendenin, *Orthodox*, 15.
58. Neve, *Churches*, 62; Schaff, *Creeds*, 2:495.
59. Schaff, *Creeds*, 2:495.
60. Larere, *Lord's Supper*, 32–34, 36.
61. Larere, *Lord's Supper*, 34.
62. Larere, *Lord's Supper*, 34, 35.
63. Larere, *Lord's Supper*, 35, 37.
64. Larere, *Lord's Supper*, 91, 92.
65. Schaff, *Creeds*, 2:497; Schaff, *History*, 3:513.
66. Neve, *Churches*, 62.
67. Schaff, *History*, 3:517.
68. Schaff, *Creeds*, 2:496.
69. Neve, *Churches*, 62.
70. Larere, *Lord's Supper*, 32, 33.
71. Neve, *Churches*, 60.
72. Schaff, *Creeds*, 2:496.
73. Neve, *Churches*, 62.
74. Schaff, *History*, 3:517.
75. Neve, *Churches*, 62.
76. Schaff, *Creeds*, 2:497.
77. *Orthodox Study Bible*, 264.
78. Larere, *Lord's Supper*, 35.
79. Hopko, "Children," 34; Neve, *Churches*, 62; Sasse, *Body*, 55; Schaff, *History*, 4:569.
80. Martin Chemnitz, *Examination of the Council of Trent: Part Two,* trans. Fred Kramer (St. Louis: Concordia, 1978), 353.
81. Larere, *Lord's Supper*, 36.
82. Clendenin, *Orthodox*, 23; Larere, *Lord's Supper*, 65.
83. Larere, *Lord's Supper*, 66.

STUDY QUESTIONS

1. True or false: Early Eastern Orthodox fathers variously held both realistic and symbolic views of the Lord's Supper.

2. The Eastern Orthodox teaching of transubstantiation as an unsearchable mystery effected by the Holy Spirit in which the bread and wine become the body and blood of Christ comes from what major Eastern father?

3. What do Orthodox Christians say about the difference between their doctrine of transubstantiation and that of the Roman Catholic Church?

4. Instead of the term "sacrament," what word do many Orthodox Christians use to refer to the Lord's Supper, Holy Baptism, and the like? How many "sacraments" are there in the Eastern Orthodox Church and what are they?

5. What four reasons from the Liturgy of Chrysostom are given for receiving the mystery of the Lord's Supper?

6. True or false: The Orthodox church believes that the Lord's Supper is not a continuation of Christ's sacrifice on the cross.

7. True or false: Orthodox Christians do not consider the Lord's Supper to be as necessary for salvation as Holy Baptism.

8. True or false: Infants receive Chrism and the Lord's Supper immediately after Holy Baptism in the Orthodox church.

9. What three regimens do Eastern Orthodox Christians undertake before receiving the Lord's Supper?

10. What does the frequency of celebrating the Lord's Supper in the Orthodox church have in common with the ancient Church?

11. What liturgy do most Eastern Orthodox churches use in which the Lord's Supper plays the central role?

12. Do Orthodox Christians use leavened or unleavened bread in the Lord's Supper?

13. What is the name of the method of distribution used in the Orthodox church, in which the bread is dipped in the wine and then given to the communicant?

14. What Communion practice is observed by the Orthodox church?

6 | THE MEDIEVAL ROMAN CATHOLIC CHURCH

Part A: The Development of Transubstantiation

T he time between the ancient and modern eras in the Western world and in the Western church is known as the medieval period. It was a time of transition between the Greco-Roman and the Romano-Germanic civilizations. Some have dated the medieval era in the church from the accession of Pope Gregory the Great on September 3, A.D. 590 to Martin Luther's posting of the Ninety-Five Theses in 1517.[1] Others consider the revolution in literature, art, and scholarship that was the Italian Renaissance, heralded by the work of Petrarch (1304–74), as the beginning of the end of the Middle Ages.

Gregory the Great made a significant pronouncement regarding the Lord's Supper that continued to have an influence throughout the medieval period and beyond. Gregory said that the Eucharistic sacrifice is the most solemn mystery of the church. It fills the faithful with holy awe. The sacrifice in the Lord's Supper is not a new sacrifice that is added to that of Jesus on the cross. It is a daily, unbloody repetition and perpetual application of that sacrifice. The sacrifice in the Lord's Supper is the *antitype* (see Chapter 5) of the Old Testament Mosaic sacrifice, and was foreshadowed by Melchizedek's unbloody offering of bread and wine. The body of Jesus Christ is the subject of this sacrifice. As His body was present on the altar of the cross, so it is present on the altar of the church, and is offered to God through the priest. Offering the sacrifice is the exclusive prerogative of the priest. It is efficacious for all in the church, including those who have died in the faith.[2] Although the Lord's Prayer had been included in Eucharistic services from very early times, Gregory is credited with officially placing it in the liturgy of the Latin Mass.[3] Gregory also wrote many prayers for the Mass and his influence on the divine service cannot be underestimated.

For a time, early church customs continued, including the carrying of elements to the homes of members and to other places. Pope Innocent III (Pope 1198–1216) commanded that leftover consecrated elements, including those reserved for the sick at home, should be kept at the church under lock and key. A little later Pope Honorius III (Pope 1216–1227) ordered that when the Sacrament was taken from the church to the sick, the people should bow reverently and lights should be carried before it.[4] The giving of wine to newly baptized infants also continued as an accepted practice until about the year A.D. 1200.[5] A debate about this lasted well beyond the end of the medieval period. On the conviction that a person must receive the Lord's Supper in order to be saved, some advocated continuing this practice. Others held to the belief that a thorough self-examination is necessary, something that is not possible in the case of infants and small children.[6] There was a controversy in the eighth century as to whether leavened or unleavened bread should be used in the celebration of the Lord's Supper. Differing from the Eastern church, the church in the West favored the use of unleavened bread, and it became the standard practice in the Western church to use it in the form of wafers.[7]

Scholars vigorously disputed the manner in which Christ's body and blood were present in the Lord's Supper in the middle of the ninth century.[8] This dispute revolved about the debate between Radbertus and Ratramnus, as detailed below. Theologians were divided primarily between two views from the ancient church. Some followed Ambrose, who held to a realistic sacramental view of the presence. Others followed Augustine, who taught a spiritual understanding of the presence in the Supper.[9] Again, one is cautious in using terms like "real" and "spiritual" because spiritual things are not simply unreal. The terms are the result of conventional, academic use. The reader, if unsure, should consider the discussion of these terms in Chapter 4 to review the understanding of the meanings and how the fathers spoke on the issue.

In A.D. 844 a French Benedictine monk, Paschasius Radbertus, published a book entitled *On the Body and Blood of the Lord*. In this book, thought to be the first full treatise on the subject,[10] he clearly taught the doctrine of transubstantiation, although he did not use that term.[11] Radbertus said that "the substance of bread and wine is effectively changed into the body and blood of Christ."[12] This is the very body and blood of Christ who was born of the Virgin, crucified, and raised from the dead.[13] After the elements have been consecrated by the priest there is nothing else in the Lord's Supper but "the flesh and blood of Christ." However, as far as the senses of sight, touch, and taste are concerned "the figure of bread and wine remain."[14] If these did not remain, there would be no room for faith. Also, the actual eating of flesh would be at variance with human custom.[15] The Holy Spirit brings about this miraculous change. As the Spirit created Christ's body in the Virgin's womb without cohabitation, so whenever the

Lord's Supper is celebrated He creates the body and blood of Christ out of the substance of bread and wine.[16] Persons who eat this "flesh" participate in the life of the mystical body of Christ in the church.[17] In what seems to be inconsistent with other things said in his book, Radbertus believed that only the faithful receive the body and blood of Christ.[18] He interpreted the words of institution literally. His teachings were further based on certain passages in John 6 and on stories of marvelous appearances of the body and blood of Christ drawn from traditional stories. For instance, Radbertus tells of the bread on the altar being in the shape of a lamb or a little child, depending on the story. When the priest would reach out to break the bread, an angel would descend from heaven with a knife, slaughter the lamb or the child and let the blood run into a cup.[19] In medieval times people readily believed such stories.

Emperor Charles the Bald asked a monk by the name of Ratramnus to write an evaluation of Radbertus's book. Ratramnus was Radbertus's monastic superior. He disagreed with Radbertus's theory. Ratramnus considered the question of whether the elements are called the body and blood of Christ in a mysterious or a literal sense. He concluded that the bread and wine remain what they were before consecration.[20] He contended that the elements are only the body and blood of Christ in a spiritual sense to those who believe.[21] He used the terms "figure,"[22] "pledge,"[23] "image,"[24] and "symbol"[25] in describing the relationship between the bread and wine and Christ's body and blood. Henry Mayr-Harting of Oxford University says that to Ratramnus's mind "the sacrament was primarily a memorial of Christ's passion."[26] A key verse for him was John 6:63, where Jesus said, "It is the Spirit that quickeneth; the flesh profiteth nothing." He distinguished the body in the Lord's Supper from the body of the historic Christ.[27] Ratramnus believed that in the Communion the souls of believers are nourished by the Word of God dwelling visibly in Christ's natural body and invisibly in the Lord's Supper.

Only those who believe can receive Christ. Ratramnus viewed the sacrifice of the Mass as a commemorative celebration of Christ's sacrifice by which Christians are assured of redemption.[28] One point of agreement between Radbertus and Ratramnus is the necessity that the priest should consecrate the elements before Christ can be present in any sense in the Lord's Supper.[29] As time went by, Radbertus's theory of the change in substance brought about by the Holy Spirit through the priest's consecration became even more popular.[30]

In the tenth century, the debate was whether or not the consecrated elements pass from the bodies of the communicants in the ordinary way of nature. Those who held to the change in substance indignantly denied this while those who believed in only a spiritual presence affirmed it.[31] As the church moved closer to the official position of transubstantiation, an eleventh century French scholar named Berengar (ca. 1000–1088) caused a new controversy. On the basis of his study of the Scripture and opinions of some church fathers, Berengar concluded that the doctrine of the Lord's Supper advocated by Radbertus two centuries earlier was superstition and contrary to the Bible, to the ancient fathers, and to reason.[32] His theory was that bread and wine are not changed into the body and blood of Christ, but are merely emblematic of His body and blood. Through the consecration a spiritual power is added to the elements. This power is apprehended by faith. Without faith, the elements remain empty, powerless signs. It is not possible for Christ to be corporeally present in the Lord's Supper, because to so be present He must be present spatially, and then His body must at one and the same time be present in separate celebrations of the Lord's Supper in a variety of places.[33] Berengar's strongest reason for rejecting the real presence was that this teaching is logically impossible. Sasse says that as far as we know Berengar was the first to interpret the word "is" in the words of institution as meaning "signifies."[34] Berengar created a considerable sensation when he shared his views with his many students in France and Germany.[35] As news of his ideas spread throughout the church he was widely denounced. In 1050, a Roman synod condemned Berengar and threatened him with severe punishment or death. Later he was forced to recant and throw his books into the fire.[36] He spent the last years of his life in strict ascetic seclusion on an island near Tours in France.[37] Berengar had a tremendous long-term influence on the church, an influence he never intended. He raised challenging questions that caused his opponents to earnestly develop the theory of transubstantiation.

The desire to clarify the nature of the presence of the body and blood of Christ in the Lord's Supper in light of sacramental eating versus materialistic eating led to several hypothetical questions and answers. For example, "What happens if an animal, a mouse or a dog, eats a consecrated host?"[38] One answer was that mice and dogs were not created to use the bread sacramentally, so they cannot eat Christ's body in a sacramental way. The mouse or dog would only eat the accidents of the elements in the same way as a person who ate consecrated bread—not knowing that it was consecrated. Another answer was that the body of Christ would be withdrawn in such cases. Still another left the matter open, claiming that animals do not receive the body of Christ when eating consecrated bread, but what they do receive, God only knows. In the cases of animals eating consecrated bread, the bread being destroyed by fire or desecrated in some other way, there was general agreement that in any such occurrences no violation of the body of Christ occurred. Some thought Christ's body was miraculously removed by angels, or in some other fashion. It was believed that in such circumstances only the species remained.[39] Thomas Aquinas (ca. 1224–1274) dealt with the question, "What happens if a consecrated host falls into the mire?" He contended that in such a case the body and blood of Christ would not be withdrawn, because God allowed Christ's body even to be crucified.[40] Disagreeing with some who preceded him, on the basis that the substance of the body remains as long as the species exists, Aquinas held that a violation of the species was an indirect violation of the body of Christ. According to his logic, a mouse or dog would eat the body with the species, but the eating would not be sacramental in nature.[41]

The celebration of private Masses with only the priest present, begun in the sixth century, increased in the medieval period. By the seventh century these Masses were so common that churches began having more than one altar for such use. The altars were placed against a wall so that others would not be disturbed by the celebration.[42] Stookey speaks of churches with as many as twenty altars. He says, "The resulting cacophony dictates that rather than speaking or chanting in a clearly audible voice, the priest shall use hushed tones, sometimes whispering the Mass or even totally silent. There is no congregation present on most days, so it matters little if anyone hears."[43] The private Mass is sometimes referred to as the silent Mass.[44]

The emphasis and action in the Lord's Supper had shifted from a sacramental and fellowship meal to a rite for the prayers of the priest.[45] The prayers spoken at these celebrations were primarily intercessory prayers for the living and the dead. Ordering such a Mass came to be considered a meritorious deed.[46] The doctrine of the "fruits of the Mass," the benefits of the spoken prayers, was developed. The faithful wished to have the "fruits of the Mass" applied to their individual salvation and to the salvation of their departed loved ones. This also marked the beginning of the Mass stipend, the giving of money or gifts to the clergy for saying Masses. Individuals giving the stipend asked that the "fruits" of a particular Mass be applied to themselves, relatives, and friends.

The private Mass not only became a daily function of priests, to be repeated over and over again, ofttimes with hardly any liturgy and without a sermon,[47] but it also had a profound effect on the Sunday worship of congregations. By the thirteenth century it had become the normative form of celebration. Even when a congregation was assembled, it was the personal function of the priest.[48] There existed almost no communication between the priest at silent prayer and the silent church members.[49] Some would have brought personal prayer books with them. Others might silently recite memorized prayers using the rosary.[50] The people were usually only observers. Their main action, as regards the Sacrament, became worship of the sacred objects of the Mass. They watched and adored the elements while the priest performed the private Mass.[51] Just before the moment when the bread and wine were to be changed into the body and blood of Christ, a server at the altar (or sometimes the priest himself) would ring a bell. Upon hearing the bell the worshipers would kneel reverently as "the miracle" occurred. Stookey says, "This is why they have come—to see the mystery of ordinary bread and wine become the body and blood of their Lord."[52] Catholic professor Regis Duffy writes that "looking at the host was considered salvific."[53] In larger cities people would run from church to church to see the elevated host as often as possible. People even started lawsuits to ensure that they got a favorable view of the altar.[54] Sometimes people gathered at a particular church for continuous prayer before a consecrated host. At times such continuous prayer lasted overnight. Again it may have been for forty unbroken hours. Ornate candelabra and incense surrounded these devotions.[55]

A Eucharistic piety, developed in the ninth century and continued in following centuries, produced several effects: The unworthiness of the common people to receive the Lord's Supper became accentuated. This emphasis led to the practice of the confession of sins before each Mass. People also began to partake of the Lord's Supper less frequently.[56] If a Christian took the Lord's Supper from two to four times a year, this was considered to be "frequent." It came to be the practice that the Sacrament was distributed to the people in a medieval parish church on the major festivals of the church year—Easter, Pentecost, and Christmas.

Sometimes the festival of the assumption of Mary was added to this schedule. Very few people made use of all of these opportunities to commune.[57] This decline in attendance increased, reaching a high point in the thirteenth and fourteenth centuries when many did not even partake of the Lord's Supper once a year.[58] Catholic author Joseph M. Champlin attributes this continued decline to "practical difficulties and poor attitudes."[59] Into the sixteenth century the Lord's Supper remained largely a private action of the priest. Eventually it was ofttimes the case that even the priest did not receive Communion during the celebration of the Mass.[60]

Another result of the Eucharistic piety emphasis was the emergence of tendencies to exercise great care in handling the bread and wine. The elements had become objects of fear.[61] The lay people were no longer permitted to take the bread into their hands. Catholic priest Paul A. Feider states, "Communion began to be received on the tongue while kneeling."[62] Some laypersons were reluctant to take the wine for fear of spilling Christ's blood.[63] There were also practical difficulties with the wine. Sasse writes that "the larger gatherings required not only much wine, but also large cups, sometimes with two handles."[64] The wine was consecrated by the priest in a small cup on the altar. The consecrated wine was then mixed with unconsecrated wine in the larger cup. The consecration of the larger amount was "by contact."[65] Fearful reluctance and practicality combined resulted in the eventual withholding of the wine from the lay people. After the Fourth Lateran Council in A.D. 1215, the withholding of the cup was made obligatory.[66]

Part B: The Effects of Lateran IV

The Fourth Lateran Council was extremely important for the doctrine of the Lord's Supper. Pope Innocent II (Pope ca. 1160–1216), in the midst of competing opinions among scholars in the church, declared transubstantiation a dogma of the church[67] and the Council officially adopted his declaration.[68] It affirmed that "in the Sacrament of the altar the body and blood of Christ are truly contained under the appearances of bread and wine, these having been transubstantiated by divine power, the bread into the body and the wine into the blood."[69]

The Council also made official the teaching that the Lord's Supper is a sacrificial meal in which Christ and the human priest-hood work together.[70] The Lord's Supper was thus regarded as "an unbloody repetition of the atoning sacrifice of Christ by the priesthood for the salvation of the living and the dead."[71] The members of an evangelical group known as the Waldensians were condemned partly because they did not accept the concept of the Lord's Supper as a sacrifice.[72] Incidentally, the Waldensians had a custom that may have been unique: They partook of a meal of fish in connection with the Lord's Supper.[73]

Because the sacraments of Penance and the Lord's Supper had fallen into disuse among the laity of the church, the Council decreed that all must make confession and receive the Lord's Sup-per at least once each year, at the time of Easter.[74] The adoration of the elements built up to a climax as a result of the official doc-trine of transubstantiation.[75] The adoration of the Eucharistic Christ believed to be present in the consecrated host increasingly replaced Holy Communion. Catholic authors have spoken of Communion with the eyes.[76] Reverence and veneration of the consecrated host became more important than the eating of the same.[77]

Due to the official doctrine of transubstantiation the Scholas-tics had an overriding desire to determine the precise moment the bread and wine were changed into the body and blood of Christ. There seemed to be agreement that when the words of institution were spoken, one substance immediately replaced the other. However, more precision was desired. They debated whether it occurred when the word "this" or the word "body" or the word "my" was spoken by the celebrant.[78] Because there were demands for more Masses than there were priests available to offer them, a practice known as the "dry Mass" developed. A priest was normally permitted to celebrate only one full Mass and personal Communion each day. If a priest needed to offer up eight Masses in a morning, he would read through the formulary to the point of consecrating the elements. Then he would back up and start over. He would only complete the service the eighth time. It was required that the priest should do all this while fasting, that is, before breakfast. Our word "breakfast" has its roots in the dry Mass. Completion of the service "breaks the fast."[79]

In view of the doctrine of transubstantiation the consecrated bread was considered so sacred that it was stored in a locked container called a "tabernacle." The name "tabernacle" was based on a literal translation of "the Word became flesh and tabernacled among us" (John 1:14).[80] A new reason given for continuing to call the church building the house of God was that Christ was thought to be dwelling in the tabernacle that was kept there.[81] A candle, or sanctuary lamp, was placed near the tabernacle to identify the location of the reserved bread, thought to be the living body of Christ. When the faithful would come near the tabernacle they would genuflect reverently. Out of respect some even doffed the hat when passing the exterior of the church building.[82]

After the Fourth Lateran Council the lay people were barred from receiving the consecrated wine.[83] The chief reason given was that the transubstantiated wine might be spilled "and cause scandal."[84] As time went by a number of additional arguments for withholding the cup were advanced. At the Council of Constance some 200 years later (1414–1418) it was stated that if the contents of the cup were to be spilled as the wine was being distributed to the laity, "great offenses of profanation of holy things would spring, and so to avoid such dangers and offenses, the cup must be forbidden to the lay people."[85] In addition to spilling, the dangers listed by the Council included the following: The risk involved in carrying the wine from place to place—the vessels might become polluted if handled and touched indiscriminately by lay people; the long beards of men; the problem of preserving the wine for the sick, because vinegar could develop in the container, in summer flies or midges might be generated, and in certain cases it might even become putrid; the great amount that would be needed to commune large congregations of people, especially at Easter; the danger of freezing; some might foster a false doctrine that the laity were equal with the priests; people might get the idea that the lay persons had always received the cup and that it would be necessary also for them; some might believe that the power and efficacy of the Lord's Supper is in the receiving, rather than in the consecration; it would follow that the church and the Council had erred regarding the Sacrament, with schisms in Christendom resulting; and the great expense that would be involved, because in some places wine can hardly be found.[86] Commenting on the reasons for withholding the wine, Champlin mentions that it was in northern countries where wine was scarce.[87]

Another indirect result of making transubstantiation the official doctrine was the appointing of the Corpus Christi festival in 1264 by Pope Urban IV (Pope 1261–1264).[88] Before Urban was pope, a nun by the name of Julianna of Leige, who led a secluded and contemplative life, reported that she had received a revelation that such a festival should be started and celebrated throughout the church. When Urban became pope he instituted the eight-day festival.[89] He commissioned Thomas Aquinas to prepare an office (*Liturgy of the Hours*) for it.[90] At first some did not accept the new festival,[91] but it eventually spread throughout the Western church.[92] At first the festival concerned a more solemn use and participation in the Lord's Supper. It was a time of reverence and devotion, and of thanking Christ for the benefits that He gives in the Lord's Supper.[93] At some time in the fourteenth century the nature of the festival began to change. The consecrated bread was enclosed in a transparent receptacle so it would be visible to the multitudes. It was then carried through the streets in a procession for the people to adore.[94] Chemnitz tells of a papal Corpus Christi procession in Rome in which a richly ornamented white horse was led, carrying the consecrated bread in a repository resting on a beautiful pillow. The horse had a beautifully sounding bell attached to its neck. Twelve papal servants carrying twelve torches, and two other servants carrying silver lanterns preceded the horse. The pope followed a short distance behind the horse.[95]

The measure of reverence for the "transubstantiated" elements is reflected in the 1217 order of Pope Honorius III, which made it obligatory for a bell to be rung at the moment of consecration so that the worshipers might kneel and adore the host. In 1281 the Lambeth Synod gave the order that the church bells be rung at the moment of consecration in order that field laborers and women doing their domestic duties might bow and worship.[96] In view of transubstantiation, provisions were made for the disposition of spilled wine and dropped bread. If a crumb of bread or a drop of wine fell on the priest's garments, the affected part was to be cut out and burned. The ashes were to be thrown into the sacrary. If the linen cover on the altar became wet with wine it was to be washed three times. The water used in the washing was to be drunk by a priest. In the event that a drop fell on a stone, a piece of wood, or hard earth it was to be licked up by a priest or some other pious person.[97] If a fly or spider was found in the wine after it had been consecrated, it was to be taken out and washed and burned. The water used and the ashes were to be thrown into the sacrary. If poison was found in the consecrated wine, the contents of the cup were to be poured out and kept in a container along with the relics.[98]

Such teachings corresponded with those of Peter Lombard (ca. 1100–ca. 1160) who taught in Paris,[99] and Thomas Aquinas who taught in Paris and Italy.[100] They held that the sacraments, including the Lord's Supper, confer grace simply by being performed. But they said that through unbelief people receiving the sacraments could put up a "barrier to grace." However, they held that it is impossible for unconscious infants and dying persons to erect such a barrier.[101] Their teaching that grace is conferred simply by the sacraments being performed came to be the accepted view of the Catholic Church.[102]

A side effect of the official doctrine of transubstantiation may be seen in the numerous reports of miraculous happenings associated with consecrated hosts. In Amsterdam the story was told of a host being vomited up by a sick person. Out of reverence for the body of Christ, an effort was made to burn everything that she expelled. Everything burned but the host. It remained suspended above the fire.[103] Another incident reported to have occurred in the Netherlands is that of a monk by the name of Adolph, who had consecrated a host. Then he saw in his hands the Virgin Mary carrying the infant Christ in her arms. He turned the host over, and on the other side he saw a lamb. Turning it over again, he saw Christ on the cross. Then there was nothing left but the form of the bread, which he then ate.[104] It was reported that a priest had refused to commune a Flemish lady. That night, Christ Himself visited her and gave her the host in His own hands.[105] In Andore the pyx was upset and five hosts that it contained were scattered. Every part of the church building was searched, but the hosts could not be found. At last they were discovered on a ledge in the wall where an angel had put them.[106] There is the account of a farmer in France who wished to become wealthy. Following the advice of a friend he placed a host in a beehive. The bees made a miniature church that contained an altar. They placed the host on the altar. Bees from throughout the neighborhood came together and sang beautifully. The farmer went to the hives expecting to find them overflowing with honey. However, he found all the hives empty except the one in which he had placed the host. The bees fiercely attacked him. He reported the incident to the priest who came in procession, found the miniature church in the hive, and carried it to the village church. The bees flew away singing songs.[107] Another story reported that in 1223 a lady in Belgium kissed her lover with a host in her mouth. She hoped this would inflame his love for her. When she found herself unable to swallow the host, she wrapped it up in a napkin. Distressed, she told her priest of her experience. The priest and the bishop came to where she was keeping the host. They found that there were three drops of blood on the napkin in which it had been wrapped. They summoned the abbot of Trond who examined the host and discovered that it was half flesh and half bread. When the bishop tried to carry away two drops of the blood sixty armed men stopped him from doing so. The sacred blood was placed in a vase and kept among the relics in St. Trond Church.[108]

After the Fourth Lateran Council Aquinas discussed the Lord's Supper in Aristotelian categories. According to the Aristotelian approach all things have two components, substance and accidents.[109] A substance is the unchangeable set of attributes that defines a species. The term "substance" is generally synonymous with "nature." For example, the human nature consists of a human body and a rational soul. Every human being has these attributes. "Accidents" comprise a set of changeable attributes that denote personal differences within a species as well as the state of individual members of a species. Accidents can be things like "tall," "short," "fair," "dark," etc. A change in accidents generally describes how thought plus action changes or actualizes matter by means of Aristotle's set of causes. The efficient cause can be described as the form in the soul of the artist that inspires a painting. The formal cause is the thought to paint whatever the subject might be. The material cause consists of the artist, paints, brushes, canvas, and the like. The final cause is the portrait or landscape that hangs in the gallery. These distinctions underlie the modern scientific method, and they enabled Aquinas to explain transubstantiation in a logical, philosophical sense. Sasse says:

> The distinction between "substance" and "accidents" in the strict sense of Aristotelian metaphysics . . . made it possible to give an accurate answer to the question as to what is changed by the consecration and what is not. It was now possible to explain how a complete conversion took place while no change in the elements was notice-able, and the "species" remained to the human sense what they had been before.[110]

The philosophical leap that he made was that in this unique case accidents could exist without substance. He substituted "quantity," another Aristotelian category, for "accidents" as the basis for the "accident." For him transubstantiation was a meta-physical miracle.[111] Because he believed that such a change could not occur except by a miracle from God, Aquinas assumed that such a miracle took place in the Lord's Supper. He fixed the time at which the bread became the body of Christ at the moment when the priest finished saying, "This is my body." Likewise, he held that the wine became the blood of Christ as the celebrant finished uttering, "This is the chalice of my blood."[112] For Aquinas the miracle of conversion was proved by the words of institution. He endeavored to base his doctrine on nothing other than Christ's words. Aquinas taught three levels of knowledge. There is a level that can be attained by reason alone. Only skilled thinkers can attain a second level by reason. Unskilled thinkers attain the second level by faith. A third level, which is the highest, is attain-able only by faith.[113] Aquinas placed transubstantiation on the third level as "an article of 'faith alone' to be believed on the authority of the Word of God."[114]

Scholars had difficulty in explaining how Christ's body could be entirely locally present in heaven and present in its substance whenever and wherever the Lord's Supper was celebrated. Thomas Aquinas and John Duns Scotus (1270–1308) represent two alternate views. Aquinas taught that Christ's celestial body is present in heaven, but that His sacramental body is substantially, though not locally, present in the Lord's Supper.[115] As the priest speaks the final words of institution, the body of Christ becomes present.[116] Duns Scotus, who taught at Oxford, Paris, and Cologne,[117] said that, "God by a miracle can cause a body to exist in different places at the same time." He came forward with the suggestion that the substance of the body of Christ, which is local in heaven, is added to the substance of the bread "at any number of places" where the Lord's Supper is celebrated.[118] Endeavoring to reconcile this idea with the official doctrine of transubstantiation, Duns Scotus and his followers assumed that the substance of the bread ceases to be, or is annihilated.[119] Other thinkers, building on the basic thought of Duns Scotus that the substance of the body of Christ is added to the substance of the bread, held that the substance of the bread remains, and is not annihilated. Their doctrine, called "consubstantiation," consists in the belief that in the consecrated host the substance of the bread and the substance of Christ's body coexist[120] and together form a third substance.[121] Some held that the body and blood of Christ are present in a natural manner, as are the bread and wine.[122]

William of Occam (ca. 1300–ca. 1349) developed a restrictive and qualified form of consubstantiation.[123] Occam was a pupil of Duns Scotus and later his rival.[124] He taught that the bread and wine and the body and blood of Christ coexist in the consecrated host.[125] Schaff summarizes this position as "the view that Christ's body is at the side of the bread."[126] Occam held that in the presence the body and blood of Christ are not bound to a certain place. The presence in the Lord's Supper is that of the glorified body.[127] In explaining Occam's position, Sasse states, "This was the presence of his body when at the Last Supper, standing before his disciples, he gave them with bread and wine his true body and blood. This miracle, like all miracles of Jesus, must be understood as a manifestation of his hidden glory."[128] In some passages

Occam also tentatively suggested that the presence of Christ's body may come under the category of divine omnipresence, but as a rule he held to the concept of the glorified body of Christ.[129] Occam believed that transubstantiation cannot be proved or defended logically from Scripture. However, he accepted and defended the doctrine of transubstantiation because of the authority of the church.[130] Occam was imprisoned at Avignon, France, for his teachings. He escaped, but was later excommunicated from the church.[131]

Part C: Later Attempts at Reform

Two important forerunners of the Protestant Reformation were John Wycliffe (1320–1384) of England and John Huss (ca. 1370–1415) of Bohemia. Wycliffe rejected the doctrine of transubstantiation.[132] Huss contended that communicants should receive both the bread and the wine in the Lord's Supper.[133]

In A.D. 1381 Wycliffe prepared 12 theses in which he declared the church's teachings regarding the Lord's Supper to be unscriptural and misleading. This was the first time since the Fourth Lateran Council that a theological expert seriously called into question the doctrine of transubstantiation. A trial was held at Oxford in which, without mentioning Wycliffe by name, the judges condemned his beliefs that the bread and wine remain after the consecration and that Christ's body is only figuratively present in the Lord's Supper. Wycliffe continued promulgating his views. In 1382 a synod condemned 24 conclusions ascribed to Wycliffe, some as errors and some as heresy.[134] The first four of these conclusions pertained to the Lord's Supper. They read as follows:

> I. That the material substance of bread and wine remains, after the consecration, in the sacrament of the altar. II. That the accidents do not remain without the subject, after the consecration, in the same sacrament. III. That Christ is not in the sacrament of the altar identically, truly, and really in his proper corporeal presence.

IV. That if a bishop or priest lives in mortal sin he does not ordain, or consecrate, or baptize.[135]

An earthquake occurred during the synodical meeting, referred to in English history as "the Earthquake Synod." The Archbishop of Canterbury interpreted this as a favorable sign regarding what they were doing.[136] Wycliffe gave a different interpretation to the quake, saying that the Lord had sent it "because the friars had put heresy upon Christ in the matter of the sacrament, and the earth trembled as it did when Christ was damned to bodily death."[137] Wycliffe continued to write, calling the monks who opposed him "the tail of the dragon, ravening wolves, the sons of Satan, the emissaries of anti-Christ and Luciferians."[138] He suffered a stroke while attending Mass on Holy Innocents Day, December 28, 1384 and died three days later.[139]

Wycliffe's basic position was that the body of Christ is spiritually present in the Lord's Supper. In reality Christ's body "as far as its dimensions are concerned" is in heaven. Efficaciously or virtually it is in the host as a symbol. This symbol represents His body.[140] Wycliffe said, "The consecrated Host we priests make and bless is not the body of the Lord but an effectual sign of it. It is not to be understood that the body of Christ comes down from heaven to the Host consecrated in every church."[141] Christ is in the bread in the same way as a king is present in all parts of his domain. He is present in the bread in the same manner as the soul is in the body. Speaking of the breaking of the bread, Wycliffe maintained that Christ's body is no more broken than a sunbeam is broken when a piece of glass is shattered. In describing Christ's presence he used the words "sacramentally," "spiritually," and "efficiently."[142] Wycliffe believed that the words of institution should be taken in a figurative sense.[143] He said that in a similar manner Jesus spoke of Himself as the seed and of the world as the field. When Jesus called John Elijah He did not mean that they were one and the same person.[144] When Jesus called Himself the vine He meant that the vine was a symbol of Him, as did St. Paul when he said that Christ is a rock.[145] Wycliffe stated that "you will meet with such modes of expression constantly in Scripture and in these expressions, without a doubt, the production is made figuratively."[146] Wycliffe believed that the physical eating in the Lord's Supper profits nothing unless the soul is fed by love.[147] To him the determining factor regarding the presence and reception of Christ was the faith of the individual participating.[148] Wycliffe held that the value of a celebration of the Lord's Supper depended on the character of the priest. He thought that a pious layman could consecrate the elements.[149]

Wycliffe called transubstantiation a dogma of moderns and of the recent church. He said it was the greatest of all heresies and declared it to be subversive of logic, grammar, and natural science. Regarding the controversy as to whether a mouse eating consecrated bread would partake of Christ's body, Wycliffe held that the primary assumption behind the question is false, for Christ is not corporeally present in the Lord's Supper.[150] He described a number of matters as shocking, including the following: the notion that the priest actually breaks Christ's body, and in doing so breaks His neck, arms, and other body parts;[151] that every day the priest should "make" and consecrate the body of Christ;[152] that those partaking of the Sacrament would actually eat the very flesh of Christ and drink His very blood; that the priest carries God in bodily form on the tips of his fingers.[153] Contrary to the position of Aquinas, Wycliffe maintained that the substance of a thing may not be separated from its accidents.[154] If it were possible for accidents to exist by themselves, one would be unable to tell what a thing is or if it exists at all. He contended that transubstantiation would logically demand transaccidentation.[155] Wycliffe believed transubstantiation to have been an invention of the anti-Christ.[156]

Jan Hus of Prague preached the Word of God in the language of the people. He tried to restore true devotion among Christians. Fearlessly he attacked corruption of all kinds in the church.

Because he defended Wycliffe's ideas of reform he was suspected of heresy. Although he did not accept all of Wycliffe's views, he was accused of Wycliffe's alleged errors. Forbidden to preach and having been excommunicated, he went into hiding and turned to writing. Hus was summoned to appear before the Council of Constance in 1414. There he was imprisoned and asked to recant his "errors." When in 1415 he refused to recant he was handed over to the secular authorities and burned at the stake.[157]

At Hus's trial before the Council of Constance he was accused of denying the doctrine of transubstantiation. He truthfully denied the charge.[158] Hus's primary difference with the established church with regard to the Lord's Supper was that he held that the persons communing should receive both the bread and the wine when partaking.[159] Shortly before he was imprisoned, Hus had written that the proper form for celebrating the Lord's Supper is that the communicants should receive both the bread and the wine.[160] His followers were divided on the matter of transubstantiation. One major group, the Utraquists, accepted it. A second major group, the Taborites, vehemently attacked the doctrine. An extreme third group, the Pickards, viewed the Lord's Supper with contempt.[161]

The demand for the chalice kept the various branches of Hussites together. It became the symbol for a common fight against the papal church. Open revolt resulted in the Hussite wars. The whole nation fought against the Germans who ruled over them and also against the hierarchy of the Roman church who supported the Germans. "Under both kinds" became both a religious and political slogan. Going into battle, Czech armies had Communion hosts affixed to their lances.[162] Inside Bohemia the people stoned the houses of the priests who opposed Hus. Churches and convents were sacked. Pope Eugene IV called together an army of some 150,000 men to deal with the situation. The papal crusaders invaded the land of Hus five times. Every time they were driven back. The Hussites took the offensive and invaded Germany.[163] As a result of the rout of the pope's army a council was called in Basel, Switzerland in 1431. At this Council a compact was made between the Hussites and the Catholic Church. The papal representatives granted the use of the cup to the Czech lay people on condition that the Hussites would agree that the whole Christ is contained in each of the elements, the bread and in the wine. The use of the cup was declared wholesome to those who partake worthily of the Lord's Supper.

The Utraquists were satisfied with the agreement. The Taborites were not. Open war broke out between these two factions. In a resulting massacre in Prague, 22,000 people were killed. The Taborites were completely defeated by 1452.[164] In 1462 the compact was declared void by Pope Pius II (pope 1458–1464). He threatened to excommunicate all priests who gave the cup to the laity. In 1485 and again in 1512, agreements were reached whereby the Utraquists were permitted to receive both bread and wine in the Lord's Supper. They continued with this privilege until 1629 when the hard and bloody Austrian king, Ferdinand II, withdrew the right of Communion in both kinds and put an end to open dissent in Bohemia.[165]

Notes

1. Lars P. Qualben, *A History of the Christian Church*, rev. ed. (New York: Nelson, 1942), 137.

2. Philip Schaff, *History of the Christian Church* (n.p.; Charles Scribner's Sons, 1958–1960), 3:507–509.

3. Richard P. McBrien, *Lives of the Popes: The Pontiffs from St. Peter to John Paul II* (San Francisco: Harper, 1997), 98.

4. Martin Chemnitz, *Examination of the Council of Trent: Part Two*, trans. Fred Kramer (St. Louis: Concordia, 1978), 310.

5. Hermann Sasse, *This is My Body: Luther's Contention for the Real Presence in the Sacrament of the Altar*, rev. ed. (Adelaide, South Australia: Lutheran Publishing House, 1977), 55.

6. Sasse, *Body*, 52.

7. Tim Dowley, et al, ed., *Eerdmans Handbook to the History of Christianity* (Grand Rapids: Eerdmans, 1977), 257.

8. Martin E. Marty, *A Short History of Christianity* (New York: Meridian, 1959), 168.

9. Sasse, *Body*, 19.

10. Marty, *History*, 168.

11. Schaff, *History*, 4:547.

12. Schaff, *History*, 4:547.

13. Sasse, *Body*, 18.

14. E. H. Klotsche, *The History of Christian Doctrine*, rev. J. Theodore Mueller and David P. Scaer (1945; reprint, Grand Rapids: Baker, 1979), 125; Schaff, *History*, 4:547.

15. Klotsche, *Doctrine*, 125.

16. Schaff, *History*, 4:547.

17. Marty, *History*, 168.

18. Sasse, *Body*, 18.

19. Schaff, *History*, 4:548.

20. Klotsche, *Doctrine*, 125; Sasse, *Body*, 18; Schaff, *History*, 4:549, 550.

21. Marty, *History*, 169; John McManners, ed. *The Oxford Illustrated History of Christianity* (New York: Oxford University Press, 1990), 103; Schaff, *History*, 4:550.

22. Schaff, *History*, 4:550.

23. Schaff, *History*, 4:550.

24. Sasse, *Body*, 18.

25. Marty, *History,* 160.

26. McManners, *Oxford*, 103.

27. Klotsche, *Doctrine*, 125; Sasse, *Body*, 18.

28. Schaff, *History*, 4:550, 551.

29. McManners, *Oxford*, 105.

30. Schaff, *History*, 4:552.

31. Schaff, *History*, 4:552.

32. Schaff, *History*, 4:555.

33. Klotsche, *Doctrine*, 126.

34. Sasse, *Body*, 26.

35. Schaff, *History*, 4:555.

36. Klotsche, *Doctrine*, 125, 126; Schaff, *History*, 4:556–559.

37. Klotsche, *Doctrine*, 126; Schaff, *History*, 4:559.

38. Sasse, *Body*, 32; Schaff, *History*, 4:719.

39. Sasse, *Body*, 32; Schaff, *History*, 4:719.

40. Schaff, *History*, 4:719.

41. Sasse, *Body*, 32.

42. Paul A. Feider, *The Sacraments: Encountering the Risen Lord* (Notre Dame: Ave Maria Press, 1986), 41, 42; Qualben, *History*, 134.

43. Laurence Hull Stookey, *Eucharist: Christ's Feast with the Church* (Nashville: Abingdon, 1993), 73, 74.

44. Johannes H. Emminghaus, *The Eucharist: Essence, Form, Celebration*, trans.

Matthew J. O'Connell. (Collegeville, Minn.: Liturgical Press, 1978), 76.

45. Feider, *Sacraments*, 42.

46. Qualben, *History*, 134.

47. Emminghaus, *Eucharist*, 75, 76.

48. Feider, *Sacraments*, 42.

49. Emminghaus, *Eucharist*, 76.

50. Stookey, *Eucharist*, 74.

51. Sasse, *Body*, 50.

52. Stookey, *Eucharist*, 74.

53. Regis Duffy, *Real Presence: Worship, Sacraments, and Commitment* (San Francisco: Harper & Row, 1982), 11.

54. Duffy, *Real Presence*, 11.

55. Joseph M. Champlin, *Special Signs of Grace: The Sacraments and Sacramentals* (Collegeville, Minn.: Liturgical Press, 1986), 58, 59.

56. Feider, *Sacraments*, 42.

57. Sasse, *Body*, 52.

58. Champlin, *Special Signs*, 55; Arthur Carl Piepkorn, *The Church: Selected Writings of Arthur Carl Piepkorn*, ed. Michael P. Plekon and Williem S. Wiecher (Delhi, NY: ALPB Books, 1993), 123.

59. Champlin, *Special Signs*, 55.

60. Feider, *Sacraments*, 44.

61. Feider, *Sacraments*, 43.

62. Feider, *Sacraments*, 42, 43.

63. Sasse, *Body*, 55.

64. Sasse, *Body*, 55.

65. Sasse, *Body*, 55.

66. Chemnitz, *Examination*, 365; Dowley, *Handbook*, 258.

67. Chemnitz, *Examination*, 254.

68. Erwin L. Lueker, ed., *Lutheran Cyclopedia: A Concise In-Home Reference for the Christian Family*, rev. ed. (St. Louis: Concordia, 1975), 460; McBrien, *Popes*, 211; Williston Walker, *A History of the Christian Church*, rev. C. C. Richardson, W. Pauck, and R. Handy (New York: Scribner, 1959), 239.

69. Chemnitz, *Examination*, 254; Marty, *History*, 169.

70. Sasse, *Body*, 15, 17.

71. Qualben, *History*, 134.

72. Lueker, *Cyclopedia*, 460; Sasse, *Body*, 14.

73. Giorgio Bouchard, "An Ancient and Undying Light," *Christian History* 8, no. 2 (1989): 9.

74. F. E. Mayer, *The Religious Bodies of America* (St. Louis: Concordia, 1954), 68; Piepkorn, *Selected Writings*, 123; Sasse, *Body*, 52.

75. Dowley, *Handbook*, 258.

76. Sasse, *Body*, 54.

77. Sasse, *Body*, 54.

78. Gaylin Schmeling, "The Theology of the Lord's Supper," *Lutheran Synod Quarterly* 28, no. 4 (1988): 26.
79. Stookey, *Eucharist*, 73.
80. Stookey, *Eucharist*, 770.
81. Sasse, *Body*, 54.
82. Stookey, *Eucharist*, 77.
83. Champlin, *Special Signs*, 55; Dowley, *Handbook*, 258; Stookey, *Eucharist*, 76.
84. Dowley, *Handbook*, 258.
85. Chemnitz, *Examination*, 365.
86. Chemnitz, *Examination*, 368, 369.
87. Champlin, *Special Signs*, 55.
88. Dowley, *Handbook*, 258; Sasse, *Body*, 54; Schaff, *History*, 4:569.
89. Chemnitz, *Examination*, 285.
90. McBrien, *Popes*, 217.
91. Chemnitz, *Examination*, 285.
92. Sasse, *Body*, 54.
93. Chemnitz, *Examination*, 287.
94. Chemnitz, *Examination*, 287.
95. Chemnitz, *Examination*, 288.
96. Schaff, *History*, 5:723.
97. Schaff, *History*, 5:723.
98. Schaff, *History*, 5:721.
99. Lueker, *Cyclopedia*, 616.
100. Lueker, *Cyclopedia*, 768.
101. Dowley, *Handbook*, 257, 258.
102. John M. Todd, *Reformation* (Garden City, N.Y.: Doubleday, 1971), 182, 183.
103. Kevin Smyth, trans., *A New Catechism: Catholic Faith for Adults* (New York: Herder and Herder, 1967), 346.
104. Schaff, *History*, 5:727.
105. Schaff, *History*, 5:727.
106. Schaff, *History*, 5:728.
107. Schaff, *History,* 5:728, 729.
108. Schaff, *History*, 5:728.
109. Stookey, *Eucharist*, 46, 47.
110. Sasse, *Body*, 37.
111. Sasse, *Body*, 38.
112. Sasse, *Body*, 37, 38.
113. Lueker, *Cyclopedia*, 768.
114. Sasse, *Body*, 38.
115. Klotsche, *Doctrine*, 151.
116. Sasse, *Body*, 37.
117. Lueker, *Cyclopedia*, 249.

118. Klotsche, *Doctrine*, 151.

119. Klotsche, *Doctrine*, 151; Sasse, *Body*, 44.

120. Sasse, *Body*, 126.

121. Lueker, *Cyclopedia*, 198.

122. Lueker, *Cyclopedia*, 198.

123. Sasse, *Body*, 44.

124. Lueker, *Cyclopedia*, 586; Schaff, *History*, 6:191.

125. Klotsche, *Doctrine*, 151; Sasse, *Body*, 44.

126. Schaff, *History*, 6:193.

127. Sasse, *Body*, 126.

128. Sasse, *Body*, 126.

129. Sasse, *Body*, 126, 127.

130. Klotsche, *Doctrine*, 151.

131. Lueker, *Cyclopedia*, 586; Schaff, *History*, 6:191.

132. Sasse, *Body*, 46.

133. Sasse, *Body*, 61.

134. Donald L. Roberts, "John Wycliffe and the Dawn of the Reformation," *Christian History* 2, no. 2 (1983): 13; Schaff, *History*, 6:320, 321.

135. Eugen Weber, *The Western Tradition: From the Renaissance to the Present*, 4th ed. (Lexington, Mass.: D. C. Heath and Company, 1990), 2:324.

136. Roberts, "Wycliffe," 13; Schaff, *History*, 6:321.

137. Schaff, *History*, 6:321.

138. Schaff, *History*, 6:321.

139. Roberts, "Wycliffe," 13.

140. Schaff, *History*, 6:336.

141. "From the Archives: Wycliffe Causes Controversy Over Eucharist," *Christian History* 2, no. 2 (1983): 24.

142. Schaff, *History*, 6:336; "Controversy," 24.

143. Sasse, *Body*, 45.

144. Sasse, *Body*, 46; Schaff, *History*, 6:337.

145. Schaff, *History* 6:337; "Controversy," 24.

146. "Controversy," 24.

147. Schaff, *History*, 6:337.

148. Roberts, "Wycliffe," 13.

149. Sasse, *Body*, 47.

150. Schaff, *History*, 6:336.

151. Schaff, *History*, 6:337.

152. Roberts, "Wycliffe," 13; Schaff, *History*, 6:337.

153. Schaff, *History*, 6:337.

154. Sasse, *Body*, 45; Schaff, *History*, 6:337.

155. Schaff, *History*, 6:337.

156. Sasse, *Body*, 45.

157. Lueker, *Cyclopedia*, 398.
158. Sasse, *Body*, 57.
159. Sasse, *Body*, 57, 58.
160. Sasse, *Body*, 61.
161. Sasse, *Body*, 58, 59.
162. Sasse, *Body*, 61.
163. Schaff, *History*, 6:393.
164. Schaff, *History*, 6:395, 396.
165. Schaff, *History*, 6:396, 397.

STUDY QUESTIONS

PART A: THE DEVELOPMENT OF TRANSUBSTANTIATION

1. When we speak of the medieval period in the Western Church, what is the general time frame that we consider?

2. What significant pronouncement did Pope Gregory I make that shaped the subsequent understanding of the Lord's Supper in the Roman Catholic Church?

3. How did this pronouncement enhance the status of the Roman Catholic priest?

4. How did Gregory enhance the status of the Lord's Prayer in the liturgy?

5. True or false: Reverence toward the Sacrament increased in the medieval period so that the elements were kept at the church under lock and key and the elements taken to the sick were done so in solemn procession, led by candles.

6. In the medieval Church, a debate continued regarding infant Communion. About 1200, a general consensus was reached. What was that decision?

7. How do the Eastern and Western churches differ with respect to their use of bread in the Lord's Supper?

8. What two medieval theologians captured the debate in the Western church between the realistic position regarding

the presence of the body and blood of Christ and the spiritual or symbolic position? What sides of the debate did the respective theologians represent?

9. What was the content of the doctrine of change and presence of Christ in the Lord's Supper, known later as transubstantiation, taught by Radbertus?

10. What Bible verse did both Ratramnus and Zwingli use to defend a spiritual or symbolic view of the Lord's Supper?

11. True or false: It appears that both Radbertus and Ratramnus believed that only the faithful received the body and blood of Christ in the Sacrament.

12. True or false: Berengar was possibly the first theologian to interpret the word "is" to mean "signifies" in the Words of Institution.

13. True or false: Medieval theories regarding the Lord's Supper did not spawn some apparently absurd, philosophically hypothetical arguments regarding the eating and passing of the consecrated elements.

14. True or false: The proliferation of private masses in the medieval period led to changes in church architecture and the addition of side-altars, to the belief of the sponsoring of a private mass to be a meritorious deed that granted "fruits" unto salvation, to the continuing enhancement and power of the Roman Catholic priests and hierarchy, and to the alienation of the laity from the former, essential participation in Sunday worship.

15. The doctrine of transubstantiation, the use of bells at the point of consecration, and the increase of piety in adoring the consecrated host led eventually to what kind of ritual procession and feast?

16. True or false: Medieval Eucharistic piety caused the laity to begin receiving the Lord's Supper very infrequently.

17. True or false: Medieval Eucharistic piety did not affect the manner in which the elements of the Lord's Supper were handled.

18. What manner of reception of the Lord's Supper did pressure from medieval Eucharistic piety help promote? At what council (give also the date) was this manner of reception finally mandated?

PART B: THE EFFECTS OF LATERAN IV

1. What two main doctrines regarding the nature of the elements and the role of priest and sacrifice in the Lord's Supper did Lateran IV mandate?

2. What two sacraments were required at least once per year by Lateran IV?

3. What practice, related to the Corpus Christi procession, gradually replaced the Lord's Supper for the general laity as a form of "communion"?

4. What kind of Mass, required to be done while fasting, helped provide the source for our word "breakfast"?

5. From what Bible verse is the concept of the tabernacle, the repository for the consecrated host in the Roman Catholic Church, drawn?

6. What council, some 200 years after Lateran IV, offered a long list of reasons why the laity should not receive the wine? Comment on one of those reasons that seems the most interesting to you.

7. What pope appointed the Corpus Christi celebration?

8. True or false: The Corpus Christi celebration changed in the fourteenth century (1301–1400) from a more solemn occasion for celebrating the Lord's Supper into a regal procession of the consecrated host.

9. What pope made it obligatory in the Roman Catholic Church for a bell to be rung at the moment of the consecration of the elements?

10. True or false: Among other things, priests had to drink the wash water used to clean stains from Communion wine and had to lick up spilled wine.

11. What two Roman Catholic theologians taught that the sacraments confer grace simply by being performed—ex opere operato?

12. True or false: The doctrine of transubstantiation did not spawn a host of occasionally bizarre legends regarding the consecrated host.

13. Thomas Aquinas used what philosopher's system of thought to work out in precise detail when the elements changed from bread and wine into body and blood, and how the change occurred?

14. True or false: Aquinas's philosophical leap was to assert that a substance could be present without its own accidents, yet with those of another. This constituted the metaphysical miracle of the Eucharist.

15. How did Aquinas account for the presence of the heavenly body of Christ in the Lord's Supper?

16. Duns Scotus later taught that the substance of Christ's body is added to the bread, then the substance of the bread is annihilated. Others following him, including William of Ockham (Occam) said that the substance of the bread is not annihilated, yielding bread plus body. What is this later view of the Lord's Supper, of which Luther has been falsely accused?

PART C: LATER ATTEMPTS AT REFORM

1. What kind of presence did John Wycliffe teach regarding the body of Christ in the Sacrament?

2. What did Wycliffe say about Aristotelian substances and accidents? How would this make Aquinas's doctrine of transubstantiation illogical and impossible?

3. Did John Hus deny the doctrine of transubstantiation? Who among his followers denied that doctrine?

4. What was Hus's chief grievance against the Roman Church with respect to the reception of the Lord's Supper?

5. Describe and name the three groups that followed Hus.

6. At what council were the Hussites granted Communion in both kinds?

THE LORD'S SUPPER AMONG THE PROTESTANT REFORMERS

7 | LUTHER'S SACRAMENTAL UNION

On October 31, 1517 Martin Luther, an Augustinian monk, posted 95 theses on the door of the Castle Church in Wittenberg, Germany. In doing this, Luther challenged fellow scholars to debate with him regarding the Roman Catholic sacrament of penance, the sale of indulgences, and how one could receive forgiveness of sins. This marked the beginning of the Protestant Reformation. Word of the theses and their contents spread like wildfire throughout the church. The debates that ensued eventually involved not only indulgences and forgiveness but also the whole of Christian doctrine, including the Lord's Supper. Protestants, so named after the protest of the revocation of religious liberties at the Second Diet of Speyer (1529), found themselves in disagreement with the Roman Church, and in many cases, with each other. Over time the several doctrinal positions coalesced primarily about the work of three individuals: Martin Luther (1483–1546), Ulrich Zwingli (1484–1531), and John Calvin (1509–1564). In addition to other doctrinal differences, these three confess different doctrines of the Lord's Supper.

Martin Luther's confession of the Lord's Supper changed somewhat over time. In his early career, Luther accepted the doctrine of transubstantiation. In a sermon that he preached in 1519 he told the congregation, "The bread is changed into his true natural body, and the wine into his true blood."[1] In the following year he rejected transubstantiation and adopted the view of his "dear master"[2] William of Occam and others, that the substance of the bread and wine remain after the consecration, and that at the same time the body and blood of Christ are given.[3] Luther first defended the withholding of the cup from the laity. In his *Treatise on the Blessed Sacrament* he said, "It is enough that the people . . . receive one kind . . . as the Christian Church ordains and offers."[4] Then, on the basis of his study of the words of institution, Luther came to the conclusion that all who participate should receive both the bread and the wine.[5] He states in *The Babylonian Captivity of the Church* that "it is wicked and despotic to deny both kinds to the laity."[6]

Luther also went from believing the chief purpose of the Lord's Supper to be fellowship to seeing the forgiveness of sins as being the most important goal of the Sacrament. Early in his career he expressed the opinion that "the significance or purpose of this sacrament is the fellowship of all the saints."[7] Luther later held and repeatedly stated that the main purpose in the Lord's Supper is that Christ gives the forgiveness of sins and life everlasting to those who receive it.[8] In an Easter sermon preached in 1534 Luther spoke concerning the forgiveness of sins received in the Lord's Supper, saying, "This is a benefit, indeed, it is the greatest and best one. We derive it from this testament."[9]

In his mature years Luther taught a sacramental presence of the body and blood of Christ in the Lord's Supper. He and his co-workers were the first to use the term "sacramental union."[10] Luther frequently employed a three-word combination when he spoke of this sacramental union. The body of Christ is "in, with and under" the bread, and His blood is "in, with and under" the wine.[11] Thus, four things are really and truly present, distributed, and received by those who commune—bread and body, wine and blood. That is the common understanding of "real presence" among Lutherans since they began using the term in the nineteenth century. How this is possible is beyond human comprehension. Luther did not attempt to explain the sacramental union or "real presence," but left it a mystery proclaimed, but not philosophically explained, by Scripture. He stated, "It is enough to know that it is a divine thing, in which Christ's body and blood are truly present—how and where we leave to him."[12]

Luther had a definite confession regarding the presence of the body and blood of Christ in this union. As we noted above, the chief purpose of the Lord's Supper confessed by Luther was the forgiveness of sins. In order to receive such forgiveness without any doubt, one could not, according to Luther, bring a meaning to Jesus' words of institution that was foreign to their literal sense. To engage in a manner of analyzing the Lord's words that does not discern the body of the Lord (1 Corinthians 11:29) according to the criterion given us by the Lord, namely, His literal words, brings one into judgment upon unworthy reception. That assertion grates against modern pluralism because it asserts that not all celebrations of the Lord's Supper are salutary for those that receive it, given the confession regarding the Lord's words.

What is this confession? It takes the Words of Institution in their literal sense and affirms that which the Lord has given us. The tenth article of the Augsburg Confession states: "It is taught among us that the true body and blood of Christ are really present in the Supper of our Lord under the form of bread and wine and are there distributed and received. The contrary doctrine is therefore rejected."[13] Article XXIV also includes, "Whoever uses the sacrament unworthily is guilty of the body and blood of Christ."[14] The Lutheran Formula of Concord, written after Luther's death, gives a more complete perspective of the confession followed by Luther:

> The other eating of the body of Christ is oral or sacramental, when all who eat and drink the blessed bread and wine in the Lord's Supper receive it as a certain pledge and assurance that their sins are truly forgiven, that Christ dwells and is efficacious in them; unbelievers receive it orally, too, but to their judgment and damnation.[15]

Luther and the Lutherans, following the confession of the literal sense of the Words of Institution, as well as the union of the two natures in Christ, assert that all recipients eat the body and blood of Christ orally, *manducatio oralis*. That some receive it to their forgiveness and blessing while others receive it to their judgment continues to grate against pluralistic sensibilities. Although many people today might ascribe the worthiness of the communicant as being individual faith and piety, the Scriptures tell us that worthiness exists in one grasping the public confession of the faithful Christian church that "this is My body" means literally what it says in the mouth of our Lord and of those whom He gives to speak in His stead and by His command. It is at this point that we understand the true significance of diverging confessions concerning the Lord's Supper among various denominations. A false confession of the Lord's Supper can do great spiritual harm to the communicants. If nothing else, the Lord's words must be toppled, to one's spiritual detriment, in order to carry out a pluralistic, "ecumenical" agenda.

Now that we have considered the danger faced by one that

alters the confession of the Lord's words, we continue to see how these words are not "just words" but are related to the two natures in Christ and the communication of attributes. The implication of such observations will be that if one wobbles in the confession of the Lord's Supper, one also wobbles in the confession of Christ and thus threatens to put one's salvation into doubt. The only Jesus that can save is the one proclaimed in the Scriptures and confessed in the Creeds. When one talks about the modes of Christ's presence, one thereby talks about the two natures in Christ, as the Scriptures proclaim and the Creeds confess.

When Luther used the words "in, with and under," he had in mind an illocal, supernatural union.[16] He called the "illocal" form of Christ's presence in the Lord's Supper "the incomprehensible, spiritual mode, according to which he neither occupies or vacates space, but penetrates all creatures wherever he pleases."[17] He compared this presence to the idea of a person's sight penetrating water or air or light without vacating or occupying space. (Before Newton (1642–1727), people commonly believed that sight was the result of some kind of energy going forth from one's eyes.) It is like sound being in air or water or a board or wall in the same way. Luther said Jesus used this mode when He passed through closed doors, when He rose from the closed tomb, in the bread and wine in the Lord's Supper, and, as it is believed, when He was born of His mother.[18]

Luther's Christology enabled him to believe that it is possible for Christ to be bodily present both in heaven and in the Lord's Supper at the same time. The most characteristic feature of Luther's Christology is his belief that the human nature of Christ shared in the properties of His divine nature.[19] Thus, through the communication of properties, Christ is present everywhere, not only according to His divine nature but also according to His human nature. Luther believed that where Christ is He is in His entirety. He once stated that even though Christ is seated at the right hand of God, He must be everywhere for "the right hand of

God is everywhere."[20] Although the Lutherans called this property of Christ the *genus apotelesmaticum*, the Reformed disparagingly referred to this doctrine as "ubiquity."[21]

While Luther's Christological position enabled him to believe that Christ can be present both in heaven and in the Lord's Supper at the same time, this was not his reason for holding that Christ is really present in the Sacrament.[22] His faith in the sacramental union is based on Christ's Words of Institution.[23] In this regard Luther made a distinction between Christ's general presence and the special sacramental presence. Luther held that "we can really find and apprehend him where he by his words binds himself to the bread."[24]

Luther considered the words "Given and shed for you for the forgiveness of sins" to be "the chief thing in the sacrament."[25] He said that it is through these words that "forgiveness of sins, life and salvation" are given in the Lord's Supper.[26] He believed that the bodily eating and drinking do not do the great things accomplished by the Lord's Supper. The power is in the words of Jesus. Luther also held that only those who believe the words "Given and shed for you for the remission of sins" receive the forgiveness of sins in their use of the Lord's Supper.[27] Spiritual eating must accompany bodily eating.[28] In the confessional document *The Augsburg Confession* Luther's co-worker Philip Melanchthon (1497–1560) said of Holy Baptism and the Lord's Supper: "They are rightly used when they are received in faith and for the strengthening of faith."[29] It follows that he believed that the only persons who are worthy to receive the Lord's Supper are those who have faith in the words "Given and shed for you for the remission of sins." Melanchthon said that anyone who does not believe these words, or doubts concerning them, is unworthy and unprepared to receive the Lord's Supper.[30]

Luther condemned a number of ideas regarding the Lord's Supper taught in the medieval church, including the idea that the Mass is a good work in which Christ is offered as a sacrifice to

God.[31] He believed that the notion of the Lord's Supper as a sacrifice brought by the priest for the living and the dead has no foundation in the New Testament. Luther states, "We must let the mass be a sacrament and a testament, and this is not and cannot be a sacrifice."[32] He considered the view of the Mass as a sacrifice to be "the most wicked abuse of all" and "the most dangerous error."[33] He wrote that this abuse of the Lord's Supper brought with it numerous other abuses.[34]

Luther also attacked the teaching that the Lord's Supper conveys grace simply by being performed. He says that by this doctrine the celebration of the Lord's Supper is converted into a good work on the part of the officiating priest.[35] In sermons Luther told his hearers that not the Sacrament, but faith in the Sacrament, justifies. Faith must precede, not only accompany, the reception of the Sacrament.[36] Roman Catholic historian John M. Todd says of Luther's view in this matter, "Above all it was no longer 'meritorious,' a 'good work.'"[37]

Also condemned was the idea that one can commune by oneself for one's own devotion. When someone asked Luther, "May a person commune himself?" he replied, "No! For at least two persons should always be present; one who gives, another who receives."[38] When he was in hiding in the Wartburg Castle, Luther requested that the chaplain not celebrate the Lord's Supper when there was no congregation present. His request was granted.[39]

To correct what Luther thought to be errors in the celebration of the Lord's Supper he proposed changes in the forms connected with the Sacrament. However, in some Lutheran congregations the changes that Luther felt to be necessary were not instituted until some decades later.[40] Some Lutheran churches continued medieval practices such as the adoration of the host as the body of Christ. In some cases church members were not even permitted to partake of the bread, but were satisfied only to behold it at a distance. Other practices associated with transubstantiation also remained.[41] Luther's doctrinal approach to the

Lord's Supper is evident in his pastoral practice regarding the Sacrament. He felt it imperative that congregations be changed from bodies of spectators and listeners to active participants in worship.[42] To accomplish this, in 1523 Luther created a liturgy of Holy Communion in the language of the people.[43] He held that no precise mode of administering the Lord's Supper was to be prescribed in the churches. In 1523 he wrote, "Even if different people use different forms, let no one either judge or despise the other."[44]

Luther felt that people should not be admitted to the Lord's Supper indiscriminately.[45] He said that those who commune together should all have the same faith and doctrine. In a sermon preached in 1534 he told the congregation, "By attending it every Christian confesses publicly and for himself what he believes. There those who have a different faith part ways, and those meet who have the same faith, whose hope and heart toward the Lord are one."[46] In 1523 Luther wrote a letter to a church at Frankfurt am Main warning them not to commune other Protestants who denied the sacramental union of Christ's body and blood in the Lord's Supper. He wrote that it terrified him to hear that both those who accepted the doctrine of the sacramental union and those we denied it were allowed to receive "one and the same Sacrament" at a Lutheran altar.[47]

Those wishing to commune should announce to the pastor beforehand, said Luther, "so that he many know their names and life." He held that pastors should examine "the petitioners," inquiring regarding their understanding of the Lord's Supper. He charged pastors to note whether the intendees "prove this faith and knowledge by their life and conduct." If one was seen to be a gross sinner, the instruction given to pastors was "let him absolutely exclude him from the Supper unless by some clear proof he has testified that his life is changed."[48]

NOTES

1. E. H. Klotsche, *The History of Christian Doctrine*, rev. J. Theodore Mueller and David P. Scaer (1945; reprint, Grand Rapids: Baker, 1979), 182.

2. Hermann Sasse, *This Is My Body: Luther's Contention for the Real Presence in the Sacrament of the Altar*, rev. ed. (Adelaide, South Australia: Lutheran Publishing House, 1977), 92.

3. Klotsche, *Doctrine*, 182, 183; E. G. Schweibert, *Luther and His Times: The Reformation from a New Perspective* (St. Louis: Concordia, 1950), 449.

4. Sasse, *Body*, 71.

5. Sasse, *Body*, 75–77.

6. *Works of Martin Luther with Introduction and Notes*; The Philadelphia Edition (Philadelphia: Muhlenberg Press, 1943), 2:187.

7. Sasse, *Body*, 87.

8. Elmer J. F. Arndt, ed., *The Heritage of the Reformation: Essays Commemorating the Centennial of Eden Theological Seminary* (New York: R. R. Smith, 1950), 103; *Works of Martin Luther*, 2:199.

9. Ewald M. Plass, *What Luther Says: An Anthology* (St. Louis: Concordia, 1959), 2:808.

10. Arthur Carl Piepkorn, *The Church: Selected Writings of Arthur Carl Piepkorn*, ed. Michael P. Plekon and Williem S. Wiecher (Delhi, N.Y.: ALPB Books, 1993), 123.

11. Schweibert, *Luther*, 450.

12. Schweibert, *Luther*, 450.

13. Augsburg Confession X, in *The Book of Concord*, ed. Theodore Tappert (Philadelphia: Fortress, 1959), 34.

14. Ausgburg Confession XXIV, (Tappert, *Concord*), 57.

15. Tappert, *Concord*, 581.

16. Klotsche, *Doctrine*, 183.

17. Sasse, *Body*, 126.

18. Sasse, *Body*, 126.

19. Sasse, *Body*, 121.

20. Sasse, *Body*, 125.

21. Sasse, *Body*, 124.

22. Francis Pieper, *Christian Dogmatics* (St. Louis: Concordia, 1951), 2:193.

23. Pieper, *Dogmatics*, 2:193.

24. Klotsche, *Doctrine*, 183.

25. F. Bente, ed., *Triglot Concordia: The Symbolical Books of the Evangelical Lutheran Church* (St. Louis: Concordia, 1921), 557.

26. Bente, *Triglot*, 557.

27. Bente, *Triglot*, 557.

28. From The Large Catechism of Dr. Martin Luther, in *The Book of Concord*, ed. Theodore G. Tappert (Philadelphia: Fortress Press, 1959), 450.

29. Augsburg Confession XIII, 2, (Tappert, *Concord*), 36.

30. Bente, *Triglot*, 557.
31. John Dillenberger and Claude Welch, *Protestant Christianity Interpreted Through Its Development* (New York: Scribner, 1954), 23, 24; John M. Todd, *Reformation* (Garden City, N.Y.: Doubleday, 1971), 184.
32. Sasse, *Body*, 67.
33. *Works of Martin Luther*, 2:191, 211.
34. *Works of Martin Luther*, 2:194.
35. *Works of Martin Luther*, 2:207.
36. Sasse, *Body*, 66.
37. Todd, *Reformation*, 184.
38. Plass, *What Luther Says*, 2:812.
39. Todd, *Reformation*, 195.
40. Schweibert, *Luther*, 475.
41. William H. Bartels, "The Palatinate and the Reformation" (S.T.M. thesis, Concordia Seminary, 1973), 9.
42. Sasse, *Body*, 63.
43. Fred L. Precht, ed., *Lutheran Worship: History and Practice* (St. Louis: Concordia, 1993), 96, 251, 451.
44. Precht, *Lutheran Worship*, 2:810, 811.
45. Plass, *What Luther Says*, 2:809.
46. Plass, *What Luther Says*, 2:812.
47. Plass, *What Luther Says*, 2:813.
48. Plass, *What Luther Says*, 2:809, 810.

STUDY QUESTIONS

1. True or false: In his early years, Luther taught the doctrine of transubstantiation, defended Communion in one kind, and believed that the chief benefit of the Sacrament was that of fellowship in the body of Christ. In his later years, Luther taught the sacramental union of bread and wine with Christ's body and blood, defended Communion in both kinds, and believed the chief benefit of the Sacrament to be the forgiveness of sins.

2. Both Lutheran and Reformed theologians accept the genus idiomaticum, the assertion that the specific properties of, respectively, the divine and the human natures may be ascribed to Christ. They both accept the *genus majesta-*

ticum, the assertion that the divine nature and its works show through in Christ, even though the human nature also remains and participates in those works. The parting of the ways comes at the *genus apotelesmaticum*, the assertion that the human nature can use properties of the divine nature as Christ accomplishes His works. Lutherans appeal to this third genus to argue for what kind of bodily presence of Christ in the Lord's Supper, which the Reformed derisively call "ubiquity?"

3. The above philosophical argument aside, what, for Luther and Lutherans, has been the chief reason for defending the sacramental union?

4. Who receives the benefits of the Lord's Supper?

5. Who falls under judgment when receiving the Sacrament?

6. What errors regarding the Mass did Luther condemn?

7. Since Luther condemned the teaching that the Lord's Supper is a good work done by the priest that automatically functions *ex opere operato*, what did Luther say it is that justifies in the Sacrament?

8. According to Luther, may one commune by oneself?

9. What did Luther encourage with respect to lay worship?

10. What kind of Communion practice did Luther advocate, and what was the general basis for admission to the Lord's Supper?

11. True or false: Luther advocated individual confession and absolution, whereby pastors examined those who intended to receive the Lord's Supper.

8 | ZWINGLI'S MEMORIAL MEAL

nother key Reformation figure was Ulrich Zwingli, a parish priest in Switzerland. In 1517 he became pastor of the influential Great Minster Church in Zurich. He had already taken humanist positions against church corruptions in his first two assignments. As he was recovering from the plague during a three-month period that year, he spent much time studying the Scriptures. The more Zwingli studied, the less he was able to reconcile the doctrines and rituals of the church with what he found in the Bible. His sermons began to go against accepted church teachings, spreading controversy. The Zurich city council issued a ruling supporting Zwingli. Reforms resulted, including that the Mass was replaced with a simple service in the vernacular, and the Lord's Supper was celebrated as a spiritual meal in memory of Christ.[1]

Zwingli's views regarding the Lord's Supper were very different from those held by Luther. He taught that the "real presence" in the Lord's Supper consisted of the presence of Christ in the hearts of His people as they partook of this communal fellowship meal. He held that Christ is not physically present in the Lord's Supper, but spiritually present in the hearts of those who commune in faith.[2] We see again that it is not enough to use the words "real presence" but to explain what one means by them.

Zwingli's teaching on the Lord's Supper has three stages. Early in his career Zwingli confessed the doctrine of transubstantiation. It appears, however, that he did not take it seriously.[3] He once said, "In my opinion no one has ever believed that he eats Christ's body essentially, though almost all have taught this or at least pretended to believe it."[4] In 1523 Zwingli openly denounced transubstantiation, beginning the second stage. He also spoke out against Communion in one kind, the practice of withholding the wine, and only giving the bread to the laity. He voiced his opposition to the idea that the Lord's Supper is a sacrifice and offering brought by the priests for the living and the dead.[5]

At this stage in the development of Zwingli's understanding of the Lord's Supper he taught that the believer eats Christ. He explained that Christ, who otherwise is seated at the right hand of the Father in heaven, miraculously descends in the Lord's Supper. By an inscrutable miracle Christ enters the soul of the believer. While Zwingli used familiar terminology such as "eating the body" and "drinking the blood," the meaning he gave to these was ambiguous and obscure. He maintained that the believer received Christ in the Lord's Supper by faith only. On the basis of John 6, Zwingli wrote that when one believes in the redeeming death of Christ, one's soul eats the Lord's body and drinks His blood.[6]

The final stage in the development of Zwingli's doctrine of the Lord's Supper resulted from his reading of a 1523 letter from Cornelius Hoen (died 1524) of Holland.[7] Hoen had made a careful study of the words of Christ: "This is My body." Hoen had come to the conclusion that the Lord's Supper should not be a sacrament as taught in the Catholic Church. Instead it ought to be considered to merely be a commemoration. Hoen interpreted the word "is" ("This *is* my body") to mean "represents" or "means." He used other Bible verses to show that the words "is" and "are" are often used in this sense. Zwingli wrote regarding Hoen's letter, "In this letter I found a pearl of great value: *is* has the sense of *means*."[8] He came to use the words "means," "represents," and "signifies" interchangeably. In a scholarly work published in 1525, Zwingli says that the word "is" means "signifies" and he renders the words of institution thus, "Take eat; this bread *signifies* My body, which is given for you."[9] In *A Clear Briefing About Christ's Supper*, which was written in German for the laity, he reasoned that if the word "is" in the words of institution has to be taken literally, the real body and blood would be seen and tasted. "Invisible corporeality is sheer nonsense."[10]

Under the influence of Andreas Bodenstein von Carlstadt (1480–1541), the exiled radical professor from Wittenberg, Zwingli concluded that Christ's body is in heaven and cannot be in the bread at the same time.[11] Zwingli came to believe that, like every other human being, Christ is unable to exist in more than one place at the same time.[12] Zwingli made a sharp distinction between the divine and human natures of Christ, holding that biblical statements about one nature can by applied only to that nature, and that no transfer or fusion of the two natures takes place. He rejected the doctrine of the communication of properties advocated by Luther.[13] He believed that Scriptural references to Christ's ascension and second coming apply only to the human nature, because according to the divine nature Christ is with the Father. Since after His ascension Christ is bodily in heaven, He cannot be present bodily in the bread and wine of the Lord's Supper.[14]

In his later career, Zwingli no longer considered the Lord's Supper to be a means of grace, but believed it to be a sign of the divine grace that one may receive even without the Lord's Supper. In his view, participation in the Lord's Supper is a good work as a response of faith.[15] The proposition "The finite cannot take up the infinite" was foundational to his thinking regarding the Lord's Supper. Therefore, the concept of the sacramental union of the visible earthly elements with the true body and blood of Christ was unacceptable to him.[16] Zwingli believed that the verse "It is the Spirit that quickeneth; the flesh profiteth nothing" (John 6:63) supported his spiritual view of the Sacrament. He called the phrase "the flesh profiteth nothing" his "diamond."[17] Lutheran scholar Hermann Sasse states that Zwingli believed that these words "clearly taught that Christ recognized only a spiritual eating, and expressly rejected all bodily eating as was taught by the Roman Church and Luther."[18] For Zwingli there were two major emphases or chief aspects of the Lord's Supper. The first of these was that the Lord's Supper is a celebration meal eaten in remembrance and thanksgiving for the redemption that God has provided in Christ.[19] The second aspect is that the Lord's Supper brings the congregation together in love, and when it is used the loving transformed nature of the fellowship of believers is evident and manifested.[20]

In pastoral practice, Zwingli made sweeping changes to the celebration of the Lord's Supper. He replaced the Latin Mass with a German order of service using the Zurich dialect.[21] This changed the formerly passive role of the laity to becoming active participants. He designed the service to emphasize the fellowship aspect of the Lord's Supper, employing commemoration, praise, and thanksgiving.[22] Sasse writes, "It was a beautiful rite in which man remembers Christ, but no longer a sacrament in which Christ comes to man."[23]

Zwingli introduced the new service at Great Minster Church during Holy Week of 1525. The Mass was conducted for the last time on Holy Wednesday. People filled the church to overflowing since they, apparently with mixed feelings, realized they would part from an integral part of their religious lives.[24] On Maundy Thursday Zwingli held the new service for the first time. He repeated it on Good Friday and on Easter Sunday. After the initial celebrations, the Lord's Supper according to the new order was observed four times a year—Easter, Pentecost, September 11 (church dedication day), and at Christmas.[25]

Zwingli replaced the altar with moveable long tables covered with white tablecloths. The communicants knelt at the table to receive the bread and wine. He replaced the traditional silver or gold Communion vessels with wooden plates for the bread and cans or wooden cups for the wine.[26] In the service, the pastor and his assistants communed first.[27] The deacons carried the unleavened bread to the congregation. The communicants each broke a small piece of bread from the loaf, then passed the rest of the loaf to the person next to him or her. The deacons distributed the wine. After partaking the communicants handed the cup to their neighbor at the table.[28]

A great controversy over the Lord's Supper arose between Luther and Zwingli, including other theologians in the respective camps. Luther and his associate John Bugenhagen (1485–1558) wrote pamphlets against Zwingli's position. Zwingli and his companion Johannus Oeclampadius (1482–1531) authored pamphlets denouncing Luther's views. The paper debate became quite heated, with Luther declaring that Zwingli and those with him were not Christians, and Zwingli calling the Lutherans flesh eaters and blood drinkers, saying that their Communion was a baked god.[29] Carlstadt suggested that when Christ said the word "this" He pointed to His visible body, so that the Lord's action implied, "You see my body before you, which I give for you; in commemoration thereof partake of bread and wine."[30] Oecolampadius did not use "is" as his starting point. He focused rather on the words "body" and "blood." He contended that when Christ said "body" He meant "*sign* of my body," and when He said "blood" He meant "*sign, emblem* of my blood." A third theory was that of a lay

Protestant mystic by the name of Casper Schwenkfeld von Ossig (ca. 1489–1561).[31] He claimed to know by special revelation that "this" was the predicate of the sentence, "This is My body," and that the words must be reversed, "My body is *this*, namely, the true bread for the soul; my blood is *this*, namely the true potion for the soul."[32]

A German Lutheran political leader, Landgrave Philip of Hesse (1504–1567) believed strongly that the Protestants needed to be united, not the least of which was for political reasons. In an effort to heal the breach occasioned by the Lord's Supper controversy, he invited Luther, Zwingli, and their fellow theologians to a conference at his castle in Marburg, early in October 1529, which came to be known as the Marburg Colloquy. The German and Swiss theologians met for several days discussing and disagreeing about the Lord's Supper. In the main, the debate was exegetical in nature. No arguments that had not already appeared in print were brought forward. The colloquy was primarily a recapitulation of the controversy that had preceded it.[33] The discussions between Luther and Zwingli were surprisingly cordial. The treated each other with gentlemanly courtesy.[34]

Luther took his stand on a literal interpretation of Christ's words "this is My body." He challenged Zwingli to prove to him that Christ's body and blood were not in the Lord's Supper. With a piece of chalk, he wrote the words "This is My body" on the table in large characters. He constantly returned to this quote throughout the debate, pointing his finger to the chalk written words of institution repeatedly during the proceedings.[35] In response to Luther's position, Zwingli argued that Christ had spoken these words metaphorically in the same manner as when he made such statements as "I am the vine" and "I am the bread of life." Luther countered Zwingli by stating that any metaphorical interpretation could not be assumed, but had to be proven, and that the burden of proof must fall on those who prefer a nonliteral interpretation.[36]

A basic verse of Scripture used by the Swiss was "It is the Spirit that quickeneth, the flesh profiteth nothing; the words that I have spoken unto you are spirit and are life" (John 6:63). Oecolampadius stated that this passage provides the key for interpreting the words of institution, and excludes a literal understanding.[37] Luther contended that when Christ said, "The flesh profiteth nothing," He was not speaking of His flesh, but of ours.[38] Just as Luther was a literalist regarding his favorite text, so was Zwingli about the words "Christ ascended into heaven."[39] He reasoned that Christ ascended into heaven; therefore, He cannot be on earth with His body, for a body cannot be in more than one place at a time. Luther quoted medieval scholars to claim that there are two different kinds of presence.[40] Again, they reached an impasse in the discussions.[41]

When it became evident that no consensus regarding the Lord's Supper could be achieved, Landgrave Philip asked Luther to draw up a set of articles on which there was agreement between the parties. Luther compiled and prepared 15 *Marburg Articles* dealing with fundamental teachings of the Christian faith.[42] All agreed to 14 of the articles. The fifteenth dealt with the doctrine of the Lord's Supper, recognizing the difference between the Lutherans and the Zwinglians.[43]

After Marburg, Luther and Melanchthon became more hopeful regarding the Swiss theologians than at any previous time. In addition, after Marburg, Martin Bucer of southern Germany, who was a member of Zwingli's delegation at the colloquy, regarded Luther's doctrinal views more favorably than before. Seeking a middle ground between Luther and Zwingli he proposed the formula "that the true body and the true blood of Christ are truly present in the Lord's Supper and are offered with the words of the Lord in the sacrament."[44] In 1534, three years after Zwingli's death, Bucer wrote a paper in which he endeavored to show that the Lutherans and the Zwinglians were in fundamental agreement.[45] The publication of this writing resulted in a meeting later that year in which Melanchthon endorsed Bucer's plan for concord between the two camps. Bucer and Melanchthon worked together to achieve unity regarding the Lord's Supper. Negotiations toward unity reached a climax at a 1536 meeting held in Luther's study. The Lutherans and the Zwinglians there present gave each other the hand of Christian fellowship. Melanchthon prepared a report of the discussions, known subsequently as the *Wittenberg Concord*. It explained the common belief in language both sides could accept, even though they interpreted the words differently. The *Concord* divided the Zwinglians into two groups, those who followed Bucer and those who retained the symbolic view of the Lord's Supper.[46]

Differences developed between Luther and Melanchthon regarding the Lord's Supper. Scholars remain divided regarding Melanchthon's actual position on the real presence of Christ in the Sacrament. Early in 1530 Melanchthon published a booklet in which he stated that one should consult the opinions of the church fathers because their opinions have always been the common convictions of the church, and it would not be safe to disagree with the common doctrine of the early church. Sasse writes that through his study of the writings of the fathers, Melanchthon "gradually became more broadminded, and his former view of the unanimity of the Church Fathers was shaken."[47] Consequently, he came to accept Bucer's practical view that several opinions could be tolerated in the church, if the concept of the real presence of the body and blood of Christ was generally accepted.[48] Under Bucer's influence, he increasingly felt that Luther's doctrine might lead to an adoration of the host and ultimately to a materialistic view of the sacramental union.[49]

In 1540, Melanchthon prepared an altered version of the *Augsburg Confession* known as the *Variata*. In the *Variata* he changed the wording of the article pertaining to the Lord's Supper. In the original version the article read, "Of the Supper of the Lord they teach that the Body and Blood of Christ are truly present and are distributed to those who eat in the Supper of the Lord; and they reject those that teach otherwise."[50] In the *Variata* he changed the words "the Body and Blood of Christ are truly present" to "the Body and Blood of Christ are truly offered."[51] Melanchthon also omitted the clause: "and they reject those that teach otherwise."[52] In their book, *Protestant Christianity* John Dillenberger and Claude Welch flatly state of Melanchthon's revision of the Lord's Supper article in the *Variata*, "Melanchthon rewrote the Augsburg Confession to permit a 'spiritual' interpretation."[53] The 1540 version came to be widely used throughout the Protestant lands of Germany. At a conference at Naumberg in 1561, the two editions became a great issue. Melanchthon's view did not prevail.[54] The controversy between the "Philippists" that followed Melanchthon and the "True Lutherans" resulted in the writing of the 1577 Formula of Concord by Chemnitz and others that rejected the Philippist position.

In 1531, three years before the *Wittenberg Concord*, Zwingli was killed in a battle between Protestants and Catholics near Kappel, Switzerland. His successor as pastor of Great Minster Church in Zurich was Heinrich Bullinger (1504–1575).[55] Bullinger adopted a modified view of Zwingli's position on the Lord's Supper. He rejected the *Wittenberg Concord* saying that it concealed Lutheran doctrine.[56] Bullinger held to a higher theory of the Lord's Supper than did Zwingli. He wrote that "we recognize a mystery in the Lord's Supper; the bread is not common bread, but venerable, sacred, sacramental bread, the pledge of the spiritual real presence of Christ to those who believe."[57]

NOTES

1. Erwin L. Lueker, ed., *Lutheran Cyclopedia: A Concise In-Home Reference for the Christian Family,* rev. ed. (St. Louis: Concordia, 1975), 845; "Zurich Reform Under Zwingli," *Pulpit Helps* (January 1995): 25.

2. John B. Payne, "Zwingli and Luther: the Giant vs. Hercules," *Christian History* 3, no. 1 (1984): 33.

3. Hermann Sasse, *This Is My Body: Luther's Contention for the Real Presence in*

the Sacrament of the Altar, rev. ed. (Adelaide, South Australia: Lutheran Publishing House, 1977), 96.

4. Sasse, *Body*, 96.

5. Sasse, *Body*, 96.

6. Sasse, *Body*, 96, 97.

7. "A Gallery of Family, Friends, Foes and Followers," *Christian History* 3, no. 1 (1984): 13; Sasse, *Body*, 87; Williston Walker, *A History of the Christian Church*, rev. C. C. Richardson, W. Pauck, and R. Handy (New York: Scribner, 1959), 324.

8. "Gallery of Family," 13.

9. W. H. T. Dau, ed., *Four Hundred Years: Commemorative Essays on the Reformation of Dr. Martin Luther and Its Blessed Results* (St. Louis: Concordia, 1916).

10. Ulrich Gäbler, *Ulrich Zwingli: His Life and Work*, trans. Ruth C. L. Gritsch (Philadelphia: Fortress, 1986), 133.

11. Sasse, *Body*, 100.

12. Gäbler, *Zwingli*, 134; Lowell C. Green, "Philosophical Presuppositions in the Lutheran-Reformed Debate on John 6," *Concordia Theological Quarterly* 56, no. 1 (1992): 17; E. H. Klotsche, *The History of Christian Doctrine*, rev. J. Theodore Mueller and David P. Scaer (1945; reprint, Grand Rapids: Baker, 1979), 119.

13. Gäbler, *Zwingli*, 134.

14. Gäbler, *Zwingli*, 134.

15. Green, "Philosophical," 23.

16. Green, "Philosophical," 17.

17. Sasse, *Body*, 100.

18. Sasse, *Body*, 100.

19. Klotsche, *Doctrine*, 190, 191; Payne, "Zwingli and Luther," 35.

20. Payne, "Zwingli and Luther," 35.

21. Philip Schaff, *History of the Christian Church* (n.p.; Charles Scribner's Sons, 1958–1960), 8:60.

22. John T. McNeill, *The History and Character of Calvinism* (New York: Oxford, 1954), 81; "Replacing the Mass with a New Order of Worship," *Christian History* 3, no. 1 (1984): 22, 23, 166.

23. Sasse, *Body*, 105.

24. Sasse, *Body*, 105.

25. Payne, "Zwingli and Luther," 35; Sasse, *Body*, 105; Schaff, *History*, 8:61.

26. McNeill, *Calvinism*, 86; Payne, "Zwingli and Luther," 34; Sasse, *Body*, 104; Schaff, *History*, 60.

27. "Replacing the Mass," 23.

28. "Replacing the Mass," 23.

29. Schaff, *History*, 7:626.

30. Dau, *Four Hundred Years*, 76.

31. Dau, *Four Hundred Years*, 77; Lueker, *Cyclopedia*, 707.

32. Dau, *Four Hundred Years*, 77.

33. McNeill, *Calvinism*, 50; Schaff, *History*, 7:640.

34. Schaff, *History*, 7:640.

35. Sydney E. Ahlstrom, *A Religious History of the American People* (New Haven: Yale University Press 1972), 76; McNeill, *Calvinism*, 50; Payne, "Zwingli and Luther," 34; Schaff, *History*, 7:640.

36. Payne, "Zwingli and Luther," 34.

37. Sasse, *Body*, 188; Schaff, *History*, 7:640.

38. Dau, *Four Hundred Years*, 81; Sasse, *Body*, 641.

39. Payne, "Zwingli and Luther," 34.

40. Schaff, *History*, 7:642.

41. Schaff, *History*, 7:643.

42. Sasse, *Body*, 175, 216.

43. Sasse, *Body*, 175, 216.

44. Klotsche, *Doctrine*, 193; Lueker, *Cyclopedia*, 114.

45. "Did You Know?" *Christian History* 3, no. 1 (1984): 7.

46. E. G. Schweibert, *Luther and His Times: The Reformation from a New Perspective* (St. Louis: Concordia, 1950), 736–739.

47. Sasse, *Body*, 255.

48. Sasse, *Body*, 255.

49. Sasse, *Body*, 256.

50. F. Bente, ed., *Triglot Concordia: The Symbolical Books of the Evangelical Lutheran Church* (St. Louis: Concordia, 1921), 47.

51. Klotsche, *Doctrine*, 204.

52. Klotsche, *Doctrine*, 204.

53. John Dillenberger and Claude Welch, *Protestant Christianity Interpreted Through Its Development* (New York: Scribner, 1954), 81.

54. Dillenberger, *Protestant*, 81.

55. "Gallery of Family," 15.

56. Schaff, *History*, 8:210.

57. Schaff, *History*, 8:210.

STUDY QUESTIONS

1. What did Zwingli define as the "real presence" of Christ in his teaching of the Lord's Supper as a memorial meal?

2. What did Zwingli say about the meaning of "is" in the final stage of development of his Lord's Supper doctrine?

3. What influence did Carlstadt, Luther's exiled, former col-

league who had gone over to the radical reformation, have on Zwingli's understanding of the body of Christ?

4. True or false: Zwingli eventually ceased to consider the Lord's Supper to be a sacrament or means of grace, but merely a good work, a sign of the grace that one can receive even without the Lord's Supper.

5. Zwingli used John 6:63 as well as what saying regarding things that are finite in order to argue against Luther?

6. What did Zwingli believe were the two main emphases of the Lord's Supper?

7. True or false: Zwingli's changes to the Lord's Supper liturgy were not as far-reaching as those of Luther.

8. To what location did Philip of Hesse invite Luther and Zwingli, together with their respective companions, to a colloquy in 1529 in order to attempt a rapprochement and a doctrinal consensus between the two sides.

9. Of the fifteen articles of faith that came out of the colloquy, both sides reached agreement on fourteen. What remained the one article upon which they could not reach consensus, thus preventing fellowship between them?

10. In the years 1534–1536, what southern German theologian among the Zwinglian camp took a position more favorable toward Luther than some others and worked toward agreement in the 1536 Wittenberg Concord?

11. What Lutheran theologian's position regarding the church fathers and the existence of differing doctrines among them over against the unanimity in doctrine asserted by Luther and others caused a rift between his doctrine of the Lord's Supper and that of Luther, reflected also in his greater cooperation with Roman Catholic and Reformed parties than other Lutherans would accept?

12. What kind of interpretation of the Lord's Supper did the 1540 Variata edition of the Augsburg Confession allow?

13. What 1577 document, contained in the 1580 Book of Concord, finds its historical context in the conflict between "Philippists" and "True Lutherans" that grew out of the continuing controversy spawned by the 1540 Variata and other documents?

14. Who succeeded Zwingli after his death?

9 | CALVIN'S SPIRITUAL PRESENCE

The final major figure in the Protestant Reformation was John Calvin. Some interpret his approach as an attempt at a "middle way" between Luther and Zwingli in the matter of the Lord's Supper.[1] Calvin's father was secretary to the bishop of Noyon, France. From an early age, John received training in preparation for a church vocation. Beginning in 1536, Calvin served a church in Geneva, Switzerland. He and his associate pastor were forced to leave Geneva in 1538. He went to Strasbourg in Germany where he enjoyed a fine working relationship with Martin Bucer.[2] During his time in Strasbourg he also established a friendship with Philip Melanchthon.[3] In 1541, Calvin was called back to Geneva. Martin Bucer had influenced him greatly,[4] serving as a spiritual father with respect to the doctrine of the Lord's Supper.

Early in his career, Calvin wished to be a disciple of Luther. He believed himself to be much closer to Luther than to Zwingli.[5] Luther, too, seems to have felt some closeness to Calvin. Reformed professor Roger Nicole says that at one time Luther felt so close to Calvin regarding the Lord's Supper that he stated that if Calvin's approach had been offered at the Marburg Colloquy, a separation between the Lutherans and the Reformed would not have been necessary.[6] Melanchthon and Calvin kept in touch with each other for over 20 years.[7] Lutheran pastor William H. Bartels says of them in the Strasbourg years, "They apparently found themselves to be congenial in doctrine, especially concerning the Lord's Supper."[8]

A significant step in the development of Calvin's position that had far reaching effects for the future of the Lord's Supper in Protestant churches was the *Zurich Consensus* of 1549. The two major theologians involved in this *Consensus* were John Calvin and Heinrich Bullinger.[9] The *Consensus* confesses the sacraments, Holy Baptism and the Lord's Supper, to be more than mere signs. The document calls them means of grace that actually convey the benefits of redemption. It speaks of their saving and sanctifying efficacy due to God's blessing and the working of the Holy Spirit. It calls the sacraments means of grace only to those who believe, the chosen people of God, not means of grace to all who indiscriminately receive them. The *Consensus* denies the local presence of Christ, maintaining that Christ's body is locally in heaven.[10] It maintains that one should understand "This is My body" in a figurative manner.

Calvin tried to find a middle way,[11] an "intermediary view,"[12] between Luther and Zwingli by rejecting the positions of both. Over against Luther's confession, Calvin held that the presence of Christ is spiritual, not coupled with the elements.[13] Against Zwingli he maintained that the bread is not a mere sign or figure of Christ's body, but a spiritual feeding of souls.[14] By adopting the *Consensus*, Bullinger abandoned Zwingli's position that the

Lord's Supper is a metaphorical event and conceded that the supper has the function of externally sealing an inner invisible work. Calvin moved farther from Luther when he agreed that in the Communion the Spirit of God does not bind Himself to the elements. The *Zurich Consensus* brought the German speaking Zurich church and the French speaking Geneva church together. It also widened the gap between the Lutherans and the Calvinists.[15] Reformed dogmatician Charles Hodge states, "No document . . . can have a higher claim to represent the true doctrine of the Reformed Church than this 'Consensus.'"[16]

Calvin's mature Lord's Supper theology agrees with the *Consensus*. He rejected the Roman Mass,[17] transubstantiation, private Masses, and adoration of the host. He considered private Masses to be a mockery of Communion, saying, "One person withdraws and gulps alone and there is no sharing among the faithful."[18] He disagreed with the concept of consubstantiation as taught by some medieval scholars. Calvin held that the souls of believing participants are spiritually fed with the body and blood of Christ.[19] He denied the bodily presence of Christ in the Lord's Supper, and instead maintained Christ's spiritual influence, His power and efficacy as the Redeemer.[20] Calvin said that Christ is not to be sought in the earthly and corruptible elements that we see and touch.[21] Accordingly, he maintained that the body and blood of Christ are not received orally by mouth, but spiritually by faith.[22] Calvin says that the participants at the Lord's Table must lift up their hearts to partake of the body of Christ in heaven.[23] In *The Institutes of the Christian Religion* he rebuked the Lutherans, saying, "They locate Christ in the bread, whereas we do not think it divinely lawful to drag him down from heaven."[24] With Christ in heaven and the believing participants here on earth, Calvin explained that it is the Holy Spirit who brings Christ and the believer together in the Lord's Supper.[25] Two possibilities are acceptable to his line of thought: Either the believers are raised to Communion with Christ in heaven by the power of the

Holy Spirit or Christ descends to believers by the power of His Spirit.[26]

Calvin believed that Jesus was speaking figuratively in the words of institution. Thus, he could affirm that communicants receive only bread and wine in their mouths. Unbelievers who partake of the Supper receive nothing more than bread and wine. On the other hand, through faith, the souls of believers spiritually receive the body and blood of Christ with their eating of the elements of bread and wine.[27] This spiritual understanding allowed Calvin to call the Lord's Supper "the bond of charity" that unites the faithful. He said that by it "we are joined in one body and one substance with our head."[28] As recognition of the full community of believers he called for Communion in both kinds, with all participants receiving the bread and the wine.[29] Conversely, the ultimate means that Calvin employed for keeping the church pure was excommunication. Exclusion from Communion was the immediate and most visible consequence of excommunication.[30] Continuing with this spiritual understanding, Calvin held that when the Lord's Supper was celebrated in homes for the benefit of sick and shut-in members, the congregation was to be represented by elders of the church because the Lord's Supper is an act of profession of faith, and such profession is meaningless unless it is made in public.[31]

While serving as pastor in Strasbourg, Calvin celebrated the Lord's Supper monthly with his congregation of French refugees.[32] He advocated Communion at every service in the Geneva church.[33] The majority of his parishioners, however, were accustomed to communing infrequently. Consequently, he did not get the response that he desired.[34] Calvin tried to institute monthly celebrations, but finally had to agree to quarterly celebrations.[35] Some have spoken of this as Calvin's "chief failure at Geneva."[36]

Calvin prepared a Lord's Supper liturgy in which the minister places the bread and wine on the table and reads the Words of

Institution. Next he should explain the promises that are given in these words, and "at the same time, keep back from communion all those who are debarred by the prohibition of the Lord."[37] Then he is to notify the people to come reverently to receive the Lord's Supper. He should begin the distribution by first himself receiving the bread and wine. The bread is then to be given to the deacon and to all who are communing, the pastor saying, "Take eat, the body of Jesus, which is delivered unto death for you." As he distributes the wine the deacon is to say, "This is the cup of the New Testament of the blood of Jesus, which is poured out for you." The congregation sings Psalm 138 during the distribution. A prayer of thanksgiving and aspiration follows the distribution.[38]

Persons who proposed to partake of the Lord's Supper were required to give notice in advance. When people announced for the Communion, the pastors were to see this as an opportunity to counsel, to give admonition, and to provide instruction to them.[39] On the Sunday before the celebration of the Lord's Supper, public announcement of the forthcoming Communion service was made to enable "each one to prepare himself and dispose himself to receive it worthily, and with such reverence as pertains to it."[40]

For Calvin, several matters were adiaphora, things neither forbidden nor commanded by God. He applied this label to the manner of receiving the bread, either by dividing it among the believers or by individual reception. He maintained that it makes no difference whether the communicants return the cup to the deacon or hand it to their neighbor. Calvin allowed for the use of either leavened or unleavened bread, as well as red or white wine.[41] Like Zwingli, Calvin replaced the altar with a table for the celebration of the Lord's Supper.[42]

NOTES

1. Hermann Sasse, *This Is My Body: Luther's Contention for the Real Presence in the Sacrament of the Altar*, rev. ed. (Adelaide, South Australia: Lutheran Publishing House, 1977), 261.

2. Oliver Fatio, "Pastor of Geneva," *Christian History* 5, no. 4 (1986): 9; Erwin

L. Lueker, ed., *Lutheran Cyclopedia: A Concise In-Home Reference for the Christian Family*, rev. ed. (St. Louis: Concordia, 1975), 124.

3. T. L. H. Parker, "The Life and Times of John Calvin," *Christian History* 5, no. 4 (1986): 11.

4. Julius Bodensieck, ed., *The Encyclopedia of the Lutheran Church* (Minneapolis: Augsburg, 1965), 1:354; Roger Nicole, "Calvin & Strasbourg September 1538–September 1541" *Tabletalk*, www.gospelcom.net/ligonier/tt-10-95/ttsubartnicole-10-98.html (accessed October 21, 1998); Sasse, *Body*, 261.

5. Sasse, *Body*, 261.

6. Nicole, "Calvin," 1.

7. Sasse, *Body*, 260.

8. William H. Bartels, "The Palatinate and the Reformation" (S.T.M. thesis, Concordia Seminary, 1973), 13.

9. Ulrich Gäbler, *Ulrich Zwingli: His Life and Work*, trans. Ruth C. L. Gritsch (Philadelphia: Fortress, 1986), 159.

10. Charles Hodge, *Systematic Theology* (Grand Rapids: Eerdmans, 1997), 3:632, 633.

11. Sasse, *Body*, 261.

12. Anders Nygren, et al, *This Is the Church*, trans. Carl C. Rammussen (Philadelphia: Muhlenberg Press, 1952), 257.

13. Nygren, *Church*, 257.

14. Sasse, *Body*, 262.

15. Gäbler, *Zwingli*, 159.

16. Hodge, *Systematic*, 3:631, 632.

17. John Calvin, *Institutes of the Christian Religion*, trans. Henry Beveridge (1989; reprint, Grand Rapids: Eerdmans, 1997), 606–621.

18. William J. Bouwsma, *John Calvin: A Sixteenth Century Portrait* (New York: Oxford University Press, 1988), 217.

19. John T. McNeill, *The History and Character of Calvinism* (New York: Oxford, 1954), 151.

20. E. H. Klotsche, *The History of Christian Doctrine*, rev. J. Theodore Mueller and David P. Scaer (1945; reprint, Grand Rapids: Baker, 1979), 242, 243; Sasse, *Body*, 262.

21. McNeill, *Calvinism*, 152.

22. Klotsche, *Doctrine*, 242, 243.

23. Sasse, *Body*, 262, 263.

24. Lowell C. Green, "Philosophical Presuppositions in the Lutheran-Reformed Debate on John 6," *Concordia Theological Quarterly* 56, no. 1 (1992): 34.

25. Sasse, *Body*, 262.

26. Klotsche, *Doctrine*, 243.

27. Klotsche, *Doctrine*, 243; Sasse, *Body*, 266.

28. Bouwsma, *John Calvin*, 216.

29. Bouwsma, *John Calvin*, 217.

30. Bouwsma, *John Calvin*, 219.

31. F. E. Mayer, *The Religious Bodies of America* (St. Louis: Concordia, 1954), 212.

32. Nicole, "Calvin," 1.

33. Bouwsma, *John Calvin*, 217.

34. James F. White, *Protestant Worship: Traditions in Transition* (Louisville: Westminster/John Knox Press, 1991), 65.

35. John M. Todd, *Reformation* (Garden City, N.Y.: Doubleday, 1971), 325.

36. White, *Protestant*, 65, 66.

37. Calvin, *Institutes*, 600.

38. McNeill, *Calvinism*, 152.

39. Bouwsma, *John Calvin*, 218, 219.

40. White, *Protestant*, 66.

41. Calvin, *Institutes*, 599.

42. Calvin, *Institutes*, 600.

STUDY QUESTIONS

1. Calvin's two great influences in his early years included one Lutheran theologian and one Reformed theologian, both of Germany. Who were they?

2. What 1549 document had far-reaching effects for the future of the Lord's Supper in Protestant churches?

3. According to the Zurich Consensus, who receives the benefits of the Sacrament?

4. In describing Calvin's middle way, what does he believe regarding the presence of the body of Christ, in contrast with Luther's sacramental union, and what does he believe about the Lord's Supper as a meal, in contrast with Zwingli's memorial?

5. What role did Calvin assign the Holy Spirit in the Lord's Supper?

6. For Calvin, what did unbelievers receive in the Lord's Supper?

7. What did Calvin say of private Communion?

8. What was Calvin's "chief failure" at Geneva?

9. True or false: Calvin required prior announcement, pastoral counsel, and self-preparation before receiving the Lord's Supper.

10. True or false: Calvin regarded several aspects of the Sacrament as adiaphora, those things neither forbidden nor commanded by God, such as the manner of receiving the bread, the handling of the chalice, the type of bread, and the kind of wine.

THE LORD'S SUPPER AMIDST DOCTRINAL DISCORD

10 | WHERE ARE WE NOW? INNOVATIONS FROM THE REFORMATION TO THE PRESENT

The Roman Catholic Church

• See Chapter 6 for a fuller discussion of the context for these changes.

• The council of Trent gave the Pope discretion to allow the bishops near or in Protestant lands to grant the Lord's Supper in both kinds. Pius IV (Pope from 1559–1565) permitted this in Germany, Austria, and Hungary.[1]

• According to the request of the Council of Trent, Pius V issued the *Missal* in 1570 that would dominate the liturgy of the church for almost four centuries. [2] Bishops previously authorized the liturgical forms used in their respective dioceses. In the later Middle Ages, excesses became the cause for revision.[3] Some believe that the changes were inadequate because the clergy continued to dominate the Mass, with the people as silent spectators.[4] Communion often became infrequent and separated from the Mass.[5]

• While the basic doctrine of the Lord's Supper has remained fixed, shifts in emphasis have occurred since the Council of Trent. In 1905, Pope Pius X (Pope from 1903–1914) encouraged Catholic people to commune more frequently. He also emphasized the importance of the people's participation. In the 1940's and 1950's, the church undertook further studies of the Lord's Supper, setting the stage for the renewal achieved in Vatican II (1962–1965).[6]

• Through changes made by Vatican II, or the Second Vatican Council, the Catholic Church continued the process of restoring the celebration of the Lord's Supper to its original form and meaning in that church. A key change was that of conducting the liturgy and reading the Scriptures in the language of the people.[7] Vatican II encouraged frequent reception of the Lord's Supper. It restored the Eucharist in both kinds to the laity in specific cases.[8] Champlin remarks that "in doing so, the Church insisted on appropriate instruction for the faithful so they would understand that no grace necessary for salvation is lost should they receive under one form only."[9] He states that the church today "views communion under two kinds as a fuller step of carrying out Jesus' command at the Last Supper."[10]

• Since Vatican II, the adoration of the host has been de-emphasized. A shift has taken the focus from outward preparation and put it on inward, spiritual preparation for the Eucharist. The current *Code of Canon Law* directs that one is "to abstain from any food or drink, with the exception only of water and medicine, for at least the period of one hour."[11] Champlin states that most Catholic young people today have never experienced the practices that for so long were connected with the Mass.[12]

• Some Catholic scholars feel the word "transubstantiation" is no longer an apt expression for explaining the change of the bread and wine into the body and blood of Christ. Leo C. Hay states that at the time of the Council of Trent the word was more fitting than it is today because the common intellectual background of the Council fathers was Scholastic philosophy and theology. He declares that "clearly the word is not intrinsic to the faith of the Church."[13] There has also been new thinking about the duration of Christ's presence in the consecrated elements. *A New Catechism: Catholic Faith for Adults* states partly that when the form of bread is no longer there, the presence ceases.[14] One must view this "progressive" thinking with caution. The *Catechism of the Catholic Church* retains the word "transubstantiation," and its citation from the Council of Trent leaves no doubt regarding the official teaching of the church. Likewise, "The Eucharistic presence of Christ begins at the moment of consecration and endures as long as the Eucharistic species subsist. Christ is present whole and entire in each of the species and whole and entire in each of their parts, in such a way that the breaking of the bread does not divide Christ."[15] Professor David P. Meyer of Concordia University in Seward, Nebraska, has correctly stated that the new Catholic catechism "calls a halt to 'progressive thinking'" regarding the Lord's Supper.[16]

Calvinist Churches—Reformed

• These churches confess Calvin's mature position on the Lord's Supper presented in Chapter 9. The emphasis remains on a spiritual presence that imparts blessing through the believer's faith.

• These churches use bread and "juice of the grape" in celebrating the Lord's Supper.[17] It does not matter whether the bread is leavened or unleavened. There is, however, widespread objection to "plastic like" wafers used by Roman Catholics and most Lutherans.[18] Johann H. Heidegger (1633–1698) and Leonard Rüseen both came out strongly against them.[19] Some use wheat wafers that are bread-like in texture and taste. Some prefer use of a whole loaf of bread, likely homemade, to better signify a "supper." The grain used is a matter of indifference, but exotic kinds are discouraged.[20] Some use wine, usually mixed with water, while others use grape juice.[21] Two reasons for mixing the wine with water are: The claim that Jesus mixed wine with water when instituting the Supper, and the water and blood that flowed from Jesus' side on the cross.[22] Some Reformed theologians allow for substitution of grain and base of fermentation where wheat and grapes are unknown.[23] However, those who approve of substitutes say that Christ's command and apostolic practice should be adhered to whenever and wherever this is possible.[24]

• Some Reformed authors divide the sacramental action into three steps: blessing, breaking, and giving.[25] Others speak of four or five parts.[26] According to the threefold action, there is an introductory, consecrating prayer. This "blessing"[27] prayer has a threefold purpose: to thank God for the gift of His Son, to prepare the hearts of those who will commune, and to consecrate the elements. Consecration is important, because in themselves bread and wine are not symbols of Christ's body and blood.[28] The second sacramental action is the breaking of the bread that understands Christ's blessing, breaking, and giving the bread as a command: "This do." They, however, do not refuse fellowship to churches that reject the rite of breaking the bread.[29] The third sacramental action is the giving of the elements to those communing. They generally reject the practice of intinction, dipping the bread into the wine and receiving both together.[30] The Reformed hold that withholding the cup from the laity is a flagrant violation of the integrity of the Lord's Supper.[31] Until the nineteenth century, Reformed churches in Europe continued to observe the Lord's Supper in the manner that Calvin and Zwingli established. In most places, "pew communion," with the recipients receiving the Lord's Supper as they are seated in the church pews, has replaced the older practice.[32]

• Reformed Christians consider that the Lord's Supper should be observed for three reasons: the institution of Christ, the function of the visible elements as signs for our benefit, and the action of the Holy Spirit to confirm and increase faith.[33] There are distinct schools of thought among the Reformed regarding self-examination in connection with the Lord's Supper. Some hold that worthy participation follows self-examination. Others understand the "body" of Christ to be the community of believers, thus seeing a requirement in 1 Corinthians 11:27–29 for a corporate post-Communion self-examination.[34]

• Reformed churches from Continental Europe use the *Heidelberg Catechism* (1563) and the *Second Helvetic Confession* (1566). The *Heidelberg Catechism* recapitulates the Calvinist doctrine of the Lord's Supper.[35] Heinrich Bullinger wrote the *Second Helvetic Confession*, which was adopted by the Reformed in most Swiss cantons. It has been well received by Reformed Christians in many lands.[36] It represents the Bullinger-Calvin compromise position.

• In 1817, King Frederick William III of Prussia desired to unite Lutheran and Reformed congregations in a national church. Several other smaller German states followed suit. Immigrants from union churches formed the Evangelical Synod of North America in 1840. "Reformed theology gained control in this church body."[37] Open Communion became a doctrinal mandate.[38] This group is now a part of the United Church of Christ.

• The Moravian Church, influenced by Hus and Jerome of Prague, withdrew in 1457 from the Bohemian national church and organized the Brethren of the Law of Christ in 1467.[39] They later established the Herrnhut colony in 1722 on the estate of Count Nikolaus von Zinzendorf (1700–1760).[40] They, with Calvin, emphasize the Lord's Supper as a "pledge of allegiance."[41] The Moravians continue to partake of the love feast, or *agape* meal, in connection with the celebration of the Lord's Supper.[42] At Herrnhut in 1727 this meal consisted simply of fresh-baked bread and coffee.[43] Today the elements of this meal may vary greatly. In some places it consists of fruit punch and cookies.[44]

Calvinist Churches—Church of England

• The Church of England came into being when Henry VIII threw off the supremacy of the pope in 1534 for political reasons, including his divorce from Catherine of Aragon.[45] Parliament declared Henry and those who would succeed him "the only supreme head on earth of the Church of England."[46] Henry did not intend to introduce Protestant doctrine or practice in England.[47] Thomas Cranmer (1489–1556), the first Protestant Archbishop of Canterbury,[48] did not share the king's views.[49] Cranmer first believed in a more Lutheran confession of the Lord's Supper but later changed to a confession similar to that of Calvin and Bucer.[50] In collaboration with others, Cranmer authored the *Book of Common Prayer*. He was also the chief author of the *Thirty Nine Articles* of 1562.[51] With the other two documents, the *Anglican Catechism* of 1529 continues to express a Calvinist position on the Lord's Supper.

• In the seventeenth century, rails were first erected surrounding Communion tables in Anglican churches in America. Dogs would sometimes stray into the worship services, and the purpose of the Communion rail was to keep wandering dogs away from the expensive paraments.[52]

• In American colonial times, the Lord's Supper was celebrated three or four Sundays a year. In the nineteenth century, both in England and in America, a trend toward more frequent celebrations of the Lord's Supper developed. Anglicans were changing from a minimally sacramental church to one that made the Sacrament central in worship, which is the current state of affairs.[53]

• Customs vary widely among Episcopalians in celebrations of the Lord's Supper. In low-church congregations, the focus is on fellowship. In high-church parishes, the emphasis is on the sacramental aspects of the meal.[54] Whether the service is simple or elaborate, four acts are always included. The priest or president (presiding minister) takes the bread and wine, gives thanks over them (including the words spoken by Jesus at the Last Supper), breaks the bread, and distributes the elements to the communicants.[55] Since 1972, any Christian baptized in the name of the Triune God and a communicant member of another Christian church is welcome to receive the Lord's Supper in the Church of England.[56]

Calvinist Churches—Presbyterian

• During the reign of Catholic Mary Tudor, John Knox (ca. 1505–1572) fled England and became pastor of congregations at Frankfort am Main, Germany, and in Geneva, Switzerland. In Geneva, he met John Calvin[57] and also became acquainted with Heinrich Bullinger of Zurich. In 1559, Knox returned to Scotland where he opposed Roman Catholicism with vigor, and promoted the establishment of the Presbyterian church as the official religion of Scotland.

• Knox and his fellow reformers made radical and sweeping changes in worship forms and practices. They discontinued oral confession and masses for the dead. They denounced the Latin Mass as being idolatrous and blasphemous because it distracted from Christ's unique sacrifice on Calvary.[58] They discontinued the use of altars and unleavened wafers. Officiating clergy no longer wore Eucharistic vestments. The Lord's Supper was viewed as a community feast as worshipers shared the elements with each other.[59]

• The first official doctrinal standard of the Reformed Church of Scotland was the *Scottish Confession of Faith*, adopted by the General Assembly in 1560. It also continues Calvin's doctrine.[60] Another significant confession for the Presbyterians is the 1647 *Westminster Confession of Faith*. In 1643, the Long Parliament called for an assembly to draw up a document for the Church of England. Those attending the assembly represented a cross section of churchmen in the British Isles, the majority being Presbyterians.[61] It replaced the *Scottish Confession* in the Church of Scotland in 1647.[62] Its contents show the influence of the Church of England on the *Scottish Confession*.[63]

• In the Scottish church, the practice of times of preparation before receiving the Lord's Supper (as had been suggested by Calvin), developed into "sacramental seasons" in which penance and preparation were emphasized.[64] They began to turn Communion into a revival meeting, reaching their peak in 1742. As Presbyterians immigrated to America, they brought revivals with them. At Cane Ridge, Kentucky in August of 1801, the Presbyterian sacramental revivals in America reached their climax.[65] Not only Presbyterians but also Methodists and Baptists were involved. Between 10,000 and 25,000 persons gathered on the church grounds during the revival.[66] By 1805, Presbyterians began withdrawing from camp meetings. Weekend Communion observances had given way to "communion Sundays."[67]

Calvinist Churches—Puritans and Congregationalists

• The Puritans and the Separatists were at first one group. In the 1560's, a split occurred as the Puritans wished to remain within the established church while the Separatists felt it better to separate from the state church.[68] The Separatists and the Puritans were, in a sense, hyper-Calvinists. However, they went beyond Calvin in what some called "a rigorous biblicism."[69]

• Many Puritans and Separatists emigrated from England to other lands where they could establish pure congregations and communities. The Separatists attached great importance to the worthiness of those who communed.[70] Even Calvin, they felt, had been too lenient in this regard. Without proper clergy, they could not celebrate the Supper, sometimes going for years without it. The Puritans objected to Eucharistic vestments. They did not kneel when receiving the Eucharist because they believed that kneeling would suggest a reverence of the bodily presence of Christ,[71] as one might kneel in front of a king or priest.

• Originally, only those who had had a conversion experience could receive the Sacrament.[72] A synod of ministers in 1662 adopted a relaxing of rigid membership standards in the *Half-Way Covenant*.[73] Children of church members that were baptized as infants were still part of the church and "could present their own children for baptism, but neither they nor their children could take the Lord's Supper unless they made a personal confession of faith."[74] Some rejected the *Half-Way Covenant* as being too lax. Others wished to go further and grant the Lord's Supper to all who lived in a Christian community.[75] That became the basis for the theological liberalism and open Communion among the Congregationalists, now a part of the United Church of Christ.

Calvinist Churches—Methodist

• The Methodists arose in the eighteenth century. John Wesley (1708–1791) never intended to start a church separate from the Church of England.[76] The first society of his followers formed in 1740.[77] In contrast to the indifference of his time, the Lord's Supper was of great importance to Wesley.[78] While students at Oxford, Wesley and his brother, Charles, founded a "Holy Club." Others ridiculed members of the club with the name "Methodists" or "sacramentarians" because of their methodical emphasis on the sacraments and daily prayer.[79]

• With apparent success, Wesley reintroduced some features of late medieval piety and practice of the Lord's Supper, including the concept of sacrifice, frequent celebrations of the Sacrament, and fasting.[80] He reintroduced the *agape*, or love feast, observed when it was not possible to celebrate the Sacrament.[81] This simple meal of bread and water "seemed to serve quasi-eucharistic functions and to carry some of the rich symbolic texture of communion."[82] Wesley also altered the *Book of Common Prayer*, incorporating some of the thinking of the Puritans. His doctrine of the Lord's Supper was probably closest to that of John Calvin.[83]

• Wesley held that only ordained clergy should administer the Lord's Supper.[84] Problems occurred because there were not sufficient Anglican clergy willing to celebrate the Lord's Supper frequently among the Methodists. Methodist societies would meet regularly for lay preaching services. Whenever a clergyman was available, the Lord's Supper was celebrated. In small class meetings consciences were examined, spiritual direction was given, testimonies regarding spiritual growth were said, and prayers were spoken together. In Methodist societies, a ticket from such a class meeting was necessary for receiving the Lord's Supper. Wesley considered the Lord's Supper to be a means of grace. In a sermon titled "The Means of Grace" he spoke of three such "means"—the Scriptures, the Lord's Supper, and prayer.[85] Ofttimes in early America, there simply was no ordained Anglican available to dispense the Sacrament. Given the circumstances of the times, itinerant preachers occasionally administered the Lord's Supper in violation of Wesley's directive.[86]

• Permitting only ordained persons to administer the Lord's Supper and to baptize was a major factor in the establishment the African Methodist Episcopal Zion Church. In the latter part of the eighteenth century, many African Americans became attracted to the Methodist church. The Methodists were the most notable abolitionists.[87] Methodist slave owners could be barred from the Lord's Supper.[88] Methodists actively evangelized blacks, both free and enslaved. Many received welcome in white congregations.[89] As a result of discrimination, African Americans who were members of the John Street Church in New York City made several requests that they be permitted to have services of their own. They asked for their own meeting place and black preachers to provide them with the sacraments.[90] The New York Conference granted their first two requests but rejected their third wish.[91] Two black congregations formed.[92] At first, the members of the new congregations had to return to the white John Street Church to receive the Lord's Supper and Baptism.[93] After continued struggle, the African Americans withdrew and started their own church body. They ruled that congregations could elect elders who could then administer the Lord's Supper and baptize.[94]

• In 1869 Dr. Thomas B. Welch (1825–1903), a pious dentist who was a former Methodist preacher, discovered a way to pasteurize grape juice that prevented its fermentation. Welch sought to produce a "non-alcoholic sacramental wine," known as Welch's grape juice today. With his apparent success, in 1876 that "pure unfermented juice of the grape" was recommended for use in Methodist churches. Largely because of the influence of the temperance movement, this order became mandatory until 1988.[95]

• Methodists practice open Communion in the sense that baptized members of all Christian denominations are welcomed at the Lord's Table. Usually children may commune as soon as they are able to grasp the elements. Historically, Methodists have not insisted on evidence for conversion of a communicant, or that he or she have a feeling of absolute assurance.[96] "Wesley's view that the Eucharist could be a 'converting ordinance' allowed that changed lives and confident profession of faith could come *through* the eucharistic means of grace."[97]

- Two denominations with Methodist roots are the Wesleyan Church and the Church of the Nazarene. The Wesleyan Church stresses Wesley's doctrine of entire sanctification, in which one may become perfectly holy in this life.[98] They hold that the Lord's Supper is not only a sign of the love Christians should have among themselves for each other, but also that it is a sacrament of our redemption by the death of Christ. For all those who receive it rightly, worthily, and with faith, God communicates grace to the heart through this medium. Through the Lord's Supper God works invisibly to quicken, strengthen, and confirm believers in their faith.[99] The Nazarenes also emphasize sanctification, adhering closely to the original doctrine of Wesley. Their *Manual* has been called "a rewritten and modified Methodist *Discipline*."[100] Concordia Seminary professor Frederick E. Mayer says the Church of the Nazarene "is essentially in accord with historic Methodism, both in doctrine and polity."[101] The Nazarene position states that the Lord's Supper is a New Testament sacrament, declarative of Christ's sacrificial death. Through it, believers have life, salvation, and the promise of all spiritual blessings.

Zwinglian Churches—Anabaptists

- Reuben Goertz, a German Menonnnonite layman in South Dakota, wrote, "Zwingli denied the real presence altogether, claiming that the Lord's Supper was purely commemorative. This is the position held by Mennonites and Hutterites to this day."[102] Some of the early Anabaptists were "disciples" of Zwingli.[103] While not all facets of their Lord's Supper theology were identical to his, they generally followed his doctrine in regard to this ordinance.[104] They shared his tendency to disassociate physical things from spiritual uses. Some went considerably farther than Zwingli in spiritualizing the Lord's Supper, so that they no longer considered the physical elements to be necessary.[105]

• Even though some may not have deemed bread and wine to be necessary, the Anabaptists still had high regard for the Lord's Supper, considering the partaking of this sacred meal to be of value as an expression of unity and fellowship. A common feature among most Anabaptists was a tendency to use the Lord's Supper largely as a communal commemorative event. They frequently referred to it as the "Lord's Memorial."[106] In partaking of this sacred memorial meal, they recalled Christ's suffering and death. As they did so they had a strong sense of the relation of the sufferings of their group with the sufferings He endured and bore for them.[107] Many of the Anabaptists were imprisoned and tortured for professing their faith.[108] They became refugees and exiles, wandering from one place to another seeking safety and a place where they could worship in peace. A large number were executed—many by drowning—and more then 1,000 were burned at the stake.[109] As they faced persecution and death, the Lord's Supper fortified their sense of unity with Christ and with one another.[110] One of their favorite themes concerning the Lord's Supper was the eucharistic line in the *Didache*: "the wheat scattered on the hills and brought together in one loaf."[111]

• The Anabaptists believed that when the Lord's Supper was celebrated, the "body of Christ" was the congregation, which had gathered to commune. As members of the body of Christ, everyone in the assembly was to be pure and undefiled.[112] To achieve this they felt it necessary that anyone who belonged to the fellowship, but who had slipped and fallen into error and sin, should be dealt with openly according to Matthew 18 before being permitted to receive the Lord's Supper or attend a service where Communion was celebrated.[113] In the *Schleitheim Confession*, which was adopted at a secret conference of Swiss Brethren in 1527,[114] these early Anabaptists say, ". . . this shall be done according to the ordering of the Spirit of God before the breaking of bread so that we may all in one spirit and in one love, break and eat from one bread and drink from one cup."[115] Frequency of celebration of the Lord's Supper varied greatly among the Anabaptists. Many groups followed Zwingli's pattern of quarterly Communion services. An extreme example of frequency was that of the Polish Brethren. They left record saying, "The Lord's Supper we attend often and, indeed, where possible every day."[116]

• When the Anabaptists celebrated the Lord's Supper, they did not employ a written liturgy or ritual. The basic outline of the Communion service was usually quite informal and commonly included hymn singing, Scripture reading, prayer, preaching by the chosen leader, lifting up and breaking of bread, and eating and drinking. The only set form was for the reading of the story of the institution of the Lord's Supper by Jesus.[117] An exception to this unwritten form of worship was *A Form of the Supper of Christ* compiled by Balthasar Hubmaier (1485–1528) in 1527. In this order of service, Hubmaier stressed the importance of partaking worthily. A period of personal self-examination is incorporated into the rite. Its purpose is to determine whether one is willing to suffer for Christ. The order also contains an exhortation to upright living.[118] Under condemnation by the Roman Catholics, Hubmaier was burned at the stake on March 10, 1528. The authorities drowned his wife in the Danube River three days later.[119]

Zwinglian Churches—Schwenkfelders

• A group closely related to the Anabaptists was the Spiritualists. Their leader was an unordained Protestant mystic, Casper Schwenkfeld von Ossig (ca. 1487–1561), who ministered in the German province of Silesia (now Poland).[120] Schwenkfeld was dismayed at the situation regarding the use of the Lord's Supper in the church of his day. Catholics, Lutherans, and Zwinglians all partook of "this central rite of Christian faith and unity" and at the same time engaged in virtual warfare with one another.

Schwenkfeld believed that they could not be observing the Lord's Supper properly or receiving it worthily. He and other ministers issued a circular letter in 1526 saying that in light of the discord and fighting in the church, and because "those who eat and drink unworthily, eat and drink damnation unto themselves, we admonish men in this critical time to *suspend for a time* the observance of the highly venerable sacrament."[121] The Schwenk-felders then discontinued celebrations of the Lord's Supper. Both Catholics and Protestants rejected them as heretics. Cruelly driven from Europe, they settled in an area near Philadelphia. They did not resume use of the Lord's Supper until 1878.[122]

Zwinglian Churches—Mennonites and Amish

• Named after Menno Simons, the Anabaptist leader in the Low Countries, the Mennonites are the modern day successors to the Anabaptists.[123] That includes the Mennonites, the Amish, and the Hutterites.[124] They prefer to call the Lord's Supper "the Breaking of Bread" in keeping with the *Schleithein Confession*.[125] Mennonites today consider the Lord's Supper to be a fellowship meal. They do not believe that Christ is in any way present in the bread and wine. Nor do they think that anything special occurs in the elements.[126] They believe that this Supper is to be done only in the community. They profess that if love and unity among the members of the congregation are lacking, it is not the Lord's Supper that is being celebrated or received.[127]

• Mennonites do not focus on the bread and wine. Instead, they feel that the lives of the persons who join in the fellowship remembrance meal and their relations to each other are of "supreme importance."[128] A related matter has to do with who may administer Breaking of Bread. Many Mennonites require no credentials, such as ordination, or other clergy stature. The quality of life of the person chosen to administer the Lord's Supper is the primary consideration.[129] Mennonites practice closed Communion because they believe that a proper observance of the Lord's Supper requires that those participating have a common faith and a common separation from the world.[130] Within Mennonite congregations, church discipline is still practiced prior to the Breaking of Bread according to the directions given in the *Schleitheim Confession*.[131]

• Mennonite author John C. Wenger has written that "the main question associated with the observance of the Lord's Supper is that of who should be admitted to the table."[132] In some Mennonite congregations individuals are admitted to the Lord's Supper for the first time when they have shown evidence that they are "born again" as Christians. In one congregation, persons who did not pass through a conversion experience were forever considered outsiders and were "tacitly denied official membership, baptism, and communion."[133]

• A distinct group of Mennonites are the Hutterian Brethren, or Hutterites, who live communally in Minnesota, the Dakotas, Montana, Washington, Alberta, British Columbia, Manitoba, and Saskatchewan.[134] They are spiritual descendants of Jacob Hutter (ca. 1500–1536) who unified Anabaptists in Tyrol and Moravia along the lines of the apostolic model of community in Acts 2–5. Like many other Anabaptists, Hutter died for his faith, being tortured, whipped, immersed in freezing water, doused with brandy, and then burned at the stake.[135] Regarding their understanding and practice of the Lord's Supper, James F. White says, "Hutterite worship was essentially Zwinglian when it came to the theology and practice of the Lord's Supper. It insisted that the elements have no power of their own but that the communal act of remembrance is all-important."[136]

• Easter Monday is the only time during the year that Hutterites celebrate the Lord's Supper.[137] Elements used are a special rich bread and wine made of grapes.[138] Later at mealtime, children are fed the same special bread that was used at Communion.[139] No confession of sins is required before an individual partakes of the Lord's Supper. It is simply assumed that they have examined themselves.[140] The Hutterites do not use the adjective "holy" when speaking of the Lord's Supper, because they feel this would imply transubstantiation.[141] They believe that both the Roman Catholics and the Lutherans make idols of the bread and wine.[142]

• In their worship services, Hutterite men and women sit on different sides of the church.[143] When the Lord's Supper is served, the minister breaks the loaf of bread in half and hands one piece to his right where the men are seated. It is received by one of the elders and then is passed from man to man down the age hierarchy ending with the youngest and most recently baptized male. In the same way the preacher hands the other half of the loaf to the oldest woman from whom it is passed woman to woman down the age hierarchy of baptized women. After the bread has been circulated, the minister pours the wine into a number of cups and these are distributed in a manner similar to that of the distribution of the bread.[144] In the seventeenth century, Hutterite bishop Andreas Ehrenpreis dealt with a "blatant error" that caused disruption when the wives of preachers and other leaders were given special separate places at the celebration of the Lord's Supper.[145]

• When they emigrated from Ukrainian Russia to southeastern South Dakota, about two-thirds of the Hutterites gave up their communal way of life. These noncommunal Anabaptists came to be known as the Prairieleut.[146] Over the years they added some Mennonites and Amish customs to their practices regarding the Lord's Supper, such as the "love chain" in which persons passed the "holy kiss" from one to another (the sexes being kept separate) and foot washing.[147] They have virtually disappeared from the church scene as a separate religious entity, and have gradually been assimilated into Mennonite churches and conferences.[148] Rod Janzen has written that "to all appearances" the Prairieleut "vanished into a Mennonite fog."[149]

• Among the Mennonites and Amish today, there are variations of practice within the general framework established by Anabaptists of an earlier day. Professor William J. Schreiber tells of customs associated with the Lord's Supper celebrations of the Old Order Amish in Ohio. They hold district plenary sessions twice a year; one in the springtime around Easter, and the other in autumn. These sessions remain closed to outsiders and include a specific day of fasting and meditation, in which purification and reconciliation take place. Foot washing and a love feast follow these preliminaries. The event culminates with the celebration of the Lord's Supper.[150]

• Educator and researcher Stephen Scott has written in some detail of the Lord's Supper practices of the New Order Amish in Holmes County, Ohio. Twice a year council meetings are held two weeks before the Lord's Supper is celebrated. All members who desire to take Communion are required to attend the council meeting.[151] If there are controversies or unresolved issues, the congregation will not celebrate the Lord's Supper until these matters are cleared up. In preparation for Communion, they observe the Sunday after the council meeting as a fast day. Sometimes the spring celebration of the Lord's Supper is held on Good Friday, but more often on a Saturday or Sunday.[152]

• The Old Order River Brethren consider that they " . . . do not observe the Lord's Supper."[153] At their love feasts men break the bread to men, and the women to each other. The River Brethren also practice foot washing in connection with the love feasts. A unique part of their feasts is a time of testimony called "the experience meeting." Any member, man or woman, may choose a hymn and witness to God's work in their lives.[154]

Zwinglian Churches—Baptist

• The Baptist denomination as it is known today originated in England.[155] Baptists were divided in two groups. The General Baptists were spiritual descendants of the Anabaptists. The Particular Baptists were part of the Separatist movement in the Church of England. The two groups united in 1891.[156] "Breaking bread" was a major element of their services in early times. They probably celebrated the Lord's Supper every Sunday.[157]

• Southern Baptist pastor Alton H. McEachern writes, "Zwingli stressed the ordinance as a remembrance of Christ's sacrifice made once and for all never needing to be repeated. He insisted that the elements were symbolic. Baptist's understanding of the Supper is similar to Zwingli's . . . This signifies my body . . . This represents my blood."[158] Professor James E. Tull says of a majority of Baptists, "The most prevalent Baptist interpretation concerning the Lord's Supper has been in line with Zwingli's memorialism."[159] The great expository preacher Alexander MacLaren stated, "There is no magic, no mystery, no 'sacrament' about it."[160] Spurgeon called the Lord's Supper, "The blessed commemorative ordinance."[161] He said, "The Lord's Supper was instituted by Christ as a memorial of his death."[162] Edward B. Cole in his book *The Baptist Heritage* says, "Baptists believe that the bread only symbolizes his body, as the wine symbolizes his blood. There is a symbolism—nothing more or less."[163]

• Some Baptists believe that the Lord's Supper is more than a memorial meal. Southern Baptist professor Bill J. Leonard says that some Baptists, especially in the southeastern part of the United States, reflect a more Calvinistic view and see the Lord's Supper as a "means of grace." They feel that the Supper brings "a special, unique blending and experience of Christ's presence." They would not hesitate to call it "an outward sign of an inward and spiritual grace," considering it "a sacramental sign of God's presence."[164] In 1948, the Council of the Baptist Union of Great Britain and Ireland adopted a statement in which they said that the Lord's Supper is a "means of grace" to those who receive it in faith. They declared that "Christ is really and truly present, not in the material elements, but in the heart and soul of the believer and in the Christian community which observes the sacrament."[165]

• Various Baptist groups in America have adopted confessional statements concerning the Lord's Supper. Notable among these is the *New Hampshire Confession of Faith* of 1830. In this document the holy meal which was instituted by Christ is defined as "the Lord's Supper, in which the members of the church, by the sacred use of bread and wine, are to commemorate together the dying love of Christ; preceded always by solemn self-examination."[166] This *Confession* has served as a model for the confessions of faith of a number of other Baptist associations and groups. The *Baptist Faith and Message* adopted by the Southern Baptist Convention in

1963 states, "The Lord's Supper is a symbolic act whereby members of the church, through partaking of the bread and the fruit of the vine, memorialize the death of the Redeemer and anticipate His second coming."[167]

• A subject on which Baptists have divided opinions is whether the Lord's Supper should be called a "sacrament" or an "ordinance." Some reject the term "sacrament." Dogmatician James P. Boyce stated that he objected to the continued use of the word "sacrament" because "it has no Scriptural authority. It has led many to attach a superstitious sacredness to these ordinances."[168] Ronald Q. Leavell of New Orleans Baptist Theological Seminary, writing about Christ's institution of the Lord's Supper, commented, "No sacrament with saving grace was intimated."[169] Some who prefer the word "ordinance" are willing to employ the word "sacrament" in a qualified way.[170] Tull informs us that a majority of Baptists reject the term "sacrament" for both Baptism and the Lord's Supper because many pedobaptists hold that sacraments convey saving grace. He says, however, that a considerable minority of Baptists prefer the word "sacrament,"[171] believing they are means of grace to those who receive them in faith. He opines that, "They are not converting sacraments, but sacraments for the converted."[172]

• Baptists view the reception of the Lord's Supper as a way in which believers affirm their allegiance to Christ. When a Baptist receives the Lord's Supper for the first time, this is a pledge of loyalty. Each time thereafter is considered a renewal of these vows. They believe that at His table, the risen Christ and His ethical claims on them confront them. They are reminded of the seriousness of their sins, are called upon to confess them, and to receive Christ's forgiveness. By receiving the Lord's Supper, they are moved to praise and gratitude for the grace from Christ which is theirs.[173]

• Baptists stress a period of self-examination before receiving the Lord's Supper. They consider it a time in which they may renew their promises to obey Christ and to let their wills be conformed to His will. At the Lord's Supper, those who commune commit themselves to live lives of righteousness. They resolve again to avoid evil, and to fill their lives with that which is good, noble, and pure.[174] McEachern urges, "Let us . . . observe the Lord's Supper as an oath of loyalty, a pledge of allegiance, and an act of dedication."[175]

• While there was agreement among early Baptists regarding the meaning of the Lord's Supper, there was controversy among them about eligibility to participate in Communion in their churches. Some practiced open Communion, permitting any professed Christian to partake of their Communion regardless of their Baptism.[176] They believed that the Lord's Supper belonged to the universal church, and therefore was to be celebrated by all persons who had an experience of faith. They referred to the Lord's Supper not as a local church ordinance but as a "kingdom ordinance."[177] Others practiced closed Communion, insisting that only those who had received believer's Baptism could participate in the Lord's Supper.[178] The term "close Communion" originated among these Baptists.[179] They seem to have used the words "close" and "closed" interchangeably.

• Controversies about open and closed Communion continually plagued the Baptists. There was a major discussion of open versus closed Communion between William Kiffin (1616–1701) and John Bunyan (1628–1688). Kiffin took a firm position for closed Communion and closed membership policies. Bunyan, who wrote *The Pilgrim's Progress*, practiced open Communion and allowed open membership in the church that he served at Belford. He did not require that persons who communed be members of the congregation.[180] He taught that since a person can be saved without Baptism, any true Christian must be welcome to come to the Lord's Table.[181] Kiffin objected to Bunyan's views due to, in his belief, both a weak handling of the Lord's Supper and the undermining of standards of church membership.[182] In the nineteenth century, a controversy between two Englishmen, Joseph Kinghorn, who argued for closed Communion, and Robert Hall, who was an exponent of open Communion, eventually involved the whole Baptist denomination.[183]

• Some early Baptists in New England practiced open or mixed Communion with other denominations, while others did not.[184] There was usually a certain degree of ambiguity in this matter.[185] For example, there was only one church in the town of Swansea, Massachusetts. The pastor, John Myles, was a Baptist. When he assumed the pastorate in 1667, he agreed to permit both Baptists and Congregationalists to be members of the congregation and to practice open, or mixed, Communion. His successor, Samuel Luther, who was also a Baptist, continued mixed Communion for a time. The Congregationalists believed in infant Baptism and the Baptists opposed it. In 1705, Luther decided that it was unscriptural to allow persons who believed in infant Baptism to be members of the church, and to partake of the Lord's Supper.[186]

• There still exists wide diversity among Baptists regarding open and closed Communion. The present situation in the Southern Baptist Convention will illustrate this. The Southern Baptist Convention has never made rules or regulations concerning Lord's Supper practices in member congregations. Consequently, member congregations follow various policies of open and closed Communion.[187] Some practice open Communion, inviting all who profess faith in Christ to come to the Lord's Table. Others welcome to the Lord's Supper all "of like faith and order." Sometimes this means all who profess an evangelical Christian faith. Sometimes it means all Baptists. In other cases, it means all Southern Baptists. Some congregations practice "close Communion," communing only members of their specific church.[188] Because some hold that only local churches possess the authority to celebrate the Lord's Supper, Southern Baptist seminaries, colleges, and other agencies do not celebrate Communion in their chapel services.[189]

• The frequency of observing the Lord's Supper varies widely among Baptists. Some celebrate as often as every Sunday, others only once or twice a year.[190] In most congregations, monthly or quarterly Communions are the usual practice.[191] In recent years some have also observed the Lord's Supper in special services on Maundy Thursday, the day Christ instituted the Supper with His disciples in the Upper Room.[192]

- Baptists use unleavened bread in their Communion celebrations.[193] This is usually baked and brought by one of the members.[194] In some churches, elders or deacons take the flat circular loaves or cakes of bread and break them into small bite-size pieces to be served to the communicants.[195] The "fruit of the vine" used in a majority of congregations is grape juice.[196] Some congregations use wine.[197] Some offer both wine and juice, with the communicants being free to select which of the two they prefer. Originally, all used wine. With the coming of the American temperance crusade in the latter nineteenth century, many Baptists became suspicious of alcoholic beverages and began using unfermented grape juice. The shift from wine to grape juice was not without controversy. A debate raged among Baptists about the drink used by Jesus and His disciples when the Lord's Supper was instituted.[198] There is still no unity on this. For example, Baptist pastor Henry Turlington writes simply and plainly in his interpretation of Mark 14:25 in the *Broadman Commentary*, "The fruit of the vine is wine."[199] Evangelist John R. Rice says, "It seems certain to me and to the most spiritual Christians that Christ did not use intoxicating wine in the Lord's Supper,"[200] and "The cup the disciples drank at the Lord's Supper is nowhere called wine but 'the fruit of the vine.' We believe it was simply grape juice."[201]

- Most Baptists distribute the "fruit of the vine" in individual Communion glasses or cups.[202] In the 1860's, the medical profession began to understand microbes as the origin of disease. Baptist theologians in Rochester, New York, wondered about the implications of this scientific discovery for the distribution of the Lord's Supper with the common cup. They designed the first individual Communion glasses.[203] They explained that by the use of the glasses it would be possible to partake of the Lord's Supper and to avoid "the maladies which are spread by mouth such as cancer, tuberculosis, influenza, and whooping cough."[204] The movement from wine to grape juice could have increased the likelihood of infection. Individual glass cups were used first at North Baptist Church in Rochester in 1854.[205]

- Some Baptist "sub-denominations" in Appalachia combine

foot washing with their celebration of the Lord's Supper. These include Old Regular Baptists, Regular Baptists, Missionary Baptists, Primitive Baptists, and Union Baptists.[206] The pattern of services is quite similar to that of the New Order Amish described earlier. The foot washing follows immediately after the celebration of the Lord's Supper. With the exception of some Regular Baptists, gender lines are not crossed in the foot washing.[207] In most congregations, men sit on one side of the church and women sit on the other.[208] In most cases, a considerable degree of emotion accompanies the foot washings—crying, shouting, singing, praying, and even preaching.[209]

• Another group that bears the Baptist name is the Old German Baptist Brethren.[210] Their roots lie in the German Brethren movement that originated in the Pietistic revival led by Philipp J. Spener (1635–1705).[211] They organized as a separate church body in 1881.[212] Foot washing and a love feast precede their celebrations of Communion.[213] The feet of all participants are washed as they are gathered around tables, and the love feast follows. Old German Baptist Brethren distinguish between what they call the Lord's Supper and what they call Communion. For them the love feast is the Lord's Supper, and Communion is in commemoration of the meal of Jesus and His disciples in the Upper Room.[214] They say of the Lord's Supper love feast that it is "a common meal taken at night as did the early Christians" and that it "beautifully shows forth the mutual fellowship and union that should characterize the people of God in this world of strife and division."[215] The simple love feast menu may consist of cooked beef, bread and broth soup, and water.[216] After the foot washing and the Lord's Supper love feast, the final action in the service is the celebration of Communion. Of Communion they say, "After supper we take the Communion as set apart as emblematical of the broken body and the shed blood of our Lord and Savior, Jesus Christ."[217] The Old German Baptist Brethren have a special way of baking the unleavened bread sticks that is symbolic, and that also makes it easy to break the bread into pieces. The dough is perforated down its entire length with holes from a fork. These holes are spaced to represent the five wounds of Christ on the cross. The "holy kiss," with men kissing men and women kissing women, is also part of their Communion observance, because Christ's followers are exhorted five times in the New Testament to greet one another in this way. There is also a symbolic action known as the "mingling of the wine" in which wine from two different bottles is poured ceremoniously together into common Communion cups. This mingling symbolizes the members of the church who were separate, but who have become one in Christ. The various activities in their service are interspersed with Scripture readings, sermons, prayers, and hymns. The entire service may last as long as five hours.[218] The Old German Baptist Brethren practice closed Communion.[219]

Zwinglian Churches—Restoration Movement

• The Christian Church (Disciples of Christ) and the Churches of Christ hold strongly to the belief that the Lord's Supper should be celebrated every Sunday, and only on Sunday.[220] They are of common origin, having been one body until a division occurred early in the twentieth century. This belief concerning the Lord's Supper is a basic tenet of these churches, inherited from their predecessors in the "Restoration movement."[221] This eighteenth century movement hoped to restore primitive Christianity and unite all Christians based on the Bible.[222] Leaders of the Restoration movement in Scotland and America advocated conducting the affairs of the church after the pattern of early Christianity, reviving such practices as the love feast, the holy kiss, and foot washing. They made the Lord's Supper the center of their Sunday Worship.[223]

• Historically, Disciples of Christ laymen were in charge of celebrating the Lord's Supper. Senior members of the congregation took turns as "president of the meeting." Among them, the participation of clergymen in the service was limited to preaching. Often this was after a layman had led the congregation in the celebration of Communion. Liturgical texts were not provided for the celebrants, but each was expected to offer "thanksgiving to the best of his ability."[224]

• In Disciples of Christ congregations, celebration of the Lord's Supper every Sunday is mandatory. It has been described as "man's act of obedience according to Christ's original plan for His Church."[225] When congregations of the Churches of Christ meet on Sunday, five items of worship are always part of the service. These are prayer, unaccompanied song, the teaching of the Word, the offering, and the Lord's Supper. The order in which these occur may vary from one church to another, but all five are always present.[226] According to their understanding of the New Testament, two of these, the Lord's Supper and the offering, should properly occur only on Sunday.[227]

• Both the Christian Church (Disciples of Christ) and the Churches of Christ are anti-creedal. Yet in 1968, the Disciples of Christ adopted a broad confessional statement entitled *Preamble to a Design for the Christian Church*. In this document they say concisely of the Lord's Supper, "At the table of the Lord we celebrate with thanksgiving the saving acts and presence of Christ."[228]

• In the 1920's some Churches of Christ churches in Oklahoma and Texas became known as "one-cuppers." "One-cup" congregations believe that the use of individual Communion glasses is an unscriptural practice. They hold that only the use of the common cup is in keeping with the pattern established by Jesus and His disciples in the Upper Room, where only one cup was used.[229] Baptism is the criterion for admission to the Lord's Supper in the Disciples of Christ and the Churches of Christ. In many cases, especially in the Churches of Christ, the Baptism must have been by immersion. Some ministers in the Churches of Christ in Texas have insisted that even if a person has been baptized by immersion, the Baptism must have been performed for the right reason for the individual to be received at the Lord's Table.[230] As time passes, more Disciples of Christ congregations are accepting the Baptism of other denominations as valid and have opened their Lord's Supper to other Christians.[231]

Zwinglian Churches—Evangelical Free

- Another body that is "Zwinglian on the Lord's Supper"[232] is the Evangelical Free Church in America. The Free Church came into being through mergers of various Swedish, Norwegian, and Danish groups that came out of the pietistic Lutheran movement in Scandinavia.[233] Considerable latitude in doctrine is allowed, with ministers being permitted to have their own convictions concerning the Lord's Supper.[234] Their *Statement of Faith*, which was adopted in 1950, is quite broad in nature. In regard to Baptism and the Lord's Supper, it reads: "That water baptism and the Lord's Supper are ordinances to be observed by the Church during the present age. They are, however, not to be regarded as means of salvation."[235] Evangelical Free Church congregations practice open Communion. They say this is because it is the Lord's Supper and not the supper of the Evangelical Free Church. All believers who are in a living fellowship with Christ are welcome to commune with them.[236] They feel the Lord's Supper is important and that all believers should share in it. Participation should be limited to those who believe.[237]

Zwinglian Churches—Quaker

- An organization that is non-creedal in nature is the Religious Society of Friends, or the Quakers. They arose under the leadership of George Fox (1624–1691), an English mystic.[238] They were the objects of severe persecution in both England and America. They openly disparaged the clergy and the sacraments.[239] The principle of the "Inner Light" or "Inner Voice"[240] dictates that God has placed a light within every person, by which He communicates directly with them in their hearts without means,[241] and by which everyone has an innate capacity to comprehend God's Word and to express opinions on spiritual matters.[242] They regard the Lord's Supper as a mere rite, or ritual, without intrinsic value, and without any real significance.[243] For them, any event in life can be considered sacramental if in truth it is an outward sign of an inward grace.

• According to some, the only reason Christ instituted the Lord's Supper was to admonish His disciples to remember Him "as oft" as they celebrated the Passover.[244] Others say that Christ ordained the Lord's Supper for a limited time for the sake of the weak. He did not mean it to survive beyond the time of the earliest Christians.[245]

• Some Quakers even reject the doctrine of the Trinity, thus placing themselves outside the Christian faith.

Zwinglian Churches—Pentecostal

• The spread and influence of Pentecostalism has been phenomenal. Born in the twentieth century, it has become the second largest Christian tradition, exceeded in numbers only by the Roman Catholic Church.[246] Pentecostal worship is unstructured, with congregations trusting the Holy Spirit to determine the sequence of what takes place. Some common occurrences in worship services are the sharing of such gifts of the Spirit as speaking in tongues, interpreting of tongues, prophesying, and ecstatic singing and dancing. As with the Quakers, emphasis in worship is placed on the immediacy of the Holy Spirit.[247]

• Frequency of celebration of the Lord's Supper in Pentecostal churches varies from weekly to occasionally. Most Pentecostals do not consider it necessary to celebrate the Lord's Supper, or to commune, frequently.[248] Many Pentecostal groups make no mention of the Lord's Supper in their creedal statements.[249] Even among those who celebrate it weekly, it is only a minor part of the service. Those who observe the Lord's Supper infrequently do so because God's gracious acts abound in many other ways. Communion seems of less importance than such matters as healing and tongues, but it is observed at least occasionally because Christ commanded it. All Pentecostal worship is seen as sacramental in showing visibly and audibly the action and presence of the Holy Spirit within the gathered community.[250]

• The largest Pentecostal group is the Assembly of God. It was founded in 1914 at Hot Springs, Arkansas, from a union of several small Pentecostal groups. Congregations of this body have strong local autonomy, but a general council determines doctrinal standards.[251] In their *Statement of Fundamental Truths* they call the Lord's Supper "the symbol expressing our sharing the divine nature of our Lord Jesus Christ (2 Peter 1:4); a memorial of His suffering and death (1 Cor. 11:26); and a prophecy of His second coming (1 Cor. 11:26); . . . enjoined on all believers 'till He come!'"[252]

• The International Church of the Foursquare Gospel rose out of the evangelistic endeavors of Aimee Semple McPherson (1890–1944). It is headquartered in Los Angeles where she built the famous Angelus Temple. Their *Declaration of Faith*, written by McPherson[253] and binding on all members, refers to bread, "fruit of the vine," an "ordinance," and self-examination.[254]

• A number of Pentecostal churches bear the name of Church of God. The Church of God (Cleveland, Tennessee) includes the Lord's Supper in its creedal statement. No comment is made, but two references from the Bible are cited, namely, Luke 22:17–20 and 1 Corinthians 11:23–26.[255] Frequent reception of the Lord's Supper "by all true believers" is stressed in the doctrinal statement of the Church of God (House of Prayer). They see the purpose of the Supper as being the showing of the Lord's death until He comes again. The elements used are bread and unfermented grape juice. Believers are encouraged to observe the ordinance quarterly, especially on the night before Good Friday and "as often as the church desires to do so."[256] Under the leadership of Ambrose J. Tomlinson (1865–1943), a group withdrew from the Church of God (Cleveland, Tennessee), and formed the Church of God of Prophecy.[257] In their document *Twenty-Nine Important Bible Truths,* the Church of God of Prophecy authors specify that the bread is to be unleavened. They use the term "wine" to mean unfermented grape juice. They observe the Lord's Supper to commemorate Christ and His death. They state, "Only sinless and consecrated Christians are eligible to partake of the Lord's Supper."[258] The Church of God (Jerusalem Acres) celebrates the Lord's Supper only once a year. This group, derived from the

Church of God (Cleveland, Tennessee), observes the Passover, including the Lord's Supper and foot washing in this annual event.[259] The Pentecostal Church of God also includes "washing of the saint's feet" as part of their observance of the Lord's Supper.[260]

• The Apostolic Faith Church, a Pentecostal body in Hawaii, holds that the Lord's Supper brings healing to our bodies if we discern the Lord's body. They partake of Communion only at night, because it was in the evening that Jesus came with the Twelve to eat the Last Supper.[261]

• Two Pentecostal bodies do not celebrate the Lord's Supper by the use of external elements, the Pentecostal Church of Zion and the Associated Brotherhood of Christians, who both speak of Communion with God through the Spirit.

• The Assemblies of the Lord Jesus Christ and the Pentecostal Assemblies of the World believe that Melchizedek, "the priest of the most high God" (Genesis 14:18), gave the first Communion consisting of bread and wine to Father Abraham. They state that Christ, who is called a "high priest forever after the order of Melchizedek" in Hebrews 6:20 and 7:21, administered the same.[262]

• Two African American Pentecostal bodies use water, rather than wine or grape juice, when they celebrate the Lord's Supper. They are the Church of the Living God (Christian Workers for Fellowship) and the Church of the Living God, the Pillar and Ground of Truth.

• A distinct group of Pentecostal churches are the loosely related and affiliated snake handling churches variously known by such names as the Free Holiness Church, the Church of Jesus with Signs Following, Church of the Lord Jesus Christ, and Holiness Church of God.[263] Dennis Covington says, "Rituals like Communion are rare in snake-handling churches."[264] Long periods of time may elapse between Communion services. For example, a congregation in Kingston, Georgia, had not celebrated the Lord's Supper for three years. After that lengthy span of time, a Lord's Supper service was held. Pastor Carl Porter apparently felt a need to instruct and catechise his people. He interspersed the words of institution with remarks of his own. After reading the words of Jesus, "Take eat; this is My body," he commented regarding our Lord and His disciples, "Now he didn't mean it was really his body. They weren't cannibals." Making an up-to-date comparison he asked, "Can you imagine me taking a bite out of Brother Junior over there, and him not even cooked?" He added about Junior that "he's forty something years old. He'd be tough as leather." After he read Jesus' words "This is my blood of the new testament," he said, "I sure ain't gonna drink nobody's blood. I ain't no vampire."[265] In these churches communicants are given unleavened bread and a choice of wine or grape juice.[266] Foot washing is an integral part of their Lord's Supper observance.[267]

Zwinglian Churches—Adventist

• Adventists believe that the only hope for the world is the second advent of Christ. At first, it was a movement among Methodists, Christians, Baptists, Presbyterians, and Congregationalists. In 1845 a call went out to Adventists to meet in Albany, New York, to organize their own church body. As a result, several like-minded groups were formed, and the Adventist denomination came into being.[268]

• The Seventh-day Adventist Church is by far the largest Adventist church body. In their literature, the Seventh-day Adventists speak of the Lord's Supper as a "memorial." They say that Jesus instituted the Lord's Supper in place of the Passover memorial, and that He did so "to memorialize His great sacrifice."[269] In His sacrifice on the cross, Christ ratified the eternal covenant of God's grace by the shedding of His own blood.[270] Participants at the Lord's Table are part of the new covenant era and, as such, have reason to celebrate. For them, "the Lord's Supper is both a memorial and a thanksgiving of the sealing of the everlasting covenant of grace."[271] They call the Lord's Supper a "commemoration," saying that it commemorates deliverance from sin. They draw a parallel between the Passover being a commemoration of the deliverance of Israel from slavery in Egypt, and the Lord's Supper commemorating deliverance "from spiritual Egypt, the bondage of sin."[272] The terms "symbol," "symbolic," and "symbolism" are also employed in their discussions of the Lord's Supper. They believe that the life of a communicant is revitalized through the sustaining power of Christ that is evidenced in the symbol. The symbolism of the Lord's Supper shows "we are dependent on Christ for spiritual life as we are on food and drink for physical life."[273]

• The Lord's Supper is celebrated "on the next to last Sabbath of the quarter" in Seventh-day Adventist churches.[274] In their writings, they note that the Bible does not specify how frequently Christians should celebrate the Lord's Supper. They have adopted the practice of many Protestants in observing the ordinance four times a year. When the early Seventh-day Adventists decided to follow this plan, they did so because they believed that if Communion services were held more often there would be danger of formality, and participants might also fail to realize the solemnity of the service. Present day Seventh-day Adventists see the quarterly plan as "a middle-of-the-road decision—between celebrating too often and leaving it for too long a period, such as once a year."[275]

• The elements used by Seventh-day Adventists are unleavened bread and the fruit of the vine. They use only unleavened bread because leaven, or yeast, is considered to be a symbol of sin. A Seventh-day Adventist author states, "Only unleavened or 'unfermented' bread could symbolize the sinless body of Christ."[276] They variously speak of the fruit of the vine as "unfermented wine" and "unspoiled fruit of the vine."[277] As only unfermented bread can properly symbolize Christ's sinless body, so also only the unfermented fruit of the vine "appropriately symbolizes the spotless perfection of the cleansing blood of the Savior."[278] Seventh-day Adventists contend that the assumption that the Jews celebrated the Passover with fermented wine is unwarranted. They are fully aware of the fact that the grape harvest in Israel was in the fall and the Passover was in the spring, but they say that throughout the ancient world various methods were used to preserve juices in an unfermented state for extended periods of time. They mention the method of reducing the juice to syrup by boiling, and say that if the syrup is kept in a cool place it will not ferment. Simply mixing this concentrate with water produces a non-alcoholic sweet wine. Raisins could also be used in making unfermented grape wine.[279]

• In Seventh-day Adventist churches, foot washing always precedes celebrations of the Lord's Supper.[280] They consider self-examination and preparation for receiving the Lord's Supper to be very important. Foot washing is part of their examination and preparation. They hold that foot washing is an ordinance instituted by Christ to assist believers in confessing and repenting of their sins, and that by confession and repentance they are enabled to be in the right spirit to have Communion with Christ in the Lord's Supper.[281] More than cleansing feet is involved in this foot washing. The ordinance of foot washing represents higher purification—a cleansing of the heart.[282]

• In addition to participation in the foot washing ceremony, those intending to receive the Lord's Supper are also urged to personally examine themselves, prayerfully reviewing their Christian experience, confessing their sins, and restoring any broken relationships.[283] The Lord's Supper service is announced in advance to enable members to have sufficient time to amply "prepare their hearts."[284]

• They believe that Christ ministers to believers through the Lord's Supper, even though those who administer it may be unworthy. The book *Seventh-day Adventists Believe . . .* states, "Hearts and hands that are unworthy may even administer the ordinance, yet Christ is there to minister to His children. All who come with their faith fixed upon Him will be greatly blessed."[285]

• Because they feel that the condition of the heart qualifies a person to participate in the Lord's Supper, not church membership, Seventh-day Adventists welcome to Communion all who are committed to Christ, and who have faith in His sacrifice.[286] Thus, they say in their doctrinal statement *Fundamental Beliefs*, "The communion service is open to all believing Christians."[287]

• Several smaller Adventist bodies celebrate the Lord's Supper once each year. Two of these, the Associated Churches of God and the Church of God Evangelistic Association, call the Lord's Supper the New Testament Passover, and believe that they should observe the anniversary of Christ's death "by partaking of the bread and wine that symbolize His broken body and shed blood."[288] The Seventh Day Church of God observes the Passover at the beginning of the fourteenth of the Hebrew month of Nisan. They hold that the Lord's Supper is a perpetual ordinance until it is fulfilled in the kingdom of God.[289] For them it is an annual memorial to Jesus' death. Elements used by the Seventh Day Church of God are unleavened bread and grape juice.[290] Foot washing is included in their observance.[291]

Zwinglian Churches—Plymouth Brethren

• The Plymouth Brethren originated in England and Ireland in the 1830's. They reject creeds, rituals, ecclesiastic organizations,[292] and wish only to be able to come together for quiet fellowship and prayer.[293] Their designation for the Lord's Supper is "the Breaking of Bread." Their simple, informal weekly services are mainly for the purpose of praise and the celebration of the ordinance of the Breaking of Bread.[294] The Breaking of Bread is celebrated on Sunday mornings, and they gather in the evening for Gospel preaching.[295] The Breaking of Bread is considered to be very important. They call it "the great occasion for worship,"[296] and refer to "the breaking of bread on every Sabbath" as "memorial of the Savior's dying love."[297] The Plymouth Brethren have no ordained clergy.[298] Any man present can preach and celebrate Communion.[299] Because they feel "the very thought of an earthly sanctuary is foreign to the genius of Christianity," their meetings for Breaking of Bread are held in private homes.[300]

Zwinglian Churches—Salvation Army

• A final group in our study is the Salvation Army, an organization which has, "a dual function of church and social agency."[301] The Salvation Army Christians, who serve so many in so many ways, are organized around the principles of their founder, William Booth (1829–1912). Their theology is Enthusiastic, and is very similar to that of the Quakers.[302] They have a low estimate of the importance of the Lord's Supper, placing it on a par with abrogated Jewish ceremonies.[303] In their opinion, Christ did not intend that the Lord's Supper be perpetually observed.[304] They feel that John's silence about the Lord's Supper, both in his Gospel and in his Epistles, evidences that no new and essential ceremony was instituted.[305] For Salvation Army Christians, true observance of the Lord's Supper consists in remembering Christ's death by engaging in spiritual conversation, particularly in connection with regular eating and drinking.[306] In an article in *The War Cry* Major David Laeger, who is an instructor at one of their training schools, says regarding the Lord's Supper, "We are His body and blood to each other . . ."[307] There is no mention of the Lord's Supper in their official statement, *Doctrines of the Salvation Army*.[308]

Lutheran Churches

• The Lutheran confession of the Lord's Supper rests upon Luther's coupling of the late medieval doctrine of the Lord's Supper with the principle of interpretation by Scripture alone. It is in this context that Luther advocated the scriptural confession of the Lord's Supper, "This is My body," referred to in chapter seven. The *Formula of Concord*, promulgated in May of 1577, continues this confession.[309] Article seven of the *Formula* deals with "the Holy Supper." The body and blood of Christ are truly present, distributed, and received with the bread and wine. The words of the testament of Christ are to be understood only in their literal sense. The presence of Christ results solely from the almighty power of Christ. Whenever the Lord's Supper is celebrated, the words of institution should be spoken publicly. The body and blood of Christ are received in a supernatural, heavenly manner. Not only worthy believers but also unworthy believers and unbelievers receive the true body and blood of Christ. The only unworthy communicants are those who do not believe. No believer, no matter how weak one may be, will receive the Lord's Supper to one's condemnation. The entire worthiness of guests at the heavenly feast is the holy and complete merit of Christ, which the believer receives through genuine faith.[310]

• Martin Chemnitz (1522–1586) was the primary author of the *Formula of Concord*.[311] His basic principle, central to *The Lord's Supper*, was that Scripture should be interpreted literally unless the context determines otherwise.[312] His *Examination of the Council of Trent* responds to and refutes, among other things, the Roman Catholic position on the Lord's Supper. Following Chemnitz, John Gerhard (1582–1637) wrote of a "sacramental" presence by which the bread is "the *exhibitive* symbol and vehicle, by which the body of Christ is communicated, or as St. Paul expresses it, it is the communication (*koinonia*) of the body of Christ."[313]

• Abraham Calov (1612–1686) refuted the charge that the Lutheran Church teaches the medieval Roman Catholic doctrine of "consubstantiation," the belief that "that the bread and the body of Christ pass into one mass"[314] in the consecrated elements. A more philosophical way of stating this claims that the substances of the bread and wine, together with the substances of Christ's body and blood, coexist and form a third substance.[315] In spite of almost universal Lutheran protests, the idea persists among some non-Lutherans that consubstantiation is the position of the Lutheran Church.[316] Lutherans simply confess what the biblical text says.

• Lutherans do not attempt to explain how the body and blood of Christ are present in the Lord's Supper. *The Use of the Means of Grace* states, "In this sacrament the crucified and risen Christ is present giving his true body and blood as food and drink. This real presence is a mystery."[317] Lutherans believe that the words of institution effect the presence of Christ.[318] Wisconsin Synod professor Adolph Hoenecke (1835–1908) said that "by virtue of the Words of Institution in the moment of partaking of the bread and wine, Christ's body and blood are under the same."[319] Gaylin Schmeling, president of Bethany Lutheran Theological Seminary, has stated that we can be certain that the chief purpose of the consecration is to effect the presence of the body and blood of Christ in the Lord's Supper.[320]

• Some Lutherans believe that the presence begins immediately following the speaking of the last syllable of the consecration. Those holding this position enlist certain statements by Luther,[321] as well as by Chemnitz and various other church fathers.[322] Bjarne W. Teigen, former president of Bethany Lutheran College, has been a present day exponent of this view.[323] Others agree with orthodox era theologian John Andrew Quenstadt (1617–1688) who wrote, "This sacramental union itself does not take place except in the distribution."[324] John Gerhard and David Hollaz supported this, as well as Adolf Hoenecke of Wisconsin and Francis Pieper of Missouri.[325] Neither view can be established conclusively on the basis of Scripture, so this question is not divisive.

• Lutherans do reject the extreme forms of these two views as heresy. The first extreme form is that the bread and wine are a complete sacrament the moment the blessing is said, that the body and blood have to be present as soon as the words of institution are spoken. The second is the opposite idea that the body and blood of Christ are present only in the eating. They quote Luther's words as being appropriate when he says, "We prescribe no moment or time to God, but are satisfied thus that we simply believe that what God says happens or occurs does certainly happen".[326]

• Lutherans believe that there is no enduring union between the body and blood of Christ and the bread and wine outside the sacramental action that consists of taking the bread and wine, blessing these elements, distributing to the communicants, receiving by those communing, and eating and drinking by the recipients.[327] There is no sacramental presence without the sacramental action. Schmeling states, "Since the remaining elements are not distributed and received, they are outside the use and therefore only bread and wine."[328]

• Lutherans bring the Lord's Supper to sick and shut-in persons who are unable to attend the celebration of the Sacrament with the worshiping congregation in the church. They are given the Lord's Supper in their homes, nursing facilities, hospitals, and other places. Some pastors consider it imperative that the entire sacramental action be completed in the presence of the person, or persons, who are communing in private, or semi-private, settings. This is in keeping with the dictum of professor C. F. W. Walther of the Missouri Synod (1811–1887) who said, "The elements consecrated by the pastor can neither be preserved nor sent to those who are absent . . . [for] the sacramental action which consists of consecration, distribution, and reception, must be completely uninterrupted."[329]

• Walther said that if for some reason the process of the sacramental action was interrupted in some way before the distribution was completed, the consecration should be repeated before distribution.[330] The Commission on Theology and Church Relations of the Missouri Synod specifies that if consecrated bread and wine are taken from the church altar to be distributed to absentees the distribution "must always include the Words of Institution in the presence of the communicant. Christ's word, the elements, and the distribution are to be Biblically held together (Mark 14:22–28)."[331]

• Although Lutherans believe that the elements left over after the Lord's Supper celebration are merely bread and wine, they still consider that these should be handled "with fitting reverence."[332] In early times, some simply stored the leftover hosts to be used again in later celebrations. Others felt that disposition of a final nature should be made of the bread and wine, due to the practice of witchcraft and other superstitious use.[333] Some congregations burned the remaining consecrated hosts and poured the leftover wine on the ground.[334] Some advised that remaining bread and wine should be consumed during the church service or following it. All of these means of disposition are still used by congregations today.[335]

• The type of bread, whether leavened or unleavened, and the grain used are left as a matter of conscience. Grape wine is ordinarily used. Color of the wine and whether the wine is pure or mixed with water are matters left to conscience, but not dictated by God.[336] The one requirement is that it be grape wine, made from the "fruit of the vine" (Matthew 26:29).[337] By virtue of His Word, the true body and blood of Christ are in and with the consecrated wine, regardless of color.[338] Some Lutherans maintain that only alcoholic wine may be used in the celebration of the Lord's Supper. However, some congregations provide non-alcoholic wine.[339] In 1991 the Department of Systematic Theology at Concordia Seminary in St. Louis gave an opinion regarding the use of non-alcoholic wine. It is genuine wine (fermented fruit of the vine) with a very low percentage of alcohol. The opinion states, "the use of 'non-alcoholic' wine should not raise doubts about the validity of the Lord's Supper."[340] A different solution to the problem experienced by persons who are alcoholics or allergic to wine is proposed in the Evangelical Lutheran Church in America's *A Statement on Communion Practices*. It affirms that it is appropriate for each individual to receive only one of the elements. "Their pastor may assure them that the crucified and risen Christ is fully present for them in, with, and under this one element."[341]

• The use of individual glasses is an innovation of the latter nineteenth century that came from American Protestantism.[342] The widespread use of such glasses in Lutheran circles seems to be based on the popular idea that this is a more sanitary means of receiving the wine. There are reliable persons in the scientific community who consider this notion to be an unfounded myth. It has been said that there exists a greater likelihood of getting sick from shaking hands and talking to people after church as from drinking wine from a common cup. Pastor Carl Stohlmann blasted the practice in his 1911 booklet *Eucharistie*, in which he declared the arguments of the day to be groundless. Other conservative Lutherans severely criticized the use of individual glasses.[343] In response, John H. C. Fritz wrote, "There is no dogmatical [sic] reason why the individual Communion cup should not be used. In many churches two cups are used, why not more?"[344] He continued, saying, "But there is no good reason why the old practice of using the common Communion cup should be discontinued."[345] Robert W. Jenson says, "It is precisely sharing a cup that is mandated."[346] Professor Carrol H. Little advanced five reasons against replacing the chalice with individual glasses. These include the use of one cup at the Last Supper; the expression of the unity of the mystical body of Christ; the disregard for historic Christian precedent; an embrace of the Reformed mode of distribution and perhaps doctrine; and the diminishing of the solemnity of the sacramental distribution.[347] R. C. H. Lenski of the Ohio Synod, who changed his congregational membership over this issue,[348] said that placing the wine "into many little individual cups . . . casts a reflection on Jesus who used a common cup." He suggests that those who do so are essentially saying, "Jesus was not clean enough."[349] In the *Manual* prepared for the use of the *Lutheran Book of Worship*, Philip H. Pfatteicher observes that various bacteriological and chemical studies have established the common cup to be hygienically safe. He reasons that by the use of pre-filled individual glasses the significance of the common cup is destroyed, such use contrary to the spirit of the Lord's Supper is expressively individualistic and completely undesirable theologically and historically.[350] He describes disposable plastic and paper cups as products of a "garbage-producing, throw away culture."[351] Those who approve of the use of individual glasses, or cups, say that the essence of the Sacrament is not that the wine is received from a common cup. Professor John R. Stephenson of Concordia Lutheran Theological Seminary in Ontario observes that "circumstances have rendered individual cups a practical adiaphoron in the life of North American Lutheranism," and that "in many cases the retention of the chalice as an option alongside individual cups is the best that can be hoped for."[352]

• Lutherans practice confession and absolution before receiving the Lord's Supper. It has been customary among Lutherans for persons who intend to attend the Lord's Supper to announce their intentions to the pastor before the service. Such announcement could provide the opportunity for private confession and absolution, though it has generally remained a matter of conscience. In liturgies used in Communion services, one often sees a general confession of sins and the subsequent absolution, spoken by the pastor. Although private confession and absolution remains a matter of conscience,[353] it used to be the norm in the early Missouri Synod. Separate confessional services have also been used before the service of Holy Communion, such as in the Pennsylvania Ministerium in the days of Henry M. Mühlenberg (1711–1787). [354] At this service, the officiating pastor pronounced absolution publicly. Before celebrating the Lord's Supper, a list of names of those who had previously announced their intent to commune was read publicly.[355] Walther spoke of "confessional announcements"[356] and stressed that this was a time for pastors to inquire into and discuss the spiritual condition of persons intending to commune. He believed pastors have a holy duty to require that those who wish to receive the Lord's Supper announce personally in advance, and that pastors should use this time wisely and faithfully for exploration and examination.[357] Today the procedure for announcing to attend the Lord's Supper is minimal.[358] A very common practice is that of handing an announcement card to the usher as the communicant is being ushered to the Lord's Table. Seminary professor David Belgum states it well when he says, "What is left of the personal relationship between the penitent and confessor is a stack of communion attendance cards which the secretary enters into the church register on Monday."[359]

• The frequency of celebrations of the Lord's Supper in Lutheran congregations has varied over the centuries. At the time of the Reformation, it was customary for congregations to do so every week. The *Apology of the Augsburg Confession* states, "In our churches Mass is celebrated every Sunday and on other festivals."[360] This level of frequency continued for 200 years.[361] Then, especially under the influence of the widespread Pietistic movement in the churches of Germany, celebrations became less frequent.[362] In the eighteenth and nineteenth centuries, the usual practice came to be a monthly or bimonthly basis. By the beginning of the nineteenth century, some Lutheran congregations were rarely celebrating the Sacrament. In such churches, the Lord's Supper was considered to be a mere appendage to the service.[363] The situation of less frequent celebrations continued into the latter half of the twentieth century, with most congregations celebrating the Sacrament only on the first Sunday of every month[364] or, in some cases, every other month. With the liturgical renewal movement in the twentieth century the situation has changed. Today, many congregations are now offering the Lord's Supper every Sunday. Members are encouraged to commune frequently, but no one is compelled to do so. Congregations are counseled not to set minimum standards of annual Communions for "members in good standing."[365] There is, however, general agreement that regular participation in the Sacrament is very important for the spiritual life and well being of believers.

• The issue of whether a pastor may commune himself has been a matter of conscience among Lutherans.[366] Those who believe that it is acceptable for a pastor to do so say that if a pastor communes himself, this should occur in the public divine service.[367] Chemnitz says that the pastor includes himself in the confession and absolution, and may, therefore, include himself in the Communion.[368] For a generation or two after the Reformation this was the common practice, but then it came into disuse. Lutheran liturgist Luther B. Reed attributes its decline to "dogmatic biblicism and pietistic subjectivism."[369] It was forbidden in many orders of worship in the seventeenth century. By the nineteenth century, opinions had largely changed.[370] The practice was considered a virtual necessity in some areas of nineteenth century frontier America. In 1932 John H. C. Fritz admitted that a man who is sole pastor in a congregation could thus legitimately commune himself, but he suggested that a better way would be if the congregation would choose a layman to distribute the elements to him. This was a novel suggestion in the Missouri Synod at the time.[371]

- Lutherans historically practiced closed Communion. That was not only a result of biblical doctrine but also a result of the territorial church structure imposed by the Peace of Augsburg (1555) and the Peace of Westphalia (1648). The unbaptized do not receive the Lord's Supper.[372] Those who have given offense and have not made amends may not partake.[373] This is based on an application of Matthew 5:23, 24 where Jesus says that if a person brings a gift to the altar and remembers that a brother has something against him, that person should first go and be reconciled. The ungodly and impenitent may not receive the Lord's Supper, lest they eat and drink condemnation to themselves.[374] Individuals who are unable to examine themselves may not receive the Lord's Supper. This includes small children, adults who have not received sufficient instruction, and persons who are in a state of unconsciousness.[375] This does not summarily exclude the mentally handicapped or elderly affected by aging, for which a judgment is made on a case-by-case basis. In support of this exclusion, Paul writes, "Let a man examine himself, and so let him eat of that bread and drink of that cup" (1 Corinthians 11:28).

- Eminent Lutheran theologian Charles Porterfield Krauth (1823–1883) drew up a statement which came to be known as the Akron Rule.[376] The rule reads as follows:

  1. Lutheran pulpits are for Lutheran ministers only. Lutheran altars are for Lutheran communicants only.

  2. The exception to this rule belongs to the sphere of privilege, not of right.

  3. The determination of the exceptions is to be made in consonance with these principles, by the conscientious judgment of pastors, as the case arises.[377]

- The General Council adopted this rule at a convention in Akron, Ohio, in 1872.[378] The General Council was an organization in which as many as 22 Lutheran synods held membership at one time or another.[379] In 1875 the General Council meeting at Galesburg, Illinois adopted a revision of the Akron Rule which was understood by some to be a setting aside of the exceptions contained in the Akron Rule.[380] The pertinent portion of the Galesburg resolution was "the rule, which accords with the Word of God and with the confessions of our Church, is: 'Lutheran pulpits for Lutheran ministers only--Lutheran altars for Lutheran communicants only.'"[381] These were the final words of the statement adopted at Galesburg. This statement has been called the Galesburg Rule. After much protracted discussion between Council members, Krauth, who was Council president, ruled that the resolution adopted at Galesburg was an amendment to the first paragraph of the Akron Rule, and that the second and third paragraphs which dealt with exceptions, remained in effect.[382] The Galesburg resolution continued to be interpreted in very different ways by various members of the Council. The conservatives believed the action at Galesburg had annulled the paragraph dealing with exceptions. Others held that the exception paragraphs were still in effect.[383] Eugene L. Fevold, who taught at Luther Theological Seminary in St. Paul, has written, "The Galesburg Rule was interpreted and applied strictly by some and flexibly by others."[384] At Pittsburgh in 1889 the General council adopted a resolution saying: "Inasmuch as the General Council has never annulled, rescinded or reconsidered the actions made at Akron, Ohio, in the year 1872, they still remain in all their parts and provisions, the action and rule of the General Council."[385]

• In essence this action by the Council gave approval to a variety in practice regarding who should be permitted to commune at Lutheran altars. A consensus developed in the more moderate wing of the Lutheran Church that variations in practice would be tolerated. The Akron-Galesburg Rule played an important role into the twentieth century, because it was accepted, either by assimilation in mergers or by formal adoption, by virtually all the Lutheran bodies which make up the present Evangelical Lutheran Church in America.[386] Fevold says, "In this way the Galesburg Rule continued to have significance in Midwestern Lutheranism long after its importance for Eastern Lutheranism had passed."[387]

• Departing from historic practice, some Lutherans in the Evangelical Lutheran Church in America (ELCA) and in the Evangelical Lutheran Church in Canada commune infants and small children.[388] In 1997, the ELCA approved a document entitled *The Use of the Means of Grace: A Statement on the Practice of Word and Sacrament*. The paper states, "The Holy Communion is given to the baptized."[389] It endorses a practice that had long been advocated by some member congregations. The Evangelical Lutheran Church in Canada had officially endorsed the practice of infant Communion in a convention in 1991.[390] At the time the Canadian Church took this action they became the only Lutheran Church in the world accepting this as permitted practice.[391] Those who believe that the Communion of infants is proper base their arguments partly on the feeding of the 5,000 and the feeding of the 4,000 by Jesus as being sacramental, in effect, celebrations of the Lord's Supper.[392] Such thinking bears striking resemblance to the Zwinglian or Calvinist understanding that sees the Eucharist primarily as a sign of fellowship, given that we have no "This is my body . . . do this" texts in these feedings. Canadian pastor J. Robert Jacobson writes, "It is important for Lutherans to come to an awareness that the Lord's Supper is more than the Last Supper."[393] Such a claim could easily expand to include any meal seen as sufficiently analogous to the Last Supper. What exists here is a clear violation of Luther's Scripture principle in favor of a human system of analogy and aesthetics determining God's Word. This matter has prompted expressions of concern on the part of other Lutherans.

• The historic practice of closed Communion among Lutherans means that members of other Christian denominations may not receive the Lord's Supper in a Lutheran Church. This is based on the concept that when persons commune, they are of one faith with those who commune with them, based on Acts 2:42 and Romans 16:17. The Prussian Union of 1817, foisted on the Lutherans by King Frederick William III, was the first major breach of closed Communion. This arrangement found a sympathetic reception among some German Lutherans in America.[394] In 1826 John A. Probst, a Lutheran pastor of the Pennsylvania Synod, published *The Reunion of Lutherans and Reformed* in which he said that Zwingli's doctrine had "become current among Lutherans and Reformed, and it has been deemed proper to abandon . . . Luther's and Calvin's opinions" in respect to it.[395] Adolph Brux, who was the first to advocate open prayer fellowship in the Missouri Synod in 1935, attacked fellowship principles based on Romans 16:17 but withdrew his position in the *Proceedings* of the 1935 synodical convention. Some Lutherans confessed the Lutheran understanding of the Lord's Supper, while others strayed from it as a detailed comparison of period editions of Luther's *Small Catechism* can show.

• Some Lutherans favored abandoning the distinctive Lutheran position on the Lord's Supper, often in the interest of ecumenical relations and "American Lutheranism." That movement found its guiding force in Samuel S. Schmucker (1799–1873).[396] Under Schmucker's influence, the Lutheran Synod of the West adopted a statement on the Lord's Supper in which they said that "the *real presence*, is so commonly admitted by the different Protestant denominations, that all dispute over the subject has subsided. God grant that on such a solemn and impressive subject, there may never again be occasion to commence it anew."[397] At a convention of the Synod of West Pennsylvania in 1837 Schmucker spoke of the Lord's Supper as an "ordinance to commemorate the dying love of the Savior, and to serve as a pledge of his spiritual presence and blessing on all worthy participants."[398] In 1855 Schmucker and others drew up and circulated a document known as the *Definite Synod Platform*. This platform contained a revised edition of the *Augsburg Confession*. There were changes in the *Augsburg Confession* that affected the orthodox Lutheran understanding of the Lord's Supper. The sanction of ceremonies during the Mass was removed. Also removed was the declaration that the blessings of the Lord's Supper are not dependent on the worthiness of the officiating minister.[399] Article ten of the *Augsburg Confession* was changed from "Of the Supper of the Lord they teach that the body and blood of Christ are truly present, and are communicated to those that eat in the Lord's Supper. And they disapprove of those that teach otherwise" to "In regard to the

Lord's Supper they teach that Christ is present with the communicants in the Lord's Supper, under the emblem of bread and wine."[400] After much controversy, the *Definite Synod Platform* was adopted by only three small synods—East Ohio, Wittenberg, and Olive Branch.[401]

- Some Lutherans in this general period practiced open Communion. Certain eastern congregations issued general invitations to the Lord's Supper.[402] An example of an entire synod extending such a welcome is that of the Lutheran Synod of the West, which said in a convention resolution, "All who are in good standing in other fundamentally orthodox denominations are always invited to partake with us."[403] Other Lutherans practiced closed Communion. Walther of the Missouri Synod, for instance, said that even if persons confessed the faith that the true body and blood of Christ are really present in the Lord's Supper, they "cannot ordinarily be admitted if he or she is and wants to be and remain, not a member of our orthodox church, but rather member of an erring fellowship."[404]

- Some predecessor bodies of the ELCA tolerated open Communion. In 1997, the ELCA entered into full altar fellowship with the United Church of Christ, the Reformed Church in America, and the Presbyterian Church (USA). In the agreement, the bodies joining in fellowship withdrew "any historic condemnation" against one another over previous doctrinal disagreements.[405] The Evangelical Lutheran Church in America also entered into full altar fellowship with the Moravian Church in America.[406] These Lutherans have since entered into full altar fellowship with the Episcopal Church.[407]

- Lutheran bodies that continue to adhere more closely with the Lutheran Confessions mandate that their member congregations practice closed Communion. These bodies include the Wisconsin Evangelical Lutheran Synod, the Evangelical Lutheran Synod, and several other smaller Lutheran groups. The Lutheran Church—Missouri Synod has a similar mandate, although it has faced considerable challenge repeatedly since 1935 (the time of the Brux case). This contributed to the dissolution of the Evangelical

Lutheran Synodical Conference of North America, a body of Lutheran churches in like confession to which the Missouri Synod once belonged. Currently, it remains difficult to ascertain the meaning of terms.[408] At one time only the terms "open" and "closed" were used among these confessional Lutherans.[409] The term "close Communion" seems to have been introduced into the Lutheran vocabulary by the *American Lutheran*, a publication of the American Lutheran Publicity Bureau which later had ties to Evangelical Lutherans in Mission, essentially those who helped form Seminex, the seminary in exile, in the 1970's. The term "close Communion" came from Baptist sources. Norman Nagel, professor at Concordia Seminary in St. Louis, says that the term "is in danger of blurring the primary reference . . . The muddle is evinced by the antonyms. 'Close' is capable of degrees; the Gospel is unfractionable."[410]

• Missouri Synod pastor William J. Stottlemyer says, "The Lord's Supper has always been for a closed group. Restricted by the Scriptures, the Lord's Supper must never be open to all but must be a Closed Communion restricted by the Word of God."[411] Professor Kurt Marquardt of Concordia Theological Seminary in Fort Wayne, Indiana, states, "If someone is prepared to have the Sacrament handed out pell-mell to everybody in attendance, like sample-bites of sausage in a supermarket, then he obviously does not believe that it is the Lord's Body and Blood . . . ."[412]

• Those who practice close Communion have a concern for those who would receive the Lord's Supper without perceiving the sacramental presence of Christ's body and blood, because they believe that such persons are cursed through receiving.[413] They quote 1 Corinthians 11:29 in support of this. There the Apostle says, "He that eateth and drinketh unworthily, eateth and drinketh damnation to himself, not discerning the Lord's body." Raymond L. Hartwig, secretary of The Lutheran Church—Missouri Synod, speaks of this concern, noting "close(d) communion is sometimes portrayed as an unloving practice." He says that really it is truly loving because it takes seriously important concerns for the good of all involved, especially those who are not "one in the faith." His words are that it is "a very loving practice for the sake of the Sacrament itself, the congregation, and perhaps especially those who would mistakenly attend."[414]

NOTES

1. Richard P. McBrien, *Lives of the Popes: The Pontiffs from St. Peter to John Paul II* (San Francisco: Harper, 1997), 388.

2. Joseph M. Champlin, *Special Signs of Grace: The Sacraments and Sacramentals* (Collegeville, Minn.: Liturgical Press, 1986), 53; Johannes H. Emminghaus, *The Eucharist: Essence, Form, Celebration,* trans. Matthew J. O'Connell. (Collegeville, Minn.: Liturgical Press, 1978), 84, 85; McBrien, *Popes,* 288, 298.

3. Champlin, *Special Signs,* 53; Emminghaus, *Eucharist,* 86.

4. Champlin, *Special Signs,* 53.

5. Emminghaus, *Eucharist,* 86, 87.

6. Paul A. Feider, *The Sacraments: Encountering the Risen Lord* (Notre Dame: Ave Maria Press, 1986), 45.

7. Feider, *Sacraments,* 45.

8. Feider, *Sacraments,* 45.

9. Champlin, *Special Signs,* 55, 56.

10. Champlin, *Special Signs,* 56.

11. Champlin, *Special Signs,* 57.

12. Champlin, *Special Signs,* 58, 59.

13. Leo C. Hay, *Eucharist: A Thanksgiving Celebration* (Wilmington, Del.: Michael Glazier, 1989), 132.

14. Kevin Smyth, trans., *A New Catechism: Catholic Faith for Adults* (New York: Herder and Herder, 1967), 345.

15. *Catechism of the Catholic Church* (Vatican City: Liberia Editrice Vaticana 1994, trans. Collegeville, Minn.: Liturgical Press, 1994), 347.

16. David P. Meyer, letter to author, 2 February 1998.

17. Charles Hodge, *Systematic Theology* (Grand Rapids: Eerdmans, 1997), 3:615.

18. Heinrich Heppe, *Reformed Dogmatics Set Out and Illustrated from the Sources,* rev. ed. trans. G. T. Thomson (London: George Allen & Unwin Ltd., 1950), 630; Laurence Hull Stookey, *Eucharist: Christ's Feast with the Church* (Nashville: Abingdon, 1993), 124.

19. Heppe, *Reformed Dogmatics,* 630.

20. Stookey, *Eucharist,* 124, 125.

21. Hodge, *Systematic,* 3:616; Stookey, *Eucharist,* 126; James F. White, *Protestant Worship: Traditions in Transition* (Louisville: Westminster/John Knox Press, 1991), 159.

22. Hodge, *Systematic,* 3:616, 617.

23. Stookey, *Eucharist,* 124, 125.

24. Hodge, *Systematic*, 3:616.

25. M. J. Bosma, *Exposition of Reformed Doctrine: A Popular Explanation of the Most Essential Teachings of the Reformed Churches*, 5th ed. (Grand Rapids: Zondervan, 1927), 275; Heppe, *Reformed Dogmatics*, 632–35; Hodge, *Systematic*, 3:617–620.

26. Heppe, *Reformed Dogmatics*, 632; Stookey, *Eucharist*, 118–122.

27. Bosma, *Reformed Doctrine*, 275.

28. Bosma, *Reformed Doctrine*, 275; Heppe, *Reformed Dogmatics*, 632–64; Hodge, *Systematic*, 3:617, 618.

29. Hodge, *Systematic*, 3:617, 618.

30. Hodge, *Systematic*, 3:620.

31. Hodge, *Systematic*, 3:620.

32. White, *Protestant*, 75.

33. Elmer J. F. Arndt, ed., *The Heritage of the Reformation: Essays Commemorating the Centennial of Eden Theological Seminary* (New York: R. R. Smith, 1950), 109.

34. Hodge, *Systematic*, 3:624; Stookey, *Eucharist*, 33, 34.

35. Philip Schaff, *The Creeds of Christendom with a History and Critical Notes*, rev. by David P. Schaff (Grand Rapids: Baker, 1966), 3:332–337.

36. Schaff, *Creeds*, 1:392–394.

37. Erwin L. Lueker, ed., *Lutheran Cyclopedia: A Concise In-Home Reference for the Christian Family*, rev. ed. (St. Louis: Concordia, 1975), 785.

38. Arndt, *Heritage*, 239.

39. F. E. Mayer, *The Religious Bodies of America* (St. Louis: Concordia, 1954), 352.

40. Mayer, *Bodies*, 353; J. L. Neve, *Churches and Sects of Christendom*, rev. ed. (Blair, Nebr.: Lutheran Publishing House, 1952), 378.

41. J. Gordon Melton, ed., *American Religious Creeds* (New York: Triumph Books, 1991), 1:258, 259.

42. Frank S. Mead, *Handbook of Denominations in the United States*, 7th ed. (Nashville: Abingdon, 1980), 189; "Moravian Glossary," *Christian History* 1, no. 1 (1982): 26.

43. "Moravian Glossary," 26.

44. *Guidelines and Worship Resources for the Celebration of Full Communion Lutheran-Moravian* (n.p.: Evangelical Lutheran Church in America; Moravian Church in America, Northern Province; Moravian Church in America, Southern Province, 1999), 12.

45. Mead, *Handbook*, 121.

46. Samuel T. Logan, "The Pilgrims and Puritans: Total Reformation for the Glory of God," *Tabletalk*, www.gospelcom.net/ligonier/tt/tt–11–96/logan.html (accessed 17 October 1998); Lars P. Qualben, *A History of the Christian Church*, rev. ed. (New York: Nelson, 1942), 321, 322.

47. Qualben, *History*, 322.

48. Qualben, *History*, 321.

49. John Dillenberger and Claude Welch, *Protestant Christianity Interpreted Through Its Development* (New York: Scribner, 1954), 69.

50. Lueker, *Cyclopedia*, 209.

51. Lueker, *Cyclopedia*, 34.

52. Mark A. Noll et al, eds., *Eerdmans Handbook to Christianity in America* (Grand Rapids: Eerdmans, 1983), 79.

53. White, *Protestant*, 110.

54. White, *Protestant*, 125.

55. "Holy Communion," Church of England, www.anglican.org (accessed 26 September 1998).

56. "Holy Communion," www.anglican.org.

57. R. Tudor Jones, "Preacher of Revolution," *Christian History* 14, no. 2 (1995): 10, 11, 13; Lueker, *Cyclopedia*, 447; White, *Protestant*, 69.

58. James Kirk, "Worship Before and After," *Christian History* 14, no. 2 (1995): 30.

59. Jones, "Preacher," 16.

60. Philip Schaff, *The Creeds of Christendom with a History and Critical Notes*, rev. by David F. Schaff (Grand Rapids: Baker, 1966), 3:468–471.

61. E. H. Klotsche, *The History of Christian Doctrine*, rev. J. Theodore Mueller and David P. Scaer (1945; reprint, Grand Rapids: Baker, 1979), 290; Lueker, Cyclopedia, 636.

62. Lueker, *Cyclopedia*, 708.

63. Schaff, *Creeds*, 3:663–667.

64. White, *Protestant*, 72.

65. Paul K. Conkin, *Cane Ridge, America's Pentecost* (Madison, Wis.: University of Wisconsin Press, 1990) 64, 68.

66. Conkin, *Cane Ridge,* 88; Mark Galli, "Revival at Cane Ridge" *Christian History* 14, no. 1 (1995): 14.

67. Conkin, *Cane Ridge*, 162.

68. Logan, "Pilgrims," 2, 3; Samuel A. Trumbore, "The Pilgrims Weren't Puritans" Unitarian Universalist Fellowship of Charlotte County, http://204.117.207.9/trumbore/sermon/e7b4.htm (accessed 17 October 1998).

69. White, *Protestant*, 115.

70. White, *Protestant*, 120, 121.

71. Edwin S. Gaustad, "Quest For Pure Christianity," *Christian History* 13, no. 1 (1994): 12.

72. Mayer, *Bodies*, 246; White, *Protestant*, 128.

73. Noll, *Handbook*, 41.

74. Noll, *Handbook*, 41, 42.

75. Noll, *Handbook*, 42.

76. "Did You Know?" *Christian History* 2: no. 1 (1983): 4.

77. Lueker, *Cyclopedia*, 812.

78. White, *Protestant*, 154.

79. White, *Protestant*, 152.

80. White, *Protestant*, 150, 151, 155.

81. White, *Protestant*, 151.

82. Russell E. Richey, *Early American Methodism* (Bloomington: Indiana University Press, 1991), 102, 103.

83. White, *Protestant*, 151.

84. White, *Protestant*, 154.

85. White, *Protestant*, 154.

86. Richey, *Methodism*, 26.

87. James Haskins, The Methodists (New York: Hippocrene Books, 1992), 96.

88. Stookey, *Eucharist*, 169.

89. Haskins, *Methodists*, 97.

90. Haskins, *Methodists*, 98, 100.

91. Haskins, *Methodists*, 100, 101.

92. Haskins, *Methodists*, 102.

93. Haskins, *Methodists*, 102.

94. Haskins, *Methodists*, 103, 104.

95. White, *Protestant*, 159, 161.

96. Stookey, *Eucharist*, 169.

97. Stookey, *Eucharist*, 169.

98. Mayer, *Bodies*, 311.

99. Melton, *American*, 1:307.

100. Mead, *Handbook*, 99.

101. Mayer, *Bodies*, 333.

102. Reuben Goertz, *Princes, Potentates, and Plain People: The Saga of the Germans from Russia* (Sioux Falls, S.Dak.: Center for Western Studies, 1994), 74.

103. Lowell C. Green, "Philosophical Presuppositions in the Lutheran-Reformed Debate on John 6," *Concordia Theological Quarterly* 56, no. 1 (1992): 22.

104. Paul Enns, *The Moody Handbook of Theology* (Chicago: Moody Press, 1989), 456; White, *Protestant*, 86.

105. White, *Protestant*, 86.

106. White, *Protestant*, 86.

107. White, *Protestant*, 87.

108. Goertz, *Princes*, 80.

109. Goertz, *Princes*, 81, 82.

110. Goertz, *Princes*, 87.

111. Goertz, *Princes*, 87.

112. Goertz, *Princes*, 86.

113. "From the Archives: The Schleitheim Confession," *Christian History* 4, no. 1 (1985): 30.

114. "Schleitheim Confession," 29.

115. "Schleitheim Confession," 30.

116. White, *Protestant*, 87, 88.

117. White, *Protestant*, 87, 88.

118. White, *Protestant*, 87.

119. "A Gallery of Factions Friends & Foes," *Christian History* 5, no. 1 (1985): 15.

120. Lueker, *Cyclopedia*, 707.

121. Peter C. Erb, "The Life and Thought of Casper Schwenckfeld Von Ossig," *Christian History* 8, no. 1 (1999): 14, 15.

122. White, *Protestant*, 79.

123. Goertz, *Princes*, 80; Mayer, *Bodies*, 396.

124. Goertz, *Princes*, 80; Mayer, *Bodies*, 396.

125. Paul M. Lederach, *A Third Way: Conversations About Anabaptist/Mennonite Faith* (Scottdale, Pa.: Herald Press, 1980), 89.

126. Dillenberger, *Protestant*, 66, 67.

127. Lederach, *Third Way*, 93.

128. Lederach, *Third Way*, 95.

129. Lederach, *Third Way*, 95.

130. John C. Wenger, "The Lord's Supper," www.bibleviews.com/lordsupper.html (accessed 6 September 1998).

131. Lederach, *Third Way*, 96.

132. Wenger, "Lord's Supper," available www.bibleviews.com/lordsupper.html.

133. Edna Boardman, *All Things Decently and in Order and Other Writings on a Germans from Russia Heritage* (Minot, N.Dak.: North American Heritage Press, 1997), 5, 6.

134. Lueker, *Cyclopedia*, 530.

135. "Gallery of Factions," 15.

136. White, *Protestant*, 90.

137. Wes Harrison, *Andreas Ehrenpreis and Hutterite Faith and Practice* (Kitchener, Ontario: Pandora Press, 1997), 168; Barbie Hofer, conversation with author, Milnor, N.Dak., 17 March 2001.

138. Peter H. Stephenson, *The Hutterian People: Ritual and Rebrith in the Evolution of Communal Life* (Lanham, Md.: University Press of America, 1991), 191.

139. Stephenson, *Hutterian People*, 192.

140. Harrison, *Andreas Ehrenpreis*, 135.

141. Stephenson, *Hutterian People*, 144.

142. Peter Rideman, *Confession of Faith: Account or our Religion, Doctrine and Faith Given by Peter Rideman of the Brethren Whom Men Call Hutterites* (Rifton, N.Y.: Plough Publishing House, 1970), 83, 84.

143. Stephenson, *Hutterian People*, 143.

144. Stephenson, *Hutterian People*, 191, 192.

145. Harrison, *Andreas Ehrenpreis*, 53, 84.

146. Rod Janzen, *The Prairie People: Forgotten Anabaptists* (Hanover, N.H.:

University Press of New England, 1999), 2.

147. Janzen, *Prairie*, 114.

148. Janzen, *Prairie*, 3.

149. Janzen, *Prairie*, 3.

150. William I. Schreiber, *Our Amish Neighbors* (Chicago: University of Chicago Press, 1962), 124.

151. Stephen Scott, *The Amish Wedding and Other Special Occasions of the Old Order Communities* (Intercourse, Pa.: Good Books, 1988), 54.

152. Scott, *Amish*, 57, 58.

153. Scott, *Amish*, 81.

154. Scott, *Amish*, 81.

155. H. Leon McBeth, *The Baptist Heritage* (Nashville: Broadman, 1987), 61, 62.

156. Lueker, *Cyclopedia*, 72.

157. McBeth, *Baptist*, 81.

158. Alton H. McEachern, *Here at Thy Table, Lord: Enriching the Observance of the Lord's Supper* (Nashville: Broadman, 1977), 18.

159. James E. Tull, "The Ordinances/Sacraments in Baptist Thought," *American Baptist Quarterly* 1, no. 2 (1982): 190.

160. Alexander Maclaren, *Maclaren's Expositions of Holy Scripture* (Eerdmans, 1959), 9:173.

161. C. H. Spurgeon, *The Metropolitan Tabernacle Pulpit* (London: Passmore & Alabaster, 1908), 2:205.

162. Spurgeon, *Tabernacle*, 5:95.

163. Edward B. Cole, *The Baptist Heritage* (Elgin, Ill.: David C. Cook, 1976), 125.

164. Bill J. Leonard, *God's Last and Only Hope: The Fragmentation of the Southern Baptist Convention* (Grand Rapids: Eerdmans, 1990), 97.

165. Tull, "Ordinances," 192.

166. Melton, *American*, 2:152.

167. Melton, *American*, 2:175.

168. James Petigru Boyce, *Abstract of Systematic Theology* (1887; reprint, den Dulk Christian Fellowship and Pompano Beach, Fla.: North Pompona Baptist Church, n.d.), 423.

169. Ronald Q. Leavell, *Studies in Matthew: The King and the Kingdom* (Nashville: Convention Press, 1962), 130.

170. McEachern, *Table*, 114.

171. Tull, "Ordinances," 191.

172. Tull, "Ordinances," 192.

173. McEachern, *Table*, 115.

174. McEachern, *Table*, 115.

175. McEachern, *Table*, 115.

176. McBeth, *Baptist*, 81.

177. Tull, "Ordinances," 191.

178. McBeth, *Baptist*, 81.

179. Norman Nagel, "Closed Communion: In the Way of the Gospel: In the Way of the Law," *Concordia Journal* 17, no. 1 (1991): 27.

180. McBeth, *Baptist*, 82.

181. McBeth, *Baptist*, 82, 83.

182. McBeth, *Baptist*, 83.

183. McBeth, *Baptist*, 196.

184. William G. McLoughlin, *Soul Liberty: The Baptists' Struggle in New England*, 1630–1833 (Hanover, N.H.: University Press of New England, 1991), 46, 94.

185. McLoughlin, *Soul*, 127, 165, 166, 250, 251, 254.

186. McLoughlin, *Soul*, 94.

187. Leonard, *Fragmentation*, 96, 97.

188. Arthur Emery Farnsley II, *Southern Baptist Politics: Authority and Power in the Restructuring of an American Denomination* (University Park, Pa.: The Pennsylvania State University Press, 1994), 4; Leonard, *Fragmentation*, 97.

189. Leonard, *Fragmentation*, 98.

190. George Clark, "This Do in Remembrance of Me," *Church Administration* 32, no. 3 (1989): 13; Howard Dorgan, *Giving Glory to Cod in Appalachia: Worship Practices of Six Baptist Subdenominations* (Knoxville: University of Tennessee Press, 1987), 140.

191. McEachern, *Table*, 21.

192. McEachern, *Table*, 21.

193. Clark, "Remembrance," 13; Dorgan, *Appalachia*, 137.

194. "From the Archives: 'This Is My Body . . . This Is My Blood.'" *Christian History* 4, no, 2 (1985): 33, 34.

195. Dorgan, *Appalachia*, 137, 142.

196. "Archives," 34; Clark, "Remembrance," 13; McEachern, *Table*, 39.

197. Dorgan, *Appalachia*, 137, 142.

198. "Archives," 34.

199. Clifton J. Allen et al, ed., *The Broadman Bible Commentary* (Nashville: Broadman, 1969–1972), 8:385.

200. John R. Rice, *Dr. Rice, Here Is My Question: Bible Answers to 294 Important Questions in Forty Years' Ministry . . .* (Murfreesboro, Tenn.: Sword of the Lord Publishers, 1962), 122.

201. John. R. Rice, *The King of the Jews: A Verse-by-Verse Commentary on the Gospel According to Matthew* (Murfreesboro, Tenn.: Sword of the Lord Publishers, 1955), 436.

202. "Archives," 34; Dorgan, *Appalachia*, 137, 138, 142.

203. "Archives," 34.

204. "Archives," 34.

205. "Archives," 34.

206. Dorgan, *Appalachia*, 114–146.

207. Dorgan, *Appalachia*, 139, 145.

208. Dorgan, *Appalachia*, 136, 137.

209. Dorgan, *Appalachia*, 129.

210. Mayer, *Bodies*, 398.

211. Lueker, *Cyclopedia*, 108.

212. Mead, *Handbook*, 65.

213. Lueker, *Cyclopedia*, 108; Scott, *Amish*, 74.

214. Scott, *Amish*, 73–75.

215. Melton, *American*, 2:117.

216. Scott, *Amish*, 74.

217. Melton, *American*, 2:117.

218. Scott, *Amish*, 75, 760.

219. Mead, *Handbook*, 65.

220. Lueker, *Cyclopedia*, 238; James S. McDonald, Jr., "Why We Take the Lord's Supper Every Sunday," Orange Park, Fla.: Lakeside Church of Christ, www.lakesidechurchofchrist.com/supper.htm (accessed 6 September 1998).

221. Paul K. Conkin, *American Originals: Homemade Varieties of Christianity* (Chapel Hill, N.C.: University Of North Carolina Press, 1997), 1.

222. Conkin, *Originals*, 2; Lueker, *Cyclopedia*, 237.

223. Conkin, *Originals*, 16.

224. White, *Protestant*, 175.

225. Mayer, *Bodies*, 382.

226. Conkin, *Originals*, 41.

227. McDonald, "Lord's Supper," 2.

228. Melton, *American*, 2:211.

229. Conkin, *Originals*, 44; Mayer, *Bodies*, 383; White, *Protestant*, 175.

230. Conkin, *Originals*, *37, 38*.

231. Conkin, *Originals*, 47.

232. Lueker, *Cyclopedia*, 281.

233. Lueker, *Cyclopedia*, 281; Mayer, *Bodies*, 349.

234. Mayer, *Bodies*, 349.

235. Melton, *American*, 1:258; "Statement of Faith: The Evangelical Free Church of America," Cheyenne Evangelical Free Church, http://pages.prodigy.com/cefc/beliefs.htm (accessed 21 November 1998).

236. "The Lord's Supper," Minocqua/Woodruff, Wis.: Faith Evangelical Free Church, http://www.we.centuryinter.net/faithfree/supper.html (accessed 21 November 1998).

237. "What We Believe," Evangelical Free Church of Fullerton, Calif., http://www.fefcf.org/believe.html (accessed 21 November 1998).

238. Lueker, *Cyclopedia*, 307, 315.

239. Lueker, *Cyclopedia*, 316.

240. Mayer, *Bodies*, 402; "Religious Society of Friends (Quakers)," www.religioustolerance.org/quaker.htm (accessed 23 November 1998).

241. Lueker, *Cyclopedia*, 316.

242. "Religious Society of Friends," online.

243. Theodore Engelder, et al, *Popular Symbolics; The Doctrines of the Churches of Christendom and of Other Religious Bodies Examined in the Light of Scripture* (St. Louis: Concordia, 1934), 384; Lueker, *Cyclopedia*, 316; Mayer, *Bodies*, 412.

244. Engelder, *Symbolics*, 348; Mayer, *Bodies*, 412.

245. White, *Protestant*, 141.

246. "Did You Know?" *Christian History* 17, no. 2 (1998): 3.

247. White, *Protestant*, 192.

248. White, *Protestant*, 201.

249. Melton, *American*, 2:1–3, 13, 14, 22–26, 32, 35, 52, 53, 71, 77–81, 83.

250. White, *Protestant*, 200.

251. Paul F. Gillespie, ed., *Foxfire 7* (Garden City, N.Y.: Anchor Press/Doubleday, 1982), 474; Mead, *Handbook*, 197, 198.

252. Melton, *American*, 2:29.

253. Mead, *Handbook*, 144.

254. Melton, *American*, 2:39.

255. Melton, *American*, 2:5.

256. Melton, *American*, 2:7.

257. Mead, *Handbook*, 85.

258. Melton, *American*, 2:10.

259. Melton, *American*, 2:8.

260. Melton, *American*, 2:46.

261. Melton, *American*, 2:51.

262. Melton, *American*, 2:54, 64.

263. Dennis Covington, *Salvation on Sand Mountain: Snake Handling and Redemption in Southern Appalachia* (Reading, Mass.: Addison-Wesley, 1995), 1, 113; David L. Kimbrough, *Taking up Serpents: Snake Handlers of Eastern Kentucky* (Chapel Hill, N.C.: University of North Carolina Press, 1995), 8, 149.

264. Covington, *Salvation*, 115.

265. Covington, *Salvation*, 115, 116.

266. Covington, *Salvation*, 116.

267. Covington, *Salvation*, 118–121.

268. Mayer, *Bodies*, 431; Mead, *Handbook*, 19, 20; Casper B. Nervig, *Christian Truths and Religious Delusions* (Minneapolis: Augsburg, 1941), 90.

269. *Seventh-Day Adventists Believe: A Biblical Exposition of 27 Doctrines* (Washington, D.C.: Ministerial Association, General Conference of Seventh-day Adventists, 1988), 195, 199.

270. *Seventh-day Adventists Believe*, 95.

271. *Seventh-day Adventists Believe*, 199, 201.

272. *Seventh-day Adventists Believe*, 199.

273. *Seventh-day Adventists Believe*, 200.

274. White, *Protestant*, 187.

275. *Seventh-day Adventists Believe*, 204.

276. *Seventh-day Adventists Believe*, 200.

277. *Seventh-day Adventists Believe*, 200.

278. *Seventh-day Adventists Believe*, 200.

279. *Seventh-day Adventists Believe*, 203, 204.

280. Engelder, *Symbolics*, 356; White, *Protestant*, 187.

281. *Seventh-day Adventists Believe*, 196.

282. *Seventh-day Adventists Believe*, 199.

283. *Seventh-day Adventists Believe*, 203.

284. White, *Protestant*, 187.

285. White, *Protestant*, 201.

286. White, *Protestant*, 203.

287. White, *Protestant*, 194.

288. Melton, *American*, 2:265, 268.

289. Melton, *American*, 2:280.

290. "The Lord's Supper," Bible Advocate Press, www.denver.net/cotgrad/Lit./LltLordSupper.html (accessed 6 September 1998).

291. "The Lord's Supper," online.

292. Lueker, *Cyclopedia*, 109.

293. Mead, *Handbook*, 65.

294. Lueker, *Cyclopedia*, 109; White, *Protestant*, 131.

295. Mead, *Handbook*, 66.

296. Mayer, *Bodies*, 387.

297. Mayer, *Bodies*, 387.

298. Mayer, *Bodies*, 387; White, *Protestant*, 131.

299. White, *Protestant*, 131.

300. Engelder, *Symbolics*, 329.

301. Mead, *Handbook*, 232.

302. Engelder, *Symbolics*, 329.

303. Engelder, *Symbolics*, 329; Mayer, *Bodies*, 344.

304. Mayer, *Bodies*, 344.

305. Engelder, *Symbolics*, 329.

306. Engelder, *Symbolics*, 329.

307. David Laeger, "Bread and Wine," *The War Cry* 120, no. 17 (2000): 16.

308. Melton, *American*, 1:304.

309. Robert D. Preus, *The Theology of Post-Reformation Lutheranism: A Study of Theological Prolegomena* (St. Louis: Concordia, 1970), 1:45.

310. Theodore G. Tappert, ed., *The Book of Concord: The Confessions of the Evangelical Lutheran Church* (Philadelphia: Fortress, 1959), 482–84.

311. J. A. O. Preus, *The Second Martin: The Life and Theology of Martin Chemnitz* (St. Louis: Concordia, 1994), 190; Preus, *Lutheranism*, 48; Gayling Schmel-

ing, "Chemnitz and the Lord's Supper," *Lutheran Synod Quarterly* 34, no. 2 (1994): 5.

312. Bjarne Wollan Teigen, *The Lord's Supper in the Theology of Martin Chemnitz* (Brewster, Mass.: Trinity Lutheran Press, 1986), 18.

313. Charles P. Krauth, *The Conservative Reformation and Its Theology* (1871; reprint, Minneapolis: Augsburg, 1963), 678.

314. Krauth, *Conservative Reformation*, 769.

315. Lueker, *Cyclopedia*, 150; Martin E. Marty, *Protestantism* (New York: Holt, Rinehart and Winston, 1972), 171; Hermann Sasse, *This is My Body: Luther's Contention for the Real Presence in the Sacrament of the Altar*, rev. ed. (Adelaide, South Australia: Lutheran Publishing House, 1977), 44.

316. Enns, *Moody*, 361; McEachern, *Table*, 19; Charles W. Ranson, "Eucharist," *Grolier Multimedia Encyclopedia*, 1996. CD-ROM.

317. *The Use of the Means of Grace: A Statement on the Practice of Word and Sacrament* (Minneapolis: Augsburg, 1997), 37.

318. Gaylin Schmeling, "The Theology of the Lord's Supper," *Lutheran Synod Quarterly* 28, no. 4 (1988): 17, 18.

319. Schmeling, "Theology," 18.

320. Schmeling, "Theology," 19.

321. Schmeling, "Theology," 32, 33.

322. Schmeling, "Theology," 18.

323. Schmeling, "Theology," 18; Teigen, *Lord's Supper*, 184.

324. Teigen, *Lord's Supper*, 84.

325. Francis Pieper, *Christian Dogmatics* (St. Louis: Concordia, 1953), 3:372, 373; Teigen, *Lord's Supper*, 184.

326. Schmeling, "Theology," 30.

327. Schmeling, "Theology," 41.

328. Schmeling, "Theology," 44.

329. C. F. W. Walther, *Walther's Pastorale, that is, American Lutheran Pastoral Theology*, trans. and abridged by John M. Drickamer (1906; New Haven, Mo.: Lutheran News, Inc., 1995), 144.

330. John H. C. Fritz, *Pastoral Theology: A Handbook of Scriptural Principles* (St. Louis: Concordia, 1932), 147, Walther, *Pastorale*, 144.

331. *Theology and Practice of the Lord's Supper* (Commission on Theology and Church Relations, The Lutheran Church—Missouri Synod, 1983), 14.

332. Norbert H. Mueller and George Kraus, ed., *Pastoral Theology* (St. Louis: Concordia, 1990), 106.

333. Schmeling, "Theology," 44, 45.

334. Schmeling, "Theology," 47.

335. Fritz, *Pastoral Theology*, 149; Mueller and Kraus, *Pastoral Theology*, 106; Philip H. Pfatteicher and Carlos R. Messerli, *Manual on the Liturgy: Lutheran Book of Worship* (Minneapolis: Augsburg, 1979), 249; *Theology and Practice of the Lord's Supper*, 17; *Use of the Means of Grace*, 50; Walther, *Pastorale*, 145. Schmeling, "Theology," 44–47.

336. Fritz, *Pastoral Theology*, 142; Armin M. Schuetze and Irwin J. Habeck, *The Shepherd Under Christ: A Textbook for Pastoral Theology* (Milwaukee: Northwestern, 1974), 90; Walther, *Pastorale*, 130.

337. *Theology and Practice of the Lord's Supper*, 16; Walther, *Pastorale*, 130.

338. Mueller and Kraus, *Pastoral Theology*, 97.

339. Sunday Bulletin (Breckenridge, Minn.: Grace Lutheran Church, 21 February 1999).

340. "Is 'Non-Alcoholic' Wine Really Wine?" *Concordia Journal* 17, no. 1 (1991): 5.

341. *Use of the Means of Grace*, 48.

342. Mueller and Kraus, *Pastoral Theology*, 105.

343. *The Pastor at Work* (St. Louis: Concordia, 1960), 170.

344. Fritz, *Pastoral Theology*, 149.

345. Fritz, *Pastoral Theology*, 149.

346. Carl E. Braaten and Robert W. Jenson, ed., *Christian Dogmatics* (Philadelphia: Fortress, 1984), 2:344.

347. John H. Stephenson, "Reflections on the Appropriate Vessels for Consecrating and Distributing the Precious Blood of Christ," *Logia* 4, no. 1 (1995): 11.

348. Stephenson, "Reflections," 17.

349. R. C. H. Lenski, *The Epistle Selections of the Ancient Church: An Exegetical-Homiletical Treatment* (Columbus: Lutheran Book Concern, 1935), 368.

350. Pfatteicher and Messerli, *Manual*, 244.

351. Pfatteicher and Messerli, *Manual*, 244.

352. Stephenson, "Reflections," 17.

353. Edward W. A. Koehler, *A Short Exposition of Dr. Martin Luther's Small Catechism, edited by the Evangelical Lutheran Synod of Missouri, Ohio, and other States, with Additional Notes for Students, Teachers, and Pastors* (River Forest, Ill.: Koehler, 1946), 289.

354. *Pastor at Work*, 163.

355. Virgilius Ferm, *The Crisis in American Lutheran Theology: A Study of the Issue between American Lutheranism and Old Lutheranism* (1927; reprint, St. Louis: Concordia, 1987), 18.

356. Walther, *Pastorale*, 116.

357. Walther, *Pastorale*, 108.

358. Mueller and Kraus, *Pastoral Theology*, 102.

359. David Belgum, *The Church and Its Ministry* (Englewood Cliffs, N.J.: Prentice-Hall, 1963), 148.

360. Apology of the Augsburg Confession XXIV, 1, in *The Book of Concord* (Tappert), 249.

361. Luther D. Reed, *The Lutheran Liturgy: A Study of the Common Service of the Lutheran Church in America* (Philadelphia: Muhlenberg Press, 1947), 233.

362. Qualben, *History*, 363.

363. Fred L. Precht, ed., *Lutheran Worship: History and Practice* (St. Louis: Concordia, 1993), 83.

364. Reed, *Lutheran Liturgy*, 234.

365. Mueller and Kraus, *Pastoral Theology*, 98.

366. Reed, *Lutheran Liturgy*, 348.

367. Walther, *Pastorale*, 151.

368. Reed, *Lutheran Liturgy*, 349.

369. Reed, *Lutheran Liturgy*, 348.

370. Reed, *Lutheran Liturgy*, 349.

371. Precht, *Lutheran Worship*, 438.

372. *Pastor at Work*, 166; Schuetze and Habeck, *Shepherd*, 800.

373. *Pastor at Work*, 167; Walther, *Pastorale*, 149.

374. Koehler, *Short Exposition*, 312.

375. Koehler, *Short Exposition*, 312; *Pastor at Work*, 167.

376. John H. Tietjen, *Which Way to Lutheran Unity?: A History of Efforts to Unite the Lutherans of America* (St. Louis: Concordia, 1966), 49, 50.

377. Neve, *History*, 160; Tietjen, *Unity*, 50.

378. Lueker, *Cyclopedia*, 321.

379. Lueker, *Cyclopedia*, 325.

380. Neve, *History*, 161.

381. Neve, *History*, 160.

382. E. Clifford Nelson, ed., *The Lutherans in North America*, rev. ed. Philadelphia: Fortress, 1980), 312.

383. Julius Bodensieck, ed., *The Encyclopedia of the Lutheran Church* (Minneapolis: Augsburg, 1965), 2:898; Nelson, *Lutherans*, 312.

384. Nelson, *Lutherans*, 312.

385. Bodensieck, *Encyclopedia*, 2:899; Neve, *History*, 161.

386. Nelson, *Lutherans*, 313.

387. Nelson, *Lutherans*, 313.

388. Ralph A. Bohlmann, letter to pastors of The Lutheran Church—Missouri Synod regarding infant Communion, 31 October 1991, 8.

389. *Use of the Means of Grace*, 41.

390. *Statement on Sacramental Practices* (n.p: Division for Parish of the Evangelical Lutheran Church in Canada, 1991).

391. Bohlmann, letter, 7.

392. J. Robert Jacobson, *Besides Women & Children: A Guide for Parents & Pastors on Infant & Child Communion*, rev. ed. (Camrose, Alberta: Concord Canada, 1981), 14.

393. Jacobson, *Besides Women and Children*, 14.

394. Ferm, *Crisis*, 45.

395. Ferm, *Crisis*, 48, 49.

396. Ferm, *Crisis*, 703.

397. Ferm, *Crisis,* 103.

398. Ferm, *Crisis*, 111.

399. J. L. Neve, *History of the Lutheran Church in America*, 3rd rev. ed. prepared

by Willard D. Allbeck.(Burlington, Iowa: The Lutheran Literary Board, 1934), 97.

400. Neve, *History*, 97, 98.

401. Neve, *History*, 99.

402. Nelson, *Lutherans*, 311.

403. Ferm, *Crisis*, 103.

404. Walther, *Pastorale*, 148.

405. *Lutheran—Episcopal, Lutheran—Reformed, and Lutheran—Roman Catholic Ecumenical Proposals Documents for Action by the 1997 Churchwide Assembly: Evangelical Lutheran Church in America* (Chicago: Evangelical Lutheran Church in America, 1996), 18.

406. *Guidelines and Worship Resources for the Celebration of Full Communion Lutheran—Moravian* (n.p. Evangelical Lutheran Church in America. Moravian Church in America, Northern Province. Moravian Church in America, Southern Province, 1999), 14.

407. Jean Coffey Lyles, "Decorum in Denver," *Christian Century* (July 10–26, 2000): 743.

408. Edward A. Engelbrecht, *Open, Close, Closed?: Lutheran Communion Practice* (Roanoke, Ill.: Angel Bright Publication), 2; *Theology and Practice of the Lord's Supper*, 20, 22.

409. Nagel, "Closed Communion," 27.

410. Nagel, "Closed Communion," 27.

411. William J. Stottlemyer, "Who May Come? A Theological and Confessional Study Concerning the Issue of Who May Receive the Lord's Supper in Our Church" (TMs. Fergus Falls, Minn.: Pastoral Conference, 1996), 10.

412. Kurt Marquart, *"Church Growth" as Mission Paradigm: A Lutheran Assessment* (Houston: Our Savior Lutheran Church, 1994), 86, 87.

413. Stottlemyer, "Who May Come," 9.

414. Raymond L. Hartwig, *Close Communion: Sharing God's Meal—Leader's Guide* (St Louis: Concordia, 1995), 25.

STUDY QUESTIONS

The Roman Catholic Church

1. What power did the Council of Trent grant to the pope with respect to the manner of celebrating the Lord's Supper in both kinds?

2. What book, issued by what pope in 1570, shaped and unified the liturgy of the Roman Church for the next four centuries?

3. What twentieth-century emphases regarding the Lord's Supper changed in the Roman Church?

4. What two changes to the liturgy and the Lord's Supper were most noted or key in Vatican II?

5. What practices were deemphasized by Vatican II?

6. True or false: Due to recent Catholic scholars finding the doctrine of transubstantiation to be idiosyncratic, belonging to a bygone era, the Roman Church no longer makes that doctrine a part of its public confession.

Calvinist Churches—Reformed, Church of England, Presbyterian, Puritans, Congreationalists, Methodist

1. What form of bread has been discouraged for use in the Lord's Supper in Reformed churches?

2. Forms of "wine" used include wine mixed with water and what other common substitute?

3. True or false: In some circumstances, replacement of grain and base of fermentation for the bread and wine may be allowed.

4. For what reasons do Reformed churches consider that the Lord's Supper should be observed?

5. What church body resulted from immigrants who came out of the Prussian union of Lutheran and Reformed churches, which mandated open Communion and later merged with other bodies to form the United Church of Christ?

6. What church body, whose understanding of the Lord's Supper is that of a pledge of allegiance, arose from the Hussite movement in Bohemia, later to find a center in Zinzendorf's Herrnhut commune and send emigrants to North America?

7. True or false: Although Thomas Cranmer, the first Protestant archbishop of Canterbury, had heard of Luther early on, he had always held a view that was more Calvinist regarding the Lord's Supper.

8. True or false: The development of the Communion rail was to keep stray animals away from the altar.

9. Whether low or high church, what four actions are common to the Episcopalian celebration of the Lord's Supper?

10. Since 1972, what form of altar fellowship have Episcopalians observed?

11. What Scottish minister, exiled during the reign of Mary Tudor and subsequently acquainted with Bullinger of Zurich, returned to Scotland to spur a reformation there that led to the rise of the Presbyterian church?

12. What phrase might be used to describe the Scottish Presbyterian understanding of the Lord's Supper?

13. What movement in America grew out of the Presbyterian sacramental seasons?

14. What was one of the most influential revivals in US history?

15. What result did that revival have on the Presbyterian church with respect to its Communion practices?

16. What is the difference between Puritans and Separatists?

17. True or false: Puritans and Separatists held some extreme views on the need for worthiness before receiving the Sacrament, sometimes going years without it.

18. What was the original position of Puritans regarding church membership and reception of the Lord's Supper?

19. When that position drained church membership over time, what solution was found and how did it work?

20. Although some thought the Half-Way Covenant to be too lax, others thought that it was too strict and wished to practice open Communion. With immigrants from the church formed by the Prussian Union, the body that practiced open Communion merged to form what church body?

21. What figure, known for his membership in the "Holy Club" at Oxford, helped found the Methodist church?

22. What aspects of ancient or medieval celebrations of the Lord's Supper were part of Methodism?

23. What problem or requirement resulted in infrequent celebrations of the Lord's Supper among Methodists?

24. What had drawn African Americans to the Methodist church early in American history, and what was the crucial request regarding clergy that led to the formation of the African Methodist Episcopal Zion Church?

25. In 1869, a dentist invented the process for making grape juice, thus allowing Methodists to opt for using grape juice instead of wine for over a century. Who is this dentist, for which a popular brand of grape juice is named?

26. What kind of altar fellowship do Methodists practice?

Zwinglian Churches—Anabaptists, Schwenkfelders, Mennonites, Amish, Baptist, Restoration Movement, Evangelical Free, Quaker, Pentecostal, Adventist, Plymouth Brethren, Salvation Army

1. What may be said of the Anabaptists, Mennonites, and Hutterites with regard to the presence of Christ in the Lord's Supper?

2. How did the Anabaptists incorporate a theology of suffering into their celebrations of the Lord's Supper?

3. True or false: The Anabaptists employed public church discipline and held, in general, quarterly celebrations of the Lord's Supper.

4. True or false: The Anabaptists used a formal liturgy when celebrating the Lord's Supper.

5. True or false: The Schwenkfelders abstained collectively from the Lord's Supper for approximately 350 years, due to the woeful condition of warring and discord that they saw among Christians.

6. The Mennonites, Amish, and Hutterites, all descendants of the movement led by Menno Simons, use what term for the Lord's Supper?

7. What is their general focus regarding the Lord's Supper, and what do they believe regarding the presence of Christ in the Sacrament?

8. What kind of altar fellowship do Mennonites practice?

9. What do River Brethren do in conjunction with their love feasts?

10. What two groups of English Baptists eventually merged in 1891 and what were their theological backgrounds?

11. Whose doctrine of the Lord's Supper is generally held among Southern Baptists?

12. Whose doctrine appears to be held by a minority of Southern Baptists and the majority of English and Irish Baptists?

13. What two terms for the Lord's Supper have generated division among Baptists?

14. How do many Baptists view the Lord's Supper with respect to the relationship of their faith to Christ?

15. According to this view of the Lord's Supper, what characterizes the self-examination period stressed by Baptists prior to receiving the Supper?

16. Controversy has existed among Baptists regarding eligibility to receive the Lord's Supper. Describe briefly the argument made by those who advocate open Communion.

17. What term arose among Baptists that rejects the argument of those opting for open Communion, who instead restrict reception to those that have received believers' baptism?

18. True or false: A lack of consensus among Baptists concerning the practice of open versus closed Communion has existed from the seventeenth century to the present day, wherein no general rules have existed to govern altar fellowship.

19. True or false: There exists relative uniformity with respect to the frequency in which many Baptists receive the Lord's Supper.

20. True or false: Although many Baptist congregations use loaves of unleavened bread and grape juice as the physical elements of the Lord's Supper, all Baptists originally used wine until the rise of the American temperance movement, and the move to grape juice did not occur without controversy.

21. The use of what type of Communion ware arose from the Baptist tradition?

22. What emotional ceremony accompanies celebrations of the Lord's Supper among some Appalachian Baptist subgroups?

23. What rites practiced by the Old German Baptist Brethren, as well as their practice of altar fellowship, recall the rites of the ancient Church?

24. The Christian Church (Disciples of Christ) and the Churches of Christ, both of a common origin in the "restoration movement," have a certain signature belief in the Lord's Supper. What is that belief?

25. What ancient practices did the restoration movement seek to revive?

26. True or false: Historically, the clergy have preached and administered the Lord's Supper among the Disciples of Christ.

27. What five elements are always parts of a Disciples of Christ worship service?

28. Although anti-creedal, what may be said broadly about the way in which the Christian Church (Disciples of Christ) and the Churches of Christ view the Lord's Supper?

29. What are "one-cuppers?"

30. What may be described as the changing nature of altar

fellowship among the Disciples of Christ?

31. What group arose from Scandinavian pietism, developed generally a Zwinglian doctrine of the Lord's Supper, and practices open Communion?

32. Who founded the Religious Society of Friends (Quakers)?

33. For Quakers, what is more important than external rites, such as the Lord's Supper?

34. True or false: Some Quakers have become Unitarian and therefore have placed themselves outside of the Christian faith and salvation.

35. What twentieth-century Christian development shares with the Quakers a strong emphasis on the inner immediacy of the Holy Spirit and has grown phenomenally to become the second-largest Christian tradition apart from Roman Catholicism?

36. What is the relative frequency and status or influence of the Lord's Supper among various Pentecostal groups?

37. The largest Pentecostal group has a confession of the Lord's Supper that is essentially a memorial meal. What is this group?

38. The International Church of the Foursquare Gospel, whose confession of faith also uses Zwinglian terms, was founded by what person?

39. True or false: Among the Pentecostal groups known as Church of God, the Lord's Supper consists of bread and grape juice, is celebrated infrequently, and accompanies foot washing in some cases.

40. True or false: The Apostolic Faith Church ascribes healing properties to the Lord's Supper.

41. True or false: Some Pentecostal groups do not celebrate the Lord's Supper.

42. True or false: Some Pentecostals believe that Melchizedek celebrated the first Holy Communion.

43. True or false: Two Pentecostal groups use water instead of wine or grape juice in the Lord's Supper.

44. True or false: Snake-handling Pentecostal groups have frequent celebrations of the Lord's Supper.

45. What is the largest of the Adventist groups that has a Zwinglian doctrine of the Lord's Supper and celebrates it quarterly?

46. What do Seventh-Day Adventists use for the elements in the Lord's Supper that are in common use among American Zwinglian churches?

47. What always precedes the Lord's Supper among them?

48. What kind of altar fellowship do Seventh-Day Adventists practice?

49. True or false: Two Adventist groups celebrate the Lord's Supper annually on the fourteenth of Nisan, the lunar anniversary of Christ's death.

50. What Zwinglian group considers the Lord's Supper to be very important and celebrates it every Sunday?

51. Who founded the church and social organization, whose theology is similar to the Quakers, known as the Salvation Army?

52. Since the Salvation Army does not believe that the rite of the Lord's Supper was intended for perpetual celebration, what does it consider to be the "Lord's Supper" among its adherents?

Lutheran Churches

1. What principle did Martin Luther apply to the late medieval doctrine of the Lord's Supper in order to arrive at the Lutheran confession of the doctrine?

2. How are the Lord's Words to be understood?

3. Who receives the body and blood of Christ in the Supper? To what effect?

4. What determines whether one receives forgiveness or judgment?

5. True or false: Lutherans allow the sacramental union to remain a mystery, confessed on the basis of Christ's words.

6. Who argued effectively against the false charge that Lutherans believe in consubstantiation?

7. Although Lutherans agree that the Words of Institution effect the bodily, supernatural presence of Christ, what has been their disagreement about when that presence takes place?

8. What do Lutherans say about the extreme views held by those involved in the disagreement over the moment that the presence occurs?

9. What have Lutherans said of the enduring presence of the body and blood of Christ in union with the physical elements?

10. What is the teaching regarding the unity of the sacramental action?

11. What are some possible means of respectfully handling the elements that remain following the celebration of the Supper?

12. What manner of bread and wine are used?

13. What is the preference in terms of the distribution of the wine?

14. What has been the historic Lutheran practice of confession and absolution prior to receiving the Lord's Supper?

15. What has changed regarding that practice?

16. What happened to the frequency of Lutheran celebrations of the Lord's Supper over the centuries?

17. True or false: The matter of a Lutheran pastor communing himself has been somewhat controversial among Lutherans throughout the centuries.

18. What has been the historic practice of altar fellowship among Lutherans? Why would that practice occur? (See Question 3 above.)

19. True or false: The Evangelical Lutheran Church in Canada and the Evangelical Lutheran Church in America have been pioneers in communing infants, thus departing from over four centuries of Lutheran witness to the effect that only those capable of discerning the body and blood of Christ may commune.

20. What was the first major breach of closed Communion among Lutherans?

21. In whom did the "American Lutheran" movement that departed from the historic Lutheran confession of the Lord's Supper find its guiding force?

22. What Lutheran body in the United States practices open Communion, as did some of its predecessors, and remains in fellowship with churches that do not confess the Lutheran doctrine of the Lord's Supper?

23. What Lutheran churches in the United States have historically practiced closed Communion and related fellowship practices?

24. Which of these three has faced significant internal challenge and debate concerning its historic fellowship practices?

25. What publication helped popularize the Baptist term "close Communion" in the Missouri Synod?

26. What belief regarding the presence of Christ's body and blood in the Lord's Supper tends to correlate with open Communion fellowship?

27. Why is the practice of closed Communion a truly loving way to serve Christians that have different beliefs regarding the Lord's Supper?

11 | CONSENSUS—DIVINE OR MERELY HUMAN?

The 1529 meeting of Martin Luther, Ulrich Zwingli, and other sixteenth-century church reformers in Marburg was a harbinger of things to come regarding human attempts to reach consensus on the Lord's Supper, even though no final agreement was reached. A second attempt took place when Martin Bucer and Philip Melanchthon worked to achieve the *Wittenberg Concord* in 1536. They explained the Lord's Supper using language that Lutherans and some Zwinglians could accept, even though they interpreted the words differently. The problem remains, however, that Christ does not abide ambiguity when He said, "This is My body." This "peace" regarding the Lord's Supper only lasted 16 years.[1] John Calvin and Heinrich Bullinger, Zwingli's successor, established the 1549 *Zurich Consensus*.[2] They agreed that Baptism and the Lord's Supper are more than mere signs, and that they are means of grace that convey the benefits of redemption.[3]

True consensus is a common confession of doctrine that leads to doctrinal fellowship. When, in 1817, Frederick Wilhelm III of Prussia proclaimed a union between Lutheran and Reformed churches in his domain, a fellowship based on human principles came into being. Frederick prescribed a new liturgy for the celebration of the Sacrament in which "he intentionally used an indefinite and ambiguous formula for the distribution in Holy Communion."[4] People who did not agree regarding the Lord's Supper were placed in Communion fellowship with each other. Lutheran and Reformed pastors were required by law to commune those of both prior churches.[5] In sizeable congregations, Lutheran and Reformed pastors were sometimes compelled to serve on the same staff. There is a story of two pastors in such a situation in the Palatinate who tried to wrest the chalice from each other's hands during a celebration, because they felt the effect of the Sacrament would depend on whether a Lutheran or a Reformed pastor administered the cup.[6] Whether in Europe or in North America, those who espoused the union concluded that differences in doctrine regarding the Lord's Supper were finally inconsequential. A vague, human consensus was the result of the human fellowship.

In Germany some fervently disagreed with the Prussian Union and refused to participate in it. Such pastors include Claus Harms, the author of the 1817 Ninety-Five Theses that inaugurated the Confessional Lutheran movement of the nineteenth century. Pastors such as Johann Scheibel in Silesia, Martin Stephan in Leipzig, and others suffered persecution for their faith.[7] Lutheran pastor August Kavel said that pastors like him who ventured to preach the Gospel and administer the sacraments according to the formula used by Lutherans for 300 years "were thrown into prison, and compelled with their families to quit their respective parishes." This was the case even if they conducted their administrations only in private homes.[8] Lutheran laypersons were subjected to fines and imprisonments. Their cattle were seized, along with their furniture and implements.[9] Some left Germany in protest and immigrated to various places, including the United States, Brazil, and Australia where they could worship without compromising their faith.[10]

A number of key events in the twentieth century have had a bearing on the matter of consensus concerning the Lord's Supper. These included the World Mission Conference of 1910 in Edinburgh, the rise of the Faith and Order movement in 1927, the founding of the World Council of Churches at Amsterdam in 1948, and the Second Vatican Council in 1962–1965.[11] Vatican II broke new ground when it acknowledged that the Body of Christ also includes Christians of other churches and Communions by making them implicit members of the Roman Church.[12] Principles underlying these events derive from the liturgical renewal movements among Roman Catholics and Protestants, coupled first with historical-critical methods and later with postmodern ones. A papal encyclical issued in 1943 made it possible for Roman Catholic scholars to engage in the same kind of biblical scholarship as was being done in Protestant churches.[13] The broad rejection of dogma that had begun among Protestants in the time of Mosheim and Lessing now engaged the paradigm of liturgy, tradition, and scripture in the Roman Church. Lutheran scholar Edmund Schlink said that the advent of the ecumenical movement "was the most significant event in the history of the church" during the twentieth century. He opined, "Recognition of the one Christ working among us demands that we advance to unity. This unity cannot be shared without fellowship in the Lord's Supper."[14] The Anglicans and the Eastern Orthodox made an early, unsuccessful attempt at unity in the 1920's.[15] Subsequent events, however, have led to organic union without agreement in doctrine.

Events on the World Stage

- Some Lutherans and the Church of South India reached an agreement on the Lord's Supper in 1955 and entered into Communion fellowship. Through their discussions with the Lutherans, the Church of South India developed a fundamental statement on the Lord's Supper for themselves.[16] A joint statement entitled *Agreed Statement on the Lord's Supper* followed.[17] The statement employed language that bridged the gap between the otherwise exclusive doctrines of the Lutherans and those bodies that had previously come together to form the church of South India—Anglicans, Methodists, and the Union Church of South India (Presbyterians and Congregationalists).[18]

- In Holland, the Dutch Reformed and Lutheran churches did so in 1956. The Lutheran-Reformed Consensus on the Holy Communion did not establish a basis for interCommunion because that had already existed for about 100 years. In this document, the Lutherans and the Reformed "simply agreed that they do not agree."[19]

- Three churches in Germany—the Lutheran, Reformed, and United—similarly came to an agreement in 1957.[20] Lutheran, Reformed, and United or Union territorial churches in Germany began a quest for consensus in 1937 when one of the United churches, the Evangelical Church of the Old Prussian Union, published a document called the Halle Resolution. They stated that "separation with regard to the Lord's Supper between Lutherans, Reformed and United is not justified by the differences of the sixteenth century."[21] During World War II, the differences between these churches were set aside in "emergency" celebrations of the Lord's Supper.[22] Postwar internal displacement only exacerbated these conditions and effectively erased old territorial boundaries.[23] After the war, the three churches joined together in a federation known as the Evangelical Church in Germany (EKD). Not all were ready to make emergency practice the basis for permanent Lord's Supper fellowship. In 1947, a commission was appointed to discuss the doctrine of the Lord's Supper and its relation to the life of the church. In 1957 this commission produced a doctrinal statement titled the Arnoldshain Theses.[24] Historical-critical analysis of the scriptural texts formed the basis of the study.[25] The historic doctrinal positions of the several churches were relegated to second place in the discussions.[26] While these theses did not result in Communion fellowship between the churches involved, progress was made toward consensus.[27]

• In 1973 the Lutheran, Reformed, and Union churches in Germany, the Waldensian Church, and the Church of the Czech Brethren signed the *Leuenberg Agreement*.[28] In this agreement, church fellowship, or full Communion, between the churches involved was declared. Since that time more than 80 churches worldwide have signed the *Leuenberg Agreement*. The document says, "In this Agreement the participating churches acknowledge that their relationship to one another has changed since the time of the Reformation."[29] They state that "with the advantage of historical distance it is easier today to discern the common elements in the witness of the churches of the Reformation."[30] This distance, characterized by new modes of life and thought, they attribute to four factors: theological wrestling with the questions of modern times, advances in biblical research, the movements of church renewal, and the rediscovery of the ecumenical horizon.[31] They define a more human-oriented definition of the Lord's Supper and affirm "the risen Jesus Christ imparts himself in his body and blood, given up for all, through his word of promise with bread and wine. He thereby grants us forgiveness of sins and sets us free for a new life of faith. He enables us to experience anew that we are members of his body. He strengthens us for service to all men."[32]

• In 1988 the Church of England and the Evangelical churches in East and West Germany adopted the *Meissen Common Statement*. This agreement led to "mutual Eucharistic hospitality" and to occasional joint celebrations of the Lord's Supper.[33] Consensus on the Lord's Supper has also been declared by Anglican churches in Great Britain and Ireland, and Evangelical Lutheran churches of Denmark, Estonia, Finland, Iceland, Latvia, Lithuania, Norway, and Sweden. In a series of meetings beginning in 1989, representatives from the churches developed the *Porvoo Declaration*, and an explanation entitled the *Porvoo Common Statement*, named for the Finnish city in which they were enacted.[34] Intercommunion between most of those bodies existed before the official Porvoo agreements,[35] but the adoption of the *Declaration* and *Common Statement* effectively merged the Anglican and Lutheran churches into one church.[36] In an evaluation of the *Porvoo Declaration* and *Common Statement* the members of the Systematic Theology departments of the two seminaries in The Lutheran Church—Missouri Synod write that the Porvoo text "as evidence of doctrinal consensus as a proper basis for pulpit and altar fellowship is to surrender the Lutheran confession in general and the Sacrament of the Altar in particular. One must not blame the Anglicans here. Porvoo does not in the least compromise their theology."[37]

• The World Council of Churches has been actively involved in the consensus movement. At their 1952 Conference of Faith and Order, held in Lund, Sweden, their central committee agreed to procedures whereby the Lord's Supper could be celebrated at World Council of Churches gatherings. They did not exclude the possibility of some holding separate services of Communion within the context of a conference.[38] The 1963 World Council on Faith and Order adopted an ecumenical consensus statement regarding the Lord's Supper: "The Lord's Supper is a gift of God to his church, is a Sacrament of the presence of the crucified and glorified Christ until he come, and a means whereby the sacrifice of the cross, which we proclaim, is operative in the church."[39] The Faith and Order Commission of the World Council of Churches presented three statements entitled *One Baptism, One Eucharist, One Ministry* to the 1975 Council assembly in Nairobi, Kenya. They asked the member churches to study the texts of these statements. Denominations not in affiliation with the World Council of Churches were also invited to respond. The evaluation of changes and responses resulted in work that was started in 1977 on a revised document entitled *Baptism, Eucharist and Ministry*.[40]

At a 1982 gathering in Lima, Peru, over 100 Christian theologians considered the final draft "ripe enough for presentation to all the churches," and the Faith and Order Commission adopted the text.[41] Max Thurian of France has written, "Since that historic day, the Lima document has become a key text for all Christians" and that "it is no longer possible to discuss baptism, eucharist and ministry without making this document the basis of reflection."[42] At least 180 official responses to the final text by both member and nonmember church bodies were submitted, included those from non-members like The Lutheran Church—Missouri Synod[43] and the Roman Catholic Church. It became the most widely discussed document in modern ecumenical history.[44] A final report on the *Baptism, Eucharist and Ministry* paper was made at the assembly of the World Council of Churches when they met in 1991 in Canberra, Australia.[45]

Events in North America

• Roman Catholics and Lutherans in the United States have met in dialogue since 1956. Two series of sessions dealt primarily with the Lord's Supper. The first, from 1966–1967, dealt with "Eucharist as Sacrifice."[46] Much time was spent in attempting to clarify words and concepts in the context of twentieth century thought. The Lutherans had questions regarding the Catholic understanding of the word "sacrifice," as did the Catholics concerning the Lutheran "real presence" doctrine.[47] The subject of "Eucharist and Ministry" was chosen for the 1968–1970 dialogue series. Meanings of terms was again a concern. It was again discovered that when Catholics and Lutherans use the same words they do not always mean the same things.[48] These dialogues did not lead to extension of altar and pulpit fellowship among the parties.

• In 1979–1981 a series of six dialogues were held between Lutherans and Baptists in the United States. A wide range of topics was discussed, including Baptism and the Lord's Supper. No consensus on the Lord's Supper was attempted or achieved, but the discussions were congenial, polite, and informative.[49]

• In 1960, the United Lutheran Church in America (ULCA), a predecessor of the LCA and ELCA, adopted a significant resolution having a long-term effect on future movements toward consensus. In the resolution entitled Statement About the Sacrament of the Altar, the ULCA said, "The time is ripe for Lutherans to initiate theological discussions with other Christian bodies regarding intercommunion."[50] Dialogues between Reformed and Lutherans in North America began in 1962–1966. There was majority agreement that during the Reformation both the Lutherans and the Reformed had evangelical intentions in their understandings of the Lord's Supper. The conferees also agreed that the total Christ, the divine-human person, is present in the Lord's Supper, but they gave no explanation as to how He is present. In their final report, they said that "as a result of our studies and discussions we see no insuperable obstacles to pulpit and altar fellowship."[51] A second dialogue series was held in 1972–1974. Subjects relative to the Lord's Supper that were discussed included the Leuenberg Agreement. A third series of dialogues between Reformed and Lutherans took place in 1981–1983. In the final report of this series of meetings entitled An Invitation to Action the participants said, "In the past Christians of the Reformed and Lutheran traditions have been deeply divided by controversy over the understanding of the Lord's Supper although both have strongly affirmed the real presence of Christ in the sacraments . . . "[52] Consequently, the American Lutheran Church, The Association of Evangelical Lutheran Churches, The Presbyterian Church (U.S.A.), the Reformed Church in America, and the United Church of Christ all took action recognizing each other as "churches in which the Gospel is proclaimed and the sacraments administered according to the ordinance of Christ," and to recognize "one another's celebration of the Lord's Supper as a means of grace in which Christ, truly present in the sacrament, is given and received."[53] The Lutheran Church in America called for more study.

• When the Evangelical Lutheran Church in America was created in 1988 by the merger of the American Lutheran Church, the

Lutheran Church in America, and the Association of Evangelical Lutheran Churches, the previous demurral by the Lutheran Church in America made null and void the official actions of the other churches involved.[54] A task force was appointed to enter into a new round of dialogues with the Reformed bodies.[55] In 1993 the results of their discussions were published in a document entitled *A Common Calling*. It acknowledged that the parties could not reconcile "the formulations of the churches' teaching on the Lord's Supper," but they said "the role of doctrinal statements in the changing churches had changed; even apparently irreconcilable language does not have to be church-dividing."[56] They recommended that the Evangelical Lutheran Church in America, the Presbyterian Church (U. S. A), the Reformed Church in America, and the United Church of Christ declare that they are in full Communion with one another.[57] A Formula of Agreement was prepared for official consideration by the four church bodies in their summer 1997 conventions. All four approved the proposed agreement; as a result, members may take the Lord's Supper in each other's churches and clergy can be shared among the denominations.

• Episcopalians and Lutherans in the United States have been engaged in dialogue concerning the Lord's Supper and other matters since 1969. The first series was held in 1969–1972. At the end of this series the participants reported that they agreed that the distinctive and central act of Christian worship consists of proclaiming the Gospel and celebrating the Sacrament. They felt that some measure of altar and pulpit fellowship between Lutherans and Episcopalians would be desirable.[58] A second series of dialogue meetings was held from 1976–1980. Mention was made of the fact that the Anglicans followed the Reformed view of "spiritual eating by faith" and that they denied that unbelievers partake of Christ.[59] They stated that the presence of Christ is proclaimed in various ways in the Lord's Supper liturgy.[60] In 1982 the *Agreement on Interim Eucharistic Sharing* initiated another round of Lutheran-Episcopal dialogue, carried on after the 1988 ELCA merger.[61] In 1996, a Lutheran-Episcopal coordinating committee made final revisions to the text of a *Concordat of Agreement*.[62] In its 1997 general convention, the Episcopal Church overwhelmingly approved the *Concordat of Agreement*.[63] The *Concordat* failed by a six-vote margin at the church-wide assembly of the Evangelical Lutheran Church in America. A Joint Lutheran-Episcopal committee revised and reissued the *Concordat* under the title *Called to Common Mission*.[64] The ELCA adopted the altered version in 1999[65] and the Episcopal Church accepted it in 2000.[66] The new relationship was celebrated at an inaugural service on January 6, 2001 at the National Cathedral in Washington.[67]

• Early in 2000, the Evangelical Lutheran Church in America and the Moravian Church in America entered into full Communion fellowship. There had long been strained feelings between these two groups (especially on the part of the Lutherans),[68] because of a negative encounter between Count Ludwig von Zinzendorf and Henry Melchior Mulenberg in 1742. The Lutheran-Moravian discussions achieved consensus on August 8, 1996.[69] Both denominations approved this, with the Moravians voting in 1998, and the Lutherans in 1999.[70] Although both churches apparently accept the *Unaltered Augsburg Confession* and Luther's Small Catechism,[71] the Lutheran confession of the body and blood of Christ "in, with and under the forms of bread and wine"[72] does not mesh with the Moravian disregard for the mode and extent of Christ's presence. They say that Jesus "is fully present with his promises and gifts in manners which God determines and actualizes through the Spirit."[73]

NOTES

1. E. H. Klotsche, *The History of Christian Doctrine,* rev. J. Theodore Mueller and David P. Scaer (1945; reprint, Grand Rapids: Baker, 1979), 193.

2. Ulrich Gäbler, *Ulrich Zwingli: His Life and Work,* trans. Ruth C. L. Gritsch (Philadelphia: Fortress, 1986), 159.

3. Charles Hodge, *Systematic Theology* (Grand Rapids: Eerdmans, 1997), 3:632.

4. A. Brauer, *Under the Southern Cross: History of the Evangelical Lutheran Church of Australia* (Adelaide, South Australia: Lutheran Publishing House, 1956), 6.

5. J. L. Neve, *Churches and Sects of Christendom,* rev. ed. (Blair, Nebr.: Lutheran

Publishing House, 1952), 380; Lars P. Qualben, *A History of the Christian Church*, rev. ed. (New York: Nelson, 1942), 396; David Schubert, *Kavel's People: From Prussia to South Australia* (Adelaide, South Australia: Lutheran Publishing House, 1956), 4, 57.

6. William H. Bartels, conversation with author, Breckenridge, Minn., 20 July 1997.

7. Brauer, *Southern Cross*, 7.

8. Schubert, *Kavel's People*, 60.

9. Brauer, *Southern Cross*, 20.

10. Julius Bodensieck, ed., *The Encyclopedia of the Lutheran Church* (Minneapolis: Augsburg, 1965), 2:1256; Brauer, *Southern Cross*, 20, 21; Eugene M. Skibbe, *Protestant Agreement on the Lord's Supper* (Minneapolis: Augsburg, 1968), 72.

11. Joseph A. Burgess, ed., *Lutherans in Ecumenical Dialogue: A Reappraisal* (Minneapolis: Augsburg, 1990), 16.

12. Ernest H. Falardeau, *One Bread and Cup: Source of Communion* (1987; reprint, Collegeville, Minn.: Liturgical Press, 1990), 95.

13. Burgess, *Lutherans*, 16.

14. Skibbe, *Protestant*, 5.

15. Neve, *Churches*, 65.

16. Neve, *Churches*, 30.

17. Neve, *Churches*, 31.

18. Neve, *Churches*, 29–44.

19. Neve, *Churches*, 46.

20. Skibbe, *Protestant*, 9.

21. Skibbe, *Protestant*, 73.

22. Skibbe, *Protestant*, 74, 75.

23. Skibbe, *Protestant*, 75.

24. Burgess, *Lutherans*, 13; Skibbe, *Protestant*, 76, 77.

25. Skibbe, *Protestant*, 78, 79.

26. Skibbe, *Protestant*, 79.

27. Skibbe, *Protestant*, 118.

28. Burgess, *Lutherans*, 37; "Leuenberg Agreement: Agreement Between Reformation Churches in Europe," *Evangelische Kirche in Deutschland (EKD)*, www.ekd.de/bekenntnisse/leuenengl.html (accessed 14 December 1998).

29. "Leuenberg Agreement," online, 1.

30. "Leuenberg Agreement," online, 1.

31. "Leuenberg Agreement," online, 3.

32. "Leuenberg Agreement," online, 6.

33. "The Porvoo Common Statement," *Concordia Theological Quarterly* 61, no. 1–2 (1997): 4.

34. "The Porvoo Declaration in Confessional Perspective," *Concordia Theological Quarterly* 61, no. 1–2 (1997), 35.

35. "Porvoo Declaration," 50, 51.

36. "Porvoo Declaration," 36.

37. "Porvoo Declaration," 46.

38. Bodensieck, *Encyclopedia*, 2:1343.

39. Bodensieck, *Encyclopedia*, 2:1343.

40. Max Thurian, ed., *Churches Respond to BEM: Official Responses to the "Baptism, Eucharist and Ministry" Text* (Geneva: World Council of Churches, 1986–88), 14; *Towards an Ecumenical Consensus on Baptism, the Eucharist and the Ministry* (Geneva: World Council of Churches, 1977), 21.

41. Thurian, *Churches Respond*, 1:2.

42. Thurian, *Churches Respond*, 1:2.

43. Thurian, *Churches Respond*, 3:131.

44. Thurian, *Churches Respond*, 4:x; 6:1x.

45. Thurian, *Churches Respond*, 6:xi.

46. Paul C. Empie and T. Austin Murphy, ed., *The Eucharist as Sacrifice: Lutherans and Catholics in Diaglue III* (Washington: Bishops' Committee for Ecumenical and Interreligious Affairs and New York: National Committee of the Lutheran World Federation, 1967), 17, 24, 25.

47. Empie, *Eucharist*, 3.

48. Empie, *Eucharist* (forward), 8.

49. Burgess, *Lutherans*, 70.

50. Skibbe, *Protestant*, 24.

51. Burgess, *Lutherans*, 34, 35.

52. Burgess, *Lutherans*, 39.

53. Burgess, *Lutherans*, 41; Karlfreid Froehlich, "Lutheran Reformed Full Communion: An Argument for Voting Yes," *Lutheran Forum* 31, no. 2 (Summer 1997): 30, 31.

54. Burgess, *Lutherans*, 41; Froehlich, "Lutheran," 30, 31.

55. Froehlich, "Lutheran," 31.

56. Froehlich, "Lutheran," 31.

57. *Lutheran—Episcopal, Lutheran—Reformed, and Lutheran—Roman Catholic Ecumenical Proposals Documents for Action by the 1997 Churchwide Assembly: Evangelical Lutheran Church in America* (Chicago: Evangelical Lutheran Church in America, 1996), 18.

58. Burgess, *Lutherans*, 111.

59. Burgess, *Lutherans*, 112.

60. Burgess, *Lutherans*, 112.

61. Burgess, *Lutherans*, 50; *Ecumenical Proposals ELCA*, 3.

62. *Ecumenical Proposals ELCA*, 4.

63. "Lutherans vote for closer ecumenical ties with three other denominations," *Daily News (Wahpeton, ND),* 19 August 1997, sec. A, p. 12.

64. Erin Hemme Froslie, "Full Speed Ahead," *The (Fargo, ND) Forum,* 14 April 2000, sec. C, p. 1.

65. "Episcopal Church considers alliance with Lutherans," *The (Fargo, ND) Forum,* 7 July 2000, sec. A, p. 6.

66. Stephen P. Wagner, "Episcopal Lutheran alliance supported," *The (Fargo, ND) Forum,* 8 July 2000, sec. A, p. 1.

67. Jean Coffey Lyles, "Decorum in Denver," *Christian Century* (July 10–26, 2000): 743.

68. *Questions & Answers related to full communion between the Evangelical Lutheran Church in America and the Moravian Church in America* (n.p.: Evangelical Lutheran Church in America, 1998), 9.

69. *Questions & Answers,* 5–7.

70. *Questions & Answers,* 2.

71. *Following Our Shepherd to Full Communion: Report of the Lutheran-Moravian Dialogue with Recommendations for Full Communion in Worship, Fellowship and Mission* (n.p.: Evangelical Lutheran Church in America, 1998), 5.

72. *Following Our Shepherd,* 5.

73. *Following Our Shepherd,* 27.

STUDY QUESTIONS

EVENTS ON THE WORLD STAGE

1. What have attempts by humans to establish a man-made, ambiguous consensus regarding the Lord's Supper had in contrast with Christ's words?

2. Although the 1529 Marburg Colloquy failed to produce a breakthrough, the 1536 Wittenberg Concord did produce a "peace" of sorts among Lutherans and some Zwinglians, yet it only lasted sixteen years. What broke that "peace?"

3. When did the next major attempt at achieving human "consensus," as opposed to true doctrinal unity, occur?

4. True or false: Elements of the Prussian Union included the religious persecution of Lutherans that held to historic beliefs, including imprisonment and seizure of property that affected both pastors and laity.

5. What major events have propelled the twentieth-century ecumenical movement?

6. What kind of "union" among churches has this movement generated?

7. Give a list of documents, with their dates and places, that have caused churches on the international stage with mutually exclusive doctrines of the Lord's Supper to cast aside their doctrinal differences and agree to a false, human "consensus."

8. True or false: Intercommunion between various signatory bodies to some of these documents existed prior to the official agreement to establish it.

EVENTS IN NORTH AMERICA

1. True or false: Roman Catholics and Lutherans in the United States have met in dialogue since 1956.

2. What important observation arose from these meetings?

3. What impact have these meetings had on fellowship?

4. What 1960 United Lutheran Church document proved to be a template and harbinger of future moves toward human "consensus?"

5. What 1993 document culminated from thirty years of dialog between mainline American Lutherans and Reformed groups, calling for mutual intercommunion?

6. What 1997 document established such intercommunion?

7. What document, a revision of the earlier *Concordat of Agreement*, established mainline Lutheran-Episcopal intercommunion in 2000?

8. True or false: The Evangelical Lutheran Church in America and the Moravian Church in America recently agreed to intercommunion even though their doctrines of the Lord's Supper do not agree.

CONCLUSION

WHAT DOES THIS MEAN?

D oes the apparent cacophony of doctrine and the human attempts to reach consensus without doctrinal agreement outlined in Unit IV seem confusing? How has it happened that four little words, "This is My body," have been so variously interpreted, resulting in such a myriad of applications and beliefs?

We only have the words of our Lord for our Christian life and for our salvation. They are enough. Jesus said, "Heaven and earth will pass away, but My words will not pass away" (Matthew 24:35). Christ's words will endure forever. That was certain for the early church and it is certain today. When some fathers in the early church attempted to use philosophical language to speak to problems and issues in their day, they sometimes helped lay the groundwork for problems in years to come. In spite of that, the church, for many centuries, held tenaciously to the Word of God.

Until the time of the late Middle Ages, there existed considerably less disagreement regarding the Lord's Supper. During the Reformation, we see Calvin and Zwingli making appeals to philosophy, saying how Christ's body may be present. We see Luther with Scripture alone: "This is My body." That is not only a shibboleth or litmus test for Wittenberg, but also for Rome, Zurich, Geneva, Canterbury, and elsewhere. Unfortunately, where the foundations have been laid on the shifting sands of human opinion, there divisions have been more prevalent. We see that most among the Zwinglians. That is less so for the Calvinists, yet it still remains present. Rome simply avoids the issue by appealing to papal authority. The Eastern Orthodox recite their liturgies. Only the Lutherans cry "Scripture alone!"

Now, even that voice is muted. In an outward appearance of unity, some Lutherans, not only overseas but also in our country, have joined together with members of other denominations and agreed to disagree with them about the Lord's Supper. While the author and his synod do not question the sincere intent and honest resolve of these Lutherans, they are sorely disappointed in their action. In an open letter to the professional church workers in his North Wisconsin District, Arleigh L. Lutz, chairman of the Council of Presidents of the Missouri Synod, wrote, "When I heard the news, I was saddened and dismayed."[1] Missourians and other orthodox Lutherans feel badly about this development for several reasons, including the fact that it is only an illusion of unity without scriptural basis. Unity based on the concept of agreeing to disagree is not the true unity of which our Lord spoke when He expressed His desire "that they may be one" (John 17:11). Nor is it the "one Lord, one faith, one baptism" unity of which St. Paul wrote to the Ephesians (Ephesians 4:5). The unity called for by Jesus and Paul is a unity based on the clear Word of God, and that Word alone. When Jesus prayed to His Father He said, "I have given them Your word" (John 17:14). There are no ambiguities in the divine words of Jesus, including those He uttered when He distributed the Lord's Supper for the first time. A Missouri Synod pastor, Charles P. Schaum, has aptly said, "The Lord's Supper of the true Church is founded on four little words: 'This is My body.'"[2] In this regard, Pastor Schaum made a timely warning lest "God's people . . . sell their inheritance for a bowl of pottage" and advised that they instead "rejoice in the gift received."[3] In our rejoicing, we sing and pray with Martin Luther:

> O Lord, we praise you, bless you, and adore you,
> In thanksgiving bow before you.
> Here with your body and your blood you nourish
> Our weak souls that they may flourish.
> O Lord, have mercy!
>
> May your body, Lord, born of Mary,
> That our sins and sorrows did carry,
> And your blood for us plead
> In all trial, fear, and need:
> O Lord, have mercy!
>
> Your holy body into death was given,
> Life to win for us in heaven.
> No greater love than this to you could bind us;
> May this feast of that remind us!
> O Lord, have mercy!
>
> Lord, your kindness so much did move you
> That your blood now moves us to love you.
> All our debt you have paid;
> Peace with God once more is made.
> O Lord, have mercy!
>
> May God bestow on us his grace and favor
> To please him with our behavior
> And live together here in love and union
> Nor repent this blest communion.
> O Lord, have mercy!

> Let not your good Spirit forsake us,
> But that heav'nly-minded he make us;
> Give your Church, Lord, to see
> Days of peace and unity.
> O Lord, have mercy![4]

NOTES

1. Arleigh L. Lutz, letter to professional church workers in the North Wisconsin District, The Lutheran Church—Missouri Synod, Wausau, Wis., September 1997, 1.

2. Charles P. Schaum, memo to author, 29 May 2003.

3. Schaum, memo.

4. *Lutheran Worship* (St. Louis: Concordia, 1982), Hymn 238.

FOR FURTHER READING

Aulén, Gustaf. *Eucharist and Sacrifice*. Translated by Eric H. Wahlstrom. Philadelphia: Muhlenberg Press, 1958.

Barth, Markus. *Rediscovering the Lord's Supper: Communion with Israel, with Christ, and Amo g the Guests*. Atlanta: John Knox Press, 1988.

Burgess, Joseph A., ed. *Lutherans in Ecumenical Dialogue: A Reappraisal*. Minneapolis: Augsburg, 1990.

Chemnitz, Martin. *Examination of the Council of Trent: Part Two*. Translated by Fred Kramer. St. Louis: Concordia, 1978.

Chemnitz, Martin. *The Lord's Supper*. Translated by J. A. O. Preus. St. Louis: Concordia, 1979.

Chytraeus, David. *Chytraeus on Sacrifice: A Reformation Treatise in Biblical Theology*. Translated and edited by John Warwick Montgomery. St. Louis: Concordia, 1962.

Conkin, Paul K. *Cane Ridge: America's Pentecost*. Madison, Wi.: The University of Wisconsin Press, 1990.

Cruz, Joan Carroll. *Eucharistic Miracles and Eucharistic Phenomena in the Lives of the Saints*. Rockford, Ill.: Tan Books and Publishers, Inc., 1987.

Dorgan, Howard. *Giving Glory to God in Appalachia: Worship Practices of Six Baptist Subdenominations*. Knoxville: University of Tennessee Press, 1987.

Elert, Werner. *Eucharist and Church Fellowship in the First Four Centuries*. Translated by N. E. Nagel. St. Louis: Concordia Publishing House, 1966.

Emminghaus, Johannes H. *The Eucharist: Essence, Form, Celebration*. Translated by Matthew J. O'Connell. Collegeville, Minn.: Liturgical Press, 1978.

Falardeau, Ernest R. *One Bread and Cup: Source of Communion*. 1987. Reprint, Collegeville, Minn.: Liturgical Press, 1990.

Hay, Leo C. *Eucharist: A Thanksgiving Celebration*. Wilmington, Del.: Michael Glazier, Inc., 1989.

Henry, Jim. *In Remembrance of Me: A Manual on Observing the Lord's Supper*. Nashville, Tenn.: Broadman & Holman Publishers, 1998.

Heppe, Heinrich. *Reformed Dogmatics Set Out and Illustrated from the Sources.* Revised and edited by Ernst Bizer. Translated by G. T. Thomson. London: George Allen & Unwin Ltd., 1950.

Higgins, A. J. B. *The Lord's Supper in the New Testament.* London: SCM, 1952.

Huebsch, Bill. *Rethinking Sacraments: Holy Moments in Daily Living.* Mystic, Conn.: Twenty-Third Publications, 1989.

Jacobson, J. Robert. *Besides Women & Children: A Guide for Parents & Pastors on Infant & Child Communion.* Rev. ed. Camrose, Alberta: Concord Canada, 1981.

Jenson, Robert W. *Visible Words: The Interpretation and Practice of Christian Sacraments.* Philadelphia: Fortress, 1978.

Jeremias, Joachim. *The Eucharistic Words of Jesus.* Translated by Norman Perrin. London: SCM Press, 1966.

Kodell, Jerome. *The Eucharist in the New Testament.* 1988. Reprint, Collegeville, Minn.: Liturgical Press, 1991.

Krauth, Charles P. *The Conservative Reformation and Its Theology.* 1871. Reprint, Minneapolis: Augsburg, 1963.

Larere, Philippe. *The Lord's Supper: Toward an Ecumenical Understanding of the Eucharist.* Translated by Patrick Madigan. Collegeville, Minn.: Liturgical Press, 1993.

LaVerdiere, Eugene. *The Eucharist in the New Testament and the Early Church.* Collegeville, Minn.: Liturgical Press, 1996.

Luther, Martin. *Luther's Works: Word and Sacrament II.* Vol. 36. Edited by Helmut T. Lehmann and Abdel Ross Wentz, Translated by Frederich C. Ahrens and Abdel Ross Wentz. Philadelphia: Fortress, 1959. This volume contains early writings by Luther on the Lord's Supper (1520–1526).

Luther, Martin. *Luther's Works: Word and Sacrament III.* Vol. 37. Edited by Helmut T. Lehmann and Robert H. Fischer, Translated by Robert H. Fischer. Philadelphia: Fortress, 1961. This volume contains treatises in which Luther discusses the positions of Zwingli and the "Fanatics" on the Lord's Supper (1527–1528).

Luther, Martin. *Luther's Works: Word and Sacrament IV.* Vol. 38. Edited by Helmut T. Lehmann and Martin E. Lehmann, Translated by Martin E. Lehmann. Philadelphia: Fortress, 1971. This volume deals with the development of Luther's concept of the Lord's Supper (1529–1544).

Mathison, Keith A. *Given for You: Reclaiming Calvin's Doctrine of the Lord's Supper.* Phillipsburg, N.J.: P & R Publishers, 2002.

McEachern, Alton H. *Here at Thy Table, Lord: Enriching the Observance of the Lord's Supper.* Nashville: Broadman Press, 1977.

Reu, Johann M. *Two Treatises on the Means of Grace.* Columbus: Wartburg Press, n. d. Reprint, Minneapolis: Augsburg, 1952.

Rordorf, Willy et al. *The Eucharist of the Early Christians.* Translated by Matthew J. O'Connell. New York: Pueblo Publishing Company, 1978.

Sasse, Hermann. *This Is My Body: Luther's Contention for the Real Presence in the Sacrament of the Altar.* Rev. ed. Adelaide, South Australia: Lutheran Publishing House, 1977.

Sasse, Hermann. *We Confess the Sacraments*. Translated by Norman Nagel. St. Louis: Concordia, 1985.

Schmeling, Gaylin R. *God's Gift to You: A Devotional Book on the Lord's Supper*. Milwaukee: Northwestern, 2001.

Schmeling, Gaylin R. "The Theology of the Lord's Supper." *Lutheran Synod Quarterly* 28, no. 4 (1988), 3.

Scott, Stephen. *The Amish Wedding and Other Special Occasions of the Old Order Communities*. Intercourse, Pa.: Good Books, 1988.

Skibbe, Eugene M. *Protestant Agreement on the Lord's Supper*. Minneapolis: Augsburg, 1968.

Stookey, Laurence Hull. *Eucharist: Christ's Feast with the Church*. Nashville: Abingdon, 1993.

Teigen, Bjarne Wollan. *The Lord's Supper in the Theology of Martin Chemnitz*. Brewster, Mass.: Trinity Lutheran Press, 1986.

Theology and Practice of the Lord's Supper. Commission on Theology and Church Relations, The Lutheran Church—Missouri Synod, 1983.

The Use of the Means of Grace: A Statement on the Practice of Word and Sacrament. Evangelical Lutheran Church in America, Minneapolis: Augsburg, 1997.

VanderWilt, Jeffrey. *Communion with Non-Catholic Christians: Risks, Challenges, and Opportunities*. Collegeville, Minn.: Liturgical Press, 2003.

Welker, Michael. *What Happens in Holy Communion?* Translated by John F. Hoffmeyer. Grand Rapids: Eerdmans, 2000.

ABOUT THE AUTHOR

Ernest Bartels is a native of Tecumseh, Nebraska. After graduating from Concordia Theological Seminary in Springfield, Illinois, he pastored congregations of The Lutheran Church—Missouri Synod for 45 years (1950–1995). The churches he served were located at Grandin, Williston, and Wahpeton in North Dakota, and at Osseo, Kaukauna, Cleghorn, and Fall Creek in northern Wisconsin. He was a vice president of the North Dakota District of his church body for a number of years. Bartels's education includes five graduate degrees: Master of Divinity, Master of Theology in Systematic Theology, Doctor of Ministry in Pastoral Ministry, Doctor of Religious Studies, and Doctor of Philosophy in Lutheran Historical Research. Concordia Theological Seminary in Fort Wayne, Indiana, gave him their *Servus Ecclesiae Christi* award, and he was recognized in the Seminary Partners program of Concordia Seminary in St. Louis, Missouri. He has authored numerous scholarly articles in *Lutheran Synod Quarterly*, and has been a contributor to three volumes of *The Concordia Pulpit*. His writings have also appeared in *Advance* and *Christian Century* magazines, and in *Affirm* and *Ministry Ideabank*. In 1950 he married Lois Juneau of Eau Claire, Wisconsin. Now retired, Dr. Bartels lives in Wahpeton, North Dakota, with his wife, Lois, and their daughter, Nancy. Their son, Robert, resides in Williston, North Dakota. Another son, John, passed away in 1980 at the early age of 28.

ANSWERS TO STUDY QUESTIONS

Unit I: The Lord's Supper in the Apostolic Era

Chapter 1: The Institution of the Lord's Supper

1. We use the term "Lord's Supper" because it occurs in the Bible and tells us who institutes, mandates, and gives us this Supper, namely, our Lord Jesus Christ. St. Paul uses the term in 1 Corinthians 11:20.

2. The accounts are found in Matthew 26:26–28; Mark 14:22–24; Luke 22:19, 20; and 1 Corinthians 11:23–25.

3. The common and essential words are "This is My body; this . . . is My blood." They are called the Words of Institution or the Dominical Words (*verba Domini*, the Lord's Words).

4. We base our findings on the evidence of the Synoptic Gospels. "Maundy" Thursday derives from the Latin for "mandate," as in Jesus' mandating and instituting the Lord's Supper before His death.

5. Jesus calls the Supper a "Passover" in Mark 22:15 and Luke 14:14.

6. True—the term was first used in the bull "Transiturus."

7. Lutherans in the United States, particularly those in the East, first began to use the term "real presence" around 1820 in their dialogues with other Protestants, while European Lutherans did not generally use it until about 1875.

8. The Roman Catholic Church teaches that the appearance of bread and wine remains, yet the substance actually changes to the body and blood of Christ. The Lutheran Church teaches that the body and blood of Christ are offered in a supernatural way, in, with, and under the visible elements of bread and wine. Calvinists teach that the body and blood are offered and received in a spiritual manner, yet they do not bind that action specifically to the natural reception of the

bread and wine, except to understand that it is a divine ordinance. Zwinglian churches believe that the Lord's Supper is a memorial ceremony, a meal in which the church remembers her Lord and His sacrifice.

9. These terms and others are linked to philosophy. Human philosophy cannot properly define God, but it can show, by means of grammar, logic, and rhetoric, how one can go into error and sinful chaos. Such terms best aid the biblical witness when they help foil human attempts, the thoughts and beliefs of the sinful world, to encroach on God's Word. These and other terms can also harm the biblical witness when used ignorantly or maliciously. Learning about these and other philosophical and theological terms helps one use the terms more wisely and helps one see when others use them improperly.

10. No, the setting does not invalidate or alter the Lord's Words, although failing to use bread and wine, the "fruit of the vine," as the elements for the Sacrament and failing to use the Lord's Words may diminish or eliminate the sacramental character of the act.

Chapter 2: The Bread of Life in the Gospel According to John

1. The Bread of Life narrative is found in John 6:35–58, following the feeding of the five thousand.

2. The turning of water into wine at the wedding in Cana (John 2:1–11) is said to be a sign that points to the Lord's Supper.

3. The Roman Catholics, Calvinists, and Zwinglians all believe that John 6 contains the doctrine of the Lord's Supper. Lutherans have generally rejected that belief.

4. Zwingli relies on John 6:63, "The flesh counts for nothing" (NIV), as the foundation of the doctrine of the Lord's Supper, not on the Words of Institution.

5. John was likely writing against the Gnostics who believed that flesh is evil and spirit is good. They doubted the physical incarnation of Jesus. Therefore, John wants to emphasize

Christ as God, the Word in human flesh that made His tabernacle among us (John 1:14).

6. They believe that Jesus is speaking of faith in the crucified Christ.

7. They understand it to be an appropriation on faith of the sacrificial death of Christ in order to receive the benefits of the Lord's Supper. They do not ascribe any benefit given through the physical eating of the consecrated bread and wine.

8. Jesus' act of foot-washing receives sacramental significance among these groups.

9. Jesus says, "I am the true vine" (NIV).

10. False—not only has this passage served to signify those two sacraments, but it has given rise to the practice among some Christians, including many in the ancient church, of mixing water and wine in the Lord's Supper.

11. The meal by the Sea of Tiberias (Galilee) in John 21:1–14 and the Emmaus meal in Luke 24:29–32 are thought by some to relate to the Lord's Supper.

Chapter 3: The Apostolic Era

1. Jesus' command is "this do in remembrance of Me" (Luke 22:19; 1 Corinthians 11:24).

2. Luke uses the term "breaking of bread" in Luke 22:19; Luke 24:13–35; Acts 2:42–46; 20:7–12; and Acts 27:33–38.

3. In the account of the Emmaus meal (Luke 24:13–35) and in the reference to a daily breaking of bread in Acts 2:46, some have suggested that these accounts do not refer properly to the Lord's Supper. Many have suggested that the breaking of bread in Acts 27 was not the Lord's Supper. Yet even those that have rejected these three references as belonging to the Lord's Supper still generally concede some kind of Eucharistic overtones.

4. Some churches adopted the agape or love feast that preceded

the celebration of the Lord's Supper. We see evidence of its abuse in 1 Corinthians 11:17–22.

5. In 1 Corinthians 11:17–22, Paul, having emphasized how Israel was set apart from the nations as the holy people of God, continues to stress the holiness of God's people in connection with the holiness of the Lord's Supper. He therefore begins to establish principles of church fellowship and closed Communion.

6. In 1 Corinthians 11:27–29, Paul instructs the church regarding the discernment of the body of Christ in order that one not drink judgment upon oneself.

7. One interpretation has been that one must recognize the presence of the body and blood of Christ in, with, and under the physical elements. That draws its basis from 1 Corinthians 10:16 and 11:23–26. Another interpretation has identified the body of Christ with the church and the act of discernment as proper conduct that respects the presence of Christ in the church at the event of the Lord's Supper. That rests mainly upon 10:31 and 11:18–22, 33.

8. That interpretation stands against the principle that the clear passages of Scripture always interpret those passages that are less clear.

9. We get "Communion" from 1 Corinthians 10:16.

10. We get "Lord's Table" from 1 Corinthians 10:21b.

11. In 1 Corinthians 11:26, Paul tells us that our eating and drinking of the Supper shows the Lord's death until He comes again.

12. Maranatha
Matthew 26:29; Mark 14:25; Luke 22:18

Unit II: The Lord's Supper in Ancient and Medieval Times

Chapter 4: The Early Church

1. The Lord's Supper was celebrated at least every Sunday and sometimes daily.

2. The Lord's Day

3. Early Christians generally worshipped in private homes.

4. Emperor Constantine

5. Such celebrations were held in cemeteries.

6. The sources are the Didache, the writings of Justin Martyr, and Hippolytus's Apostolic Tradition.

7. True

8. The Kiss of Peace

9. The ancient offerings consisted of the bread, water, and wine used in the celebration of the Lord's Supper, as well as milk and honey.

10. True

11. False

12. True

13. Secular authorities and Jewish antagonists contributed to the persecution of early Christians, thereby shaping their services to be secretive, simple, and brief. False rumors about the Christian Eucharist included allegations of homosexual drunken orgies and cannibalism by drinking the blood of infants.

14. False

15. True

16. True

17. False

18. True

19. The realistic view was also the most direct: it confessed that

the body and blood of Christ were present in the physical elements as body and blood indeed, following the consecration of the elements. The symbolic view held that the Word of God is applied to the physical elements so that the elements, with the Word, point to or serve as an allegory for that which they signify, namely, the body and blood of Christ. The metabolic view theorized that a spiritual transformation of the bread and wine into the body and blood of Christ occurred, while the bread and wine remained as bread and wine with respect to their physical substances.

20. Augustine made statements that sometimes supported the realistic view and at other times supported the symbolic view. Later theologians among different camps could cite Augustine in support of their respective positions. Each would claim to be correct and have a church father supporting him.

21. True

22. True

23. True

24. True

Chapter 5: Eastern Orthodoxy: The Lord's Supper as Liturgy

1. True

2. John of Damascus

3. They say that the Roman doctrine is a philosophical definition to which the mystery of the Lord's Supper has been subjected.

4. They use the term "mystery." They count seven sacred mysteries, including Holy Baptism, Unction (anointing) with Chrism, the Lord's Supper, Holy Orders, Marriage, and Unction with Oil.

5. The reasons are the purification of the soul, the remission of sins, the fellowship of the Holy Spirit, and the fulfillment of the kingdom of heaven.

6. False

7. False

8. True

9. They undertake self-examination (including private confession), fasting, and prayer.

10. The frequency is almost the same: Celebrations occur every Sunday and even daily in some settings and cultures.

11. Most use the Liturgy of St. John Chrysostom.

12. They use leavened bread.

13. The method is known as intinction.

14. They observe closed Communion.

Chapter 6: The Medieval Roman Catholic Church
Part A: The Development of Transubstantiation

1. The medieval period dates roughly from the ascension of Pope Gregory I in A.D. 590 to either the beginning of the Italian Renaissance or the posting of the Ninety-Five Theses (Disputation on the Power and Efficacy of Indulgences) in 1517.

2. Gregory declared that the Lord's Supper was the continuing unbloody sacrifice of Christ on the cross, foreshadowed by Old Testament sacrifices.

3. It made the offering of the unbloody sacrifice the sole prerogative of the priest.

4. He officially made it a fixed part of the liturgy in the celebration of the Lord's Supper.

5. True

6. The decision was that, based on the need for self-examination and the belief that reception of the Lord's Supper was not equal to Baptism in order that one be saved, infants would no longer receive Holy Communion.

7. The Eastern church uses leavened bread in loaves, while the Western church has used unleavened wafers since medieval times.

8. Radbertus represented the realist position and Ratramnus represented the spiritual position.

9. Radbertus taught that the Aristotelian substances of bread and wine were miraculously replaced by the substances of Christ's body and blood, while the Aristotelian accidents, the attributes of appearance, etc., remained those of bread and wine.

10. They both used John 6:63.

11. True

12. True

13. False

14. True

15. These factors led to the Corpus Christi celebration.

16. True

17. False

18. Reception in one kind, bread only on the tongue, was promoted by the fear of handling the elements and Lateran IV mandated it in 1215.

Part B: The Effects of Lateran IV

1. Lateran IV mandated the doctrines of transubstantiation and of the unbloody sacrifice of Christ by the priest in the Mass.

2. Penance and the Lord's Supper

3. The adoration of the host replaced the Lord's Supper.

4. The "Dry Mass"

5. John 1:14

6. The Council of Constance

7. Urban IV

8. True

9. Honorius III

10. True

11. Peter Lombard and Thomas Aquinas

12. False

13. He used Aristotelian metaphysics.

14. True

15. He asserted that Christ's body was present with respect to its substance but not with respect to its location, that is, illocally present.

16. Consubstantiation

Part C: Later Attempts at Reform

1. Wycliffe taught a spiritual or symbolic presence of the body of Christ.

2. He said that a substance may not be separated from its accidents because that would destroy the basic Aristotelian meaning of "substance." Transubstantiation, therefore, was not only impossible but also nonsense-talk.

3. Huss did not deny the doctrine of transubstantiation, but the Taborites rejected it.

4. Huss wanted the laity to receive the Sacrament in both kinds. The Roman Church wanted the laity to receive only one kind.

5. The Utraquists wanted both kinds in the Supper and espoused transubstantiation. The Taborites wanted both kinds and rejected transubstantiation. The Pickards held the Lord's Supper in contempt.

6. The Council of Basel

Unit III: The Lord's Supper Among the Protestant Reformers

Chapter 7: Luther's Sacramental Union

1. True

2. Lutherans appeal to this third genus to argue for an illocal presence of Christ's body and blood in the Lord's Supper that neither takes up nor evacuates space.

3. Christ's words of institution remain the surest defense of the sacramental union.

4. Those who believe the Words of Institution and "given and shed for you for the forgiveness of sins" worthily receive the benefits of the Sacrament.

5. Those who reject the Words of Institution for what they plainly say and reject or doubt "given and shed for you for the forgiveness of sins" unworthily receive the body and blood of Christ and fall under God's judgment.

6. Luther condemned the belief that the Mass was a good work, a continuing sacrifice of Christ, and a work that benefited the dead by getting them out of purgatory sooner.

7. Luther said that faith in the Sacrament justifies, not the mere doing of the Sacrament itself.

8. No, one may not self-commune; there must be at least two present.

9. He changed the role of the laity from mere observers to active participants.

10. Luther advocated closed Communion. The general basis for the Lord's Supper was the doctrinal, Lutheran confession of the sacramental union.

11. True

Chapter 8: Zwingli's Memorial Meal

1. Zwingli considered the "real presence" to be the spiritual presence of Christ in the hearts of His people as they received the Sacrament.

2. He said that "is" should be understood as "means" or "signifies."

3. Carlstadt's influence helped Zwingli to believe that Christ's body, like that of any other human, can be in only one place at one time, making any presence of Christ in the Supper only possible in a figurative or metaphorical sense.

4. True

5. The finite cannot take up the infinite.

6. The first emphasis is on the Lord's Supper as a celebration meal eaten in remembrance and thanksgiving for the redemption that God has provided in Christ. The second emphasis is the work of the Lord's Supper bringing the congregation together in love: the loving transformed nature of the fellowship of believers is evident and manifested.

7. False

8. Marburg

9. They could not agree on the Lord's Supper.

10. Martin Bucer

11. Philip Melanchthon

12. The Variata allowed a spiritual understanding of the Lord's Supper.

13. The Formula of Concord

14. Heinrich Bullinger

Chapter 9: Calvin's Spiritual Presence

1. They were Philip Melanchthon and Martin Bucer.

2. The 1549 Zurich Consensus, involving Calvin and Bullinger, established Calvin's middle way between Luther and Zwingli.

3. Only the people of God who believe receive its benefits.

4. Calvin asserts that the presence of the body of Christ is spiritual, not essential, yet he believes that the meal is an actual spiritual feeding of souls.

5. For Calvin, the Holy Spirit either lifted the soul of the believer to heaven to receive spiritually the body and blood of Christ, or provided the means for Christ to descend to spiritually feed the communicant.

6. Unbelievers only received bread and wine.

7. He believed that the Lord's Supper is, by definition, a profession of faith and therefore meaningless unless it is done publicly or in the presence of the elders of the church.

8. Calvin failed to institute frequent celebrations of the Lord's Supper.

9. True

10. True

Unit IV: The Lord's Supper Amidst Doctrinal Discord

Chapter 10: Where Are We Now? Innovations from the Reformation to the Present

The Roman Catholic Church

1. The council granted the pope the discretion to allow bishops near Protestant lands to authorize the celebration of the Mass in both kinds.

2. Pius V issued the 1570 Missal.

3. The laity were urged to more frequent Communion and to greater participation.

4. The liturgy and Scriptures were read and sung in the vernacular, while Communion in both kinds was generally permitted.

5. Fasting, adoration of the host, and other outward signs have lost importance, while inward, spiritual preparation has gained importance.

6. False

Calvinist Churches—Reformed, Church of England, Presbyterian, Puritans, Congregationalists, Methodist

1. Calvinist churches have discouraged "plastic-like" wafers.

2. Grape juice

3. True

4. The institution of Christ, the function of the visible elements as signs for our benefit, and the action of the Holy Spirit to confirm and increase faith.

5. The Evangelical Synod of North America

6. The Moravian Church

7. False: he first held a more Lutheran position, and then moved toward Calvinism.

8. True

9. The priest takes the bread and wine, gives thanks over them (including the words spoken by Jesus at the Last Supper), breaks the bread, and distributes the elements to the communicants.

10. They have observed open Communion.

11. John Knox

12. One may use "community feast" to describe it.

13. The revival movement developed from these seasons.

14. The 1801 Cane Ridge revival started the Second Great Awakening and moved the Unites States toward the religiosity commonly associated with the mid-nineteenth century.

15. They began to withdraw from revivals and move toward Communion Sundays instead of sacramental seasons.

16. Puritans chose to stay in the established church, while Separatists chose to leave it.

17. True

18. One had to have had a prior conversion experience.

19. The Half-Way Covenant was proposed, in which baptized children of church members could themselves remain members and present their children for Baptism, but could not receive the Lord's Supper.

20. They formed the United Church of Christ.

21. John Wesley

22. The concept of sacrifice, frequent celebrations of the Sacrament and fasting, as well as the agape, or love feast, were reintroduced by Wesley.

23. Wesley required that only ordained clergy could celebrate the

Lord's Supper, yet there were few Anglican clergy willing to do so among the Methodists.

24. Methodists were generally adamant abolitionists, thus attracting many blacks that were naturally opposed to slavery. Racial tension within Methodism, however, prompted blacks of that faith to request that they form their own congregations. When the request for black clergy was denied, they separated and formed what is now known popularly as the AME Church.

25. Thomas B. Welch

26. They practice open Communion.

Zwinglian Churches—Anabaptists, Schwenkfelders, Mennonites, Amish, Baptist, Restoration Movement, Evangelical Free, Quaker, Pentecostal, Adventist, Plymouth Brethren, Salvation Army

1. They believe it to be merely a commemorative feast.

2. They related their persecution and suffering to that of Christ, thus viewing the Lord's Supper as a means to strengthen the community and show solidarity.

3. True

4. False

5. True

6. They call it "the Breaking of Bread."

7. Their focus is generally on the community and the holiness of the lives of the faithful. They do not believe that there is anything that happens to the elements, so that talk of a presence of Christ is excluded.

8. Based on the criterion of holiness, they practice closed Communion.

9. They practice foot washing.

10. General Baptists formed from the Anabaptist movement in England and were Zwinglian, while Particular Baptists were Calvinists from the Separatist movement among Puritans.

11. They generally hold a Zwinglian position.

12. They hold a Calvinist position.

13. Some use the term "sacrament" and others use "ordinance," usually to the mutual exclusion of each other.

14. They view their first reception of the Lord's Supper as a pledge or making of vows to Christ, and subsequent reception of the Sacrament as a renewal of those vows.

15. The self-examination focuses on a recommitment to Christ, renewal of faith, and allegiance and eschewing of evil.

16. Those who have open Communion argue that the Lord's Supper is a so-called kingdom ordinance that belongs to the universal church and is therefore open to all Christians.

17. Close Communion

18. True

19. False

20. True

21. It was among Baptists that individual Communion glasses came to be used.

22. They perform foot washing.

23. They hold a love feast and have a foot washing prior to the celebration of the Lord's Supper. Their service includes a holy kiss. They practice closed Communion.

24. They believe that the Lord's Supper should be celebrated every Sunday, and only on Sunday.

25. Leaders sought to revive the love feast, foot washing, and the holy kiss.

26. False

27. These are prayer, unaccompanied song, the teaching of the Word, the offering, and the Lord's Supper.

28. In the tradition of Zwingli, they perceive it to be a communal act of celebration of the saving acts and presence of Christ.

29. Certain congregations among the Disciples of Christ became

known as "one-cuppers" because they rejected the use of individual Communion glasses as being contrary to Scripture.

30. Some congregations have begun to recognize the Baptisms performed in other denominations, thereby opening their Communion fellowship from only those who had received believers' baptism among them to include those whose Baptisms are now recognized as being legitimate.

31. The Evangelical Free Church

32. George Fox

33. The Inner Light or Inner Voice

34. True

35. Pentecostalism

36. Among such groups, celebration of the Lord's Supper may vary greatly in frequency, yet in most cases it has decreased status in comparison with direct experiences claimed to be of the Holy Spirit.

37. The Assemblies of God

38. Aimee Semple McPherson

39. True

40. True

41. True

42. True

43. True

44. False

45. Seventh-Day Adventists

46. They use unleavened bread and grape juice.

47. Foot washing

48. They practice open Communion.

49. True

50. The Plymouth Brethren

51. William Booth

52. For them true observance of the Lord's Supper consists in remembering Christ's death by engaging in spiritual conversation, particularly in connection with regular eating and drinking.

Lutheran Churches

1. He used interpretation by Scripture alone (sola scriptura).

2. One should understand them only in the literal sense.

3. All partakers receive Christ's body and blood. Some receive it unto their salvation, whereas others unto judgment.

4. The worthiness of the communicant rests entirely on the holy merit of Christ, which the one who believes in Christ and in His literal words of institution receives worthily and which the unbeliever, the one who rejects Christ's literal words and thereby Christ Himself, receives unto judgment.

5. True

6. Abraham Calov

7. Some say that the presence takes place after the last syllable of the Words of Institution, while others say that the presence takes place at the moment of reception.

8. Lutherans have rejected the extreme views on both sides as heresy.

9. They have repeatedly said that the presence of Christ does not endure beyond the sacramental action of consecration, distribution, and reception.

10. Lutherans teach that the sacramental action must continue unbroken, else it must be repeated from the beginning, as, for example, among Communion of the sick and shut-in, in which consecrated elements may not be distributed and received at a later time without re-consecration.

11. The bread may be stored for later sacramental use, eaten, or burned. The wine may be poured out onto the ground or into a special drain that leads to the ground, but not the

sewer, or it may be reverently consumed, as appropriate.

12. Type of bread, whether leavened or unleavened, and color of wine are left as a matter of conscience. Alcohol-bearing wine is preferred, although some permit the use of non-alcoholic wine.

13. The common cup, which is clearly the historic precedent establish by Jesus, is the preferred method. If individual glasses are used, the ideal is to make use of them as options to an available chalice.

14. The historic practice has been to have private confession and absolution.

15. During the twentieth century, announcements made by those intending to commune, which would have occurred in context with individual confession and absolution, began to occur in the form of Communion cards. The corporate confession and absolution in church services started to replace the older practice.

16. At the time of the Reformation, Lutherans communed every Sunday, even as the Lutheran Confessions state. That continued for two centuries. The pietistic movement, however, caused monthly, bimonthly, or even quarterly celebrations to become the norm. That lasted into the middle of the twentieth century, when a liturgical renewal started to occur and the original practice of weekly celebration, or at least semi-monthly celebration, became more widespread again.

17. True

18. Lutherans have historically practiced closed Communion for the benefit of those who might otherwise eat and drink the Supper to their judgment.

19. True

20. The Prussian Union of 1817

21. Samuel Schmucker

22. The Evangelical Lutheran Church in America

23. The Wisconsin Evangelical Lutheran Synod, the Evangelical

Lutheran Synod, and The Lutheran Church—Missouri Synod

24. The Lutheran Church—Missouri Synod

25. The American Lutheran, published by the American Lutheran Publicity Bureau

26. Open Communion tends to correlate with those who reject a bodily, supernatural, essential presence of the body and blood of the Lord.

27. It prevents them from eating and drinking judgment upon themselves.

Chapter 11: Consensus—Divine or Merely Human?

Events on the World Stage

1. Christ does not abide ambiguity with respect to the Lord's Supper.

2. The Zurich Consensus of 1549

3. The next attempt was the Prussian Union of 1817.

4. True

5. These include the World Mission Conference of 1910 in Edinburgh, the rise of the Faith and Order movement in 1927, the founding of the World Council of Churches at Amsterdam in 1948, and the Second Vatican Council in 1962–1965.

6. It has brought into being a "union" known as organic union, whereby unity in doctrine is not achieved, contrary to the will of God, while human "unity" is proffered as a kind of Utopia.

7. 1955 Agreed Statement on the Lord's Supper in South India
1956 Consensus on the Holy Communion in the Netherlands
1937 Halle Resolution in Germany
1957 Arnoldshain Theses in Germany
1973 Leuenberg Agreement in Germany
1988 Meissen Common Statement in Germany

1989 Porvoo Declaration and Porvoo Common Statement in Finland

1975 One Baptism, One Eucharist, One Ministry in Kenya

1983 Baptism, Eucharist and Ministry in Peru

1991 final report on Baptism, Eucharist and Ministry in Australia

8. True

Events in North America

1. True

2. It was discovered that when Catholics and Lutherans use the same words they do not always mean the same things.

3. These dialogues did not lead to extension of altar and pulpit fellowship among the parties.

4. The Statement About the Sacrament of the Altar

5. A Common Calling

6. A Formula of Agreement

7. Called to Common Mission

8. True